# THE REFERENCE SHELF

Vol. 20                                    No. 4

# REPRESENTATIVE AMERICAN
# SPEECHES: 1947-1948

Selected by
### A. CRAIG BAIRD
*Department of Speech, State University of Iowa*

## THE H. W. WILSON COMPANY
NEW YORK                          1948

Copyright 1948

By The H. W. Wilson Company

*All Rights Reserved*

Published September 1948

PRINTED IN THE UNITED STATES OF AMERICA

# PREFATORY NOTE

REPRESENTATIVE AMERICAN SPEECHES: 1947-1948 is the eleventh in this annual series. Each volume includes some thirty speeches of "representative" public speakers of the United States. These eleven volumes together include some two hundred "orators" and more than three hundred addresses.

The speeches are grouped according to content, such as International Policies, Atomic Energy, Labor and the Cost of Living, National Defense, the Political Campaigns, Personalities. An alternative classification, according to occasions or speaking types, can easily be made, such as Congressional Debates, Eulogies, Educational Lectures, Executive Speeches, Speeches of Introduction, Radio Broadcasts, Judicial Speeches, Sermons, Speeches before Business Groups. (See Introduction to *Representative American Speeches: 1945-1946*, p9-10, for detailed classifications.)

Classifications either of content or of speaking types obviously overlap. They are set forth for the reader's convenience, rather than as examples of logical scientific division.

The editor makes no claim that these are the "best" performers of each year or of this eleven-year span, but merely that these are "important" examples of a point of view and of a speech type.

This volume, like the earlier ones, is to be used as a reference text for the study of contemporary American problems; as a partial record of recent history; as material for courses in debate or extempore speaking; and as a series of speeches for the systematic study of contemporary American public speaking. Each volume, then, in addition to its service to reference workers, is especially recommended to students of extempore speaking, communication, debate, social sciences, history, and general public speaking.

The Introduction to this volume suggests specific lines of investigation for the orderly examination of each speech. The brief introductory note accompanying each provides background

facts and aims to stimulate the reader to probe more fully into the speaking methods; into the occasion and audience; and into the immediate and later effects of the address as clues for judging the total effectiveness.

The biographical notes in the Appendix are inserted partly to encourage the investigator to explore more fully the intellectual resources, the personality, and the previous speaking record of each representative.

The Table of Contents of each annual edition and the Cumulative Author Index at the end of this volume are further means for reviewing the issues and the individual speakers of the period 1937-1948.

The student of speeches in 1948-1949 will have a better appreciation of a current speech if he has before him the addresses and speakers of the preceding years. From such approach former discourses lose their character as "dated" or "unimportant" documents. The study of technique in each speech will give important clues concerning what to adopt and what to reject in the construction and presentation of the student's own performances.

The editor is heavily indebted to the various authors of these discourses for permission to make these reprints and for specific information relating to the speech occasion; and to the publishers and organizations that have graciously cooperated. Specific acknowledgment is made in the footnotes accompanying each speech.

A. CRAIG BAIRD

June 1, 1948

# CONTENTS

## The Political Campaigns

## Education and Civilization

## Personalities

## Religion

# INTRODUCTION

## How Shall We Judge a Speech?

How shall we judge the speeches and speakers contained in this anthology? How shall we test those of the ten earlier volumes in this series? In the previous Introductions I have attempted to suggest briefly the criteria for such evaluation. Here I propose to summarize systematically the methods there proposed and thus perhaps to encourage a more discerning appraisal of a given speech.

I. *Decide whether the speaker composed the speech attributed to him.* It is important to know whether the orator you are examining wrote his own discourse or whether he merely read or memorized somebody else's. Ghost writers of speeches abound. Busy and cautious government executives, military leaders, and others continually give speeches and official utterances. It is impossible for them to produce the number of talks demanded of them.

My procedure is to select, as nearly as I can do so, only those speeches created—or largely created—by the alleged authors. For the present volume I have carefully examined the authenticity of the addresses by Marshall, Vandenberg, Dulles, Lilienthal, Truman, and the others. The speech in each case, I conclude, bears the stamp of its alleged author. Truman, for example, as did Roosevelt, has had his collaborators. The Truman message of March 17, 1948, nevertheless, is largely his own—if we may judge by internal evidence and by the testimony of those observers close at hand. Your diligence in checking authorship, therefore, is not time wasted. You need to hear many speeches by the orator, note his extempore skill as repeatedly demonstrated, study his habits of composition and delivery, and get from those closely associated with him the most reliable evidence of his compositional skill.

II. *Decide whether the text duplicates what the speaker said.*
The speaker may have edited the reprint to enhance his literary
merit, or later to qualify unguarded statements made on the platform. I have frequently noted discrepancies between the text as
uttered (and recorded) and the version submitted to me for
publication. It should be added that these changes are usually
inconsequential and that these reprints are made with the cooperation of the speaker and from texts approved by him.

At best the problem of getting an accurate reproduction is
complicated. (1) The best speeches—for example, many extempore remarks—may be unrecorded. (2) Shorthand reports
are admittedly not entirely accurate. (3) Congressional speakers,
for example, have the privilege of correcting in printer's proofs
their remarks in minor and even major items. (4) A literal
transcription of extempore remarks would not always be fair to
the speakers. The broken sentences, loose structure, and even
questionable grammar may be entirely acceptable in the speaking
situation. Reduced to print, the results may invite readers' criticism. Spoken style is best understood in its setting, accompanied
by the voice and manner of the speaker himself.

What shall we do about this problem of textual accuracy?
Make electrical or other recordings wherever possible. For other
speeches, compare the various texts and select the most authentic
copy.

III. *Review the social and politcal background of the speech.*
Since speechmaking is oral communication and exists for a practical purpose, it arises in the social medium. Speeches are possible
only because an audience is present. (By definition a speech is
not a monolog delivered to empty space.) The speaker and
audience are of the times. As a student of speeches, you will
immerse yourself in the contemporary economic and political
currents. Against such background these speakers of 1947-48
have done their thinking and talking.

Each speech in this volume is accompanied by a brief summary of background events. These brief items suggest the complicated array of events that comprise the American world of this
period.

Between June 1947 and June 1948, America moved through
one international crisis or "situation" after another. The breach

with Russia widened. The Mashall Plan evolved. The Cominform arose. Communist "direct action" in France and Italy waxed and, outwardly at least, waned. Italians voted, amidst worldwide excitement, against Soviet domination. Soviet authority, however, intensified itself over Middle Europe. Sovietism engulfed Czechoslovakia. Turkey continued mobilization and Greece made doubtful headway against the guerilla-Communist rebels. Western Germany split from the Russian sector. The Allied units still clung precariously to their Berlin zone. British, French, and American deliberations over terms of peace for Germany and Austria degenerated into endless violent recriminations. Marshall and his colleagues finally ceased in despair or disgust.

In the Middle East the confusion grew. Jews and Arabs, after partition was announced, moved into open or covert combat. When America retracted her approval of the Palestine split, the role of the United Nations in this feud became more and more uncertain and controversial.

In the Far East the Communists continued to absorb northern China and so to supplant the former Japanese domination with Russian military encroachments. Korean elections (south of the thirtieth parallel) presaged a free Korea that might be only a shadow nation. In Latin America's Bogotá, too, the Inter-American Conference carried on before and after a Colombian revolt achieved only limited results. All of these international movements found wide echo in American official or spontaneous speechmaking.

On the domestic front these foreign disturbances produced parallel problems. Noticeable was our recognition of and pride in our enormous activity and prosperity. But inflation continued. Rising prices and uncontrolled rents stirred heated debate. Miners and many other organized workers struck. Lewis, as usual, was in the vortex. The railroads almost stopped. Emergency injunctions and arguments about the Taft-Hartley law accompanied the management-labor war.

Presidential politics loomed up as June-July conventions approached. Republican primaries were especially active. Stassen, Dewey, Taft, and Wallace, the avowed candidate of a Third Party, created considerable discussion. Communism continued as a foremost topic. In the early months of the campaign people talked about the "impending Russian war." Congress voted for strong national defense, and a draft bill. Congress, too, despite the President's repeated vetoes, reduced income taxes. There was much talk in Congress, but—in a national election year—not always decision.

Thus, over the radio, in Congress, in the pulpits, at business conferences and dinners, among school and college students, on farms, in villages, these events and their problems were debated, expounded, and reargued. To appraise these speeches, then, is to relive the days and nights of 1947-48 as the Americans and their speechmakers lived them.

IV. *Analyze the specific audience.* Get the facts concerning each audience. Determine the reasons for the assembly, the complexion of the audiences, their attitudes toward the speaker and his topic, their general framework of thinking, and the character of their reaction to the speech and speaker. Observe the race, politics, occupations, religion, traditions, economic level, age, and other attributes of the group. In many cases it will be a specialized audience, about which you can find not too much. In other cases, where the speaker patently appeals via radio to a nationwide audience, your problem is to fathom, as best you can, the disposition and probable attitudes of these national listeners.

Vandenberg, arguing for the European Recovery Plan, addressed his associates, many of them old friends, in the Senate. President Truman, asking for the draft, in the well of the House of Representatives, focused on the two houses in joint session. Walter Lippmann, at Williamsburg, Virginia, was lecturing to a Phi Beta Kappa audience. Senator Taft and Walter Reuther broadcast, each hoping to win to his side most of those who might be listening. Helen Douglas talked to a largely vacant House of Representatives, but appealed over their shoulders to her constituency in California and elsewhere. Henry Wallace stimulated the left-wingers and progressive face-to-face listeners, but also appealed over the radio to "all who love peace." Niebuhr spoke to a sophisticated audience at the Waldorf Astoria, New York; Goldsborough, to a courtroom audience which included John L. Lewis; Dewey, Stassen, and Taft, to audiences who would presently vote in Republican primaries.

These were representative audience types, American in their immediate and traditional associations. Each group had special traits and attitudes toward the speaker and his message. To enter somewhat imaginatively into the understanding of each audience and of the general American audiences of the time is necessary if you are to interpret properly a given speech.

V. *Classify the speech according to its occasion and purpose.* Speeches in this volume may be classified as: (1) deliberative and executive addresses, including political campaign speeches; (2) forensic or legal addresses; (3) occasional speeches, including eulogistic, anniversary, dedicatory, and similar types; and (4) sermons.[1]

These divisions, to be sure, overlap. And you may put a given speech in a somewhat different category from those suggested above. Most, for example, are "radio talks." The groupings, nevertheless, are of help in understanding the speaker's purpose in his speech and the type of speech the specific audience expects from the speaker.

VI. *Weigh the ideas or chief arguments of the speech.* Every important speech, including those in this volume, is composed of a series of ideas. What are these thoughts? How original are they? How consistent? How sensible? How clearly expressed? What appeal to those who listen? These basic concepts of the speaker almost invariably relate to current economic or other difficulties. What does the speaker have to say about policies with respect to Germany, Russia, atomic energy, strikes, drafts, inflation, civil rights, educational reform, religious principles, or similar problems? Your task is to set forth these premises or lines of argument and decide their "worth."

VII. *Evaluate the supporting evidence or details that support the central ideas.* You will note concrete details that support the

---

[1] For more detailed classifications, see *Representative American Speeches: 1945-46.* p9-10.

central pillars—the authorities, statistics, general illustrations, hypothetical or actual cases, the anecdotes, figurative or literal analogies or comparisons, the definitions, cause-to-effect reasoning, and similar materials that give body to the essential thought.

Your examination of these arguments or propositions or central ideas and their amplifications in a given speech will require you to be something of a logician. You will apply tests of acceptable definitions; of inference; of an alleged "fact"; of analogy, causal reasoning, generalization from cases, authority; of circumstanial details; of reasoning by deduction and induction; of refutation; and, in general, of sound thinking.

Such logical appraisal of a speech is difficult at best, but the effort is necessary. We need to rely on more than a hunch to decide whether a talk is based upon straight thinking.

VIII. *Evaluate the emotional elements of the speech.* The supporting materials of the speech—those that directly contribute to the speaker's logic—are "explicit"; and those that stir emotional reaction and supply "motivation for action" are "implicit." No hard and fast line can, of course, be drawn between "implicit" from "explicit" elements. An analogy, for example, may furnish proof of an idea. At the same time it may stir the imagination and emotions. We can, nevertheless, separate those prosaic, matter-of-fact speeches from the others filled with emotional expression—the typical "oration." We note the appeals to patriotism, fear, reverence, loyalty to tradition and national heroes, pride of achievement, and similar motives; the speaker's methods of developing such suggestions; the relationship of these "appeals" to the current attitudes and experiences of the listeners. We decide whether these motivational features are justified as logic, as "good psychology," and as acceptable moral practice.

IX. *Test the structure (organization) of the speech.* Organization is no mere mechanical detail of the speech pattern. The speaker's arrangement of ideas reflects his thinking. As a critic, you will outline the address. Note the materials included as well as those omitted and the clearness with which unity is achieved; the order in which the ideas are presented; the relationship of such sequence to audience needs and interests; the proportion of time and space given to an idea.

X. *Evaluate the speaker's language.* The words are to be viewed as reflectors of the speaker's thinking and of his adjustment (or failure in adjustment) to his audience. Vocabulary is important as an index of speaking effectiveness. At their worst, words may block real communication and furnish only cloudy meanings by creating logical pitfalls and by setting up bad emotional currents. At best, language conveys maximum meaning and enhances ideas by original and pleasurable expression. Each speech in the present volume has an individual oral style. A comparison and contrast of the sentence structure, phrasing, concreteness, compactness, originality, and colloquial and idiomatic elements of language in the various speeches will make clear this individual quality.

XI. *Evaluate the delivery.* What of the speaker's voice, enunciation, pronunciation, and bodily action? Does he read his speech? Give it from memory? Extemporize? Does he have adequate intellectual-emotional control through his voice and physical activity? What of his gestures, posture, platform movements? His vocal pitch? His rate of utterance? His loudness (or lack of it)? His inflection, use of pauses, and other marks of a "lively sense of communication"? His articulation and pronunciation? Does he speak like a Midwesterner or a New Englander? Is he free from bombast and declamation? At ease on a platform?

These details, however, are not ends in themselves. Each factor is to be weighed, and the total delivery is to be judged in relation to its general effect on the audience.

XII. *Evaluate the speaker's speaking personality.* Is the speaker a person of conviction, sincerity? Has he self-confidence, humor, taste, tact, generosity, good will, modesty, sincerity? Does he have self-control and emotional balance in speaking? These qualifications, intangible though they are, are important in the speaker's appeal to audiences. If he has a reputation for these virtues, and if, in addition, your appraisal of him reveals his genuine possession of them, you can gauge him as especially strong in his speaking personality.

For insight into these factors, you will collect information concerning the speaker's biography, his speech training, and his platform behavior before audiences. (See the biographical notes in the Appendix and supplement them by your more detailed investigations.)

XIII. *Evaluate the total effectiveness of the factors investigated above.* Your problem is to avoid undue stress on specific minutiae of gestures, language, or organization. Each is important, but relative to the total effect, sometimes secondary. Great speeches have no doubt been accompanied by bad grammar, loose gestures, and other shortcomings. Your approach to a just estimate is to view the speaker in relation to his purpose, his mustering of his major resources in accomplishing his speaking ends, and his general effectiveness in evoking favorable audience response. Keep before you each item. But do not settle the case by mathematical totaling of specific items. After your review of the isolated details, survey the performance in its totality and so pronounce the speaker as superior, excellent, good, standard, or below standard.

The speakers here included have merits that in certain particulars lift them above mediocrity. The critics, even though favorable, would be the first to recognize the shortcomings in the public speaking of each.

In conclusion, it should be noted that we need standards of judgment by which we can rate speakers and set goals for our own speaking performances. We need more knowledge of the facts behind the printed addresses. You need a norm by which to listen, to read, and to judge. You will therefore study English composition, psychology, logic, history, and speech itself.

# INTERNATIONAL POLICIES

## COLLAPSE OF THE LONDON BIG
## FOUR CONFERENCE [1]

### George C. Marshall [2]

Secretary of State George C. Marshall on Friday, December 19, 1947, broadcast this report of the London Conference of the Council of Foreign Ministers.

On Monday, December 15, the conference, meeting to discuss peace treaties for Germany and Austria, collapsed. Thirteen hours after his return, the Secretary of State, in his address to the nation and the world, placed full blame for the breakdown on Russia. Marshall advocated support of the European Recovery Program, and warned that the Soviet Union had made "a frank declaration of hostility and opposition" to it. Peacemaking, Marshall declared, was impossible until Europe became politically and economically stable.

This Big Four session, the fifth since 1945, carried on through seventeen meetings. Marshall, Bevin, and Bidault at no time made progress in their negotiations with Molotov. On all major issues—reparations, frontiers, a program for Austria, an economic pattern for Germany—the ministers were deadlocked.

It was literally a war of words—"interminable discussions during the weeks of debate." Several of the sessions were consumed with debates over procedure. Russia was obviously not interested in progress—except on her own terms. Her chief motive was to use the conference as a propaganda sounding-board—"only an interest in making more and more speeches intended for another audience."

The specific issue on which the negotiators broke is clearly expounded in this speech: "Should Germany be divided or should it be united?" The Western Allies outlined certain principles for unification. The Soviets categorically opposed each principle.

Marshall showed splendid skill in his broadcast in simplifying the entire controversy and expounding it so that the nationwide audience could grasp the essentials. His blunt statements, his framing of the issue, the simplicity of his language and syntax—all raise this address above mediocrity. It was in the usual Marshall unadorned style, but its

---

[1] Text supplied by the Division of Publications of the Department of State.
[2] For biographical note see Appendix.

meaning was unmistakable and its implications conclusive: "There can be no settlement until the coming months demonstrate whether or not the civilization of Western Europe [can] restore a healthy society." Without verbiage or high persuasion the speaker presented his evidence and logic and drove home his conclusion: We must get about the huge job of European recovery.

What was the problem growing out of this impasse? The Russians proceeded apace to consolidate their Eastern German zone, largely agricultural with some eighteen million Germans. The dominant Soviets rapidly converted it into a semi-socialistic state, with land reforms and a huge state monopoly of business.

The Western Allies, on their part, consolidated their zone into a Trizonia, largely industrial, with forty-six million Germans. The problem of the Western Allies was partly to get rid of the costs of occupation, some $700,000,000 annually, and, therefore, to get German production back to the 1936 level and so contribute to the European Recovery Program. The issue was this: would a revival of such German power later mean a German attack on France and Great Britain? With two Germanys thus created, would the Soviet-Germany, with Berlin as the capital, outbid the Western nations for the absorption of Trizonia? Or would the Western Germans take over their Eastern brothers and so provoke Russia to World War III? With an economically restored Western Europe (including Trizonia), it was hoped that Russia would cooperate in a genuine peace settlement with respect to both Germany and Austria.

Marshall continued to address the American public in his dry, flat tones. His was by no means a musical voice. His articulation was undistinguished. But his intellectual energy, his directness of statement, his extempore ability and soldierly forthrightness on the platform all served to make him one of the competent public speakers of 1948.

The result of the recent meeting of the Council of Foreign Ministers in London was disappointing. I realize that the many lengthy statements and the frequent and fundamental disagreements were very confusing to the general public. Also, the continuous accusations against the good faith, the integrity, and the purposes of the governments of the Western powers, particularly the United States, necessarily added greatly to the confusion. This was, as a matter of fact, one of the purposes of these attacks.

I anticipated great difficulty in reaching a comprehensive agreement, but I did have a hope that we might take three or four fundamental decisions which would permit immediate action by the Four Powers to alleviate the situation in Germany this winter and greatly improve the prospects for all of Europe. That we failed to reach any such agreements is the greatest disappointment.

The United States Delegation went to London with an open mind, as I had stated we would in Chicago, but we went with a strong determination to bring to an end the division of Germany which has existed since the German capitulation. We were also determined that any agreement reached at London should be a genuine workable agreement, and not one which would immediately involve obstruction and frustration in the Allied Control Council when it came to be put into effect in Germany.

I shall review only briefly the interminable discussions during the weeks of debate at London. To us it was but a dreary repetition of what had been said and resaid at the Moscow conference. I shall endeavor, however, to point out the main issues on which the Conference deadlocked and give you my estimate of the underlying reasons.

The basic issue, as we saw it before the opening of the London conference, was whether or not the Allies could agree among themselves to reunite Germany.

The issue in regard to the American treaty was even simpler and had already emerged clearly at the Moscow conference.

Because the two main issues which I have outlined would be the controlling factors in our discussions, three of the delegations had agreed that the Austrian treaty should be considered first and the economic principles to govern the treatment of Germany as an economic whole should come second. We felt that this order was logical and necessary if we were to debate with any prospect of success the remaining items on our agenda. The Soviet Delegation held a different view and insisted that questions on the preparation of a German peace treaty should be given precedence over the questions regarding immediate economic unity for Germany.

In order to get the Conference started, it was finally agreed to accept the Soviet request that the preparation of a German peace treaty should be item two on the agenda. As a result, with the exception of one day of discussion of Austria and the Austrian treaty, it was not until after ten days of meetings that the Conference really reached the heart of the German question. These first ten meetings were devoted to futile and somewhat unreal discussion of the mechanisms for the preparation of an eventual German peace treaty before the question of whether or not there was to be united Germany had even been considered. There was one question, however, of real substance during this phase of the discussion which had a direct application not only to a German peace treaty but also to the immediate situation in Germany. This was the question of the present and future frontiers of the German state. No serious consideration of a peace treaty could be undertaken without first considering what was to be the area of the future German state. Three delegations had already expressed their agreement that the area of the Saar should be separated from Germany and integrated into French economy. Mr. Molotov refused to commit his Government on this point.

On this vital matter of frontiers, three delegations agreed to the establishment of a frontier commission or commissions to make an expert study of any proposed changes from the prewar frontiers. Mr. Molotov refused to agree. It was impossible for me to reconcile his urgent insistence upon the necessity of expediting the preparation for a German peace treaty with his categoric refusal to agree to the appointment of boundary commissions, which three delegations considered to be an absolutely essential first step in any serious preparation for a future German peace settlement.

Many other questions concerning the actual preparation of any peace treaty were discussed without agreement.

It was during this stage of the debate that Mr. Molotov insisted that the Four Powers should agree upon the immediate establishment of a German central government. Although the United States had been, I believe, the first of the four occupying countries to suggest at Moscow the desirability for the earliest possible establishment of a German provisional central government, it was obvious that until the division of Germany had been healed and conditions created for German political and economic unity, any central government would be a sham and not a reality. This view was shared by the other Western delegations but to Mr. Molotov was completely unacceptable. This was the first clear evidence of his purpose to utilize the meeting as an opportunity for propaganda declarations which would be pleasant to German ears.

After several days of consideration by the deputies, the Austrian treaty was again brought to the conference table on December 4. The sole issue discussed was the determination of what were the true German assets in eastern Austria to which the Soviet Union was fully entitled by the Potsdam agreement. This had been the stumbling block in reaching final agreement on the treaty draft, and it was an issue which would determine whether or not Austria would be under such complete economic domination by the Soviet Union that it would be virtually a vassal state.

The French had endeavored to break the impasse by submitting a compromise proposal, but this was categorically refused by the Soviet Delegate. In the last hour of the final session of the Conference Mr. Molotov indicated an apparent willingness to accept a percentage reduction in the Soviet claims, without specifying the actual amount involved in his proposal. The matter was immediately referred to the deputies, and I was informed just prior to my departure from England that the Soviet Government would submit later a detailed proposition.

It was not until the tenth meeting that the Conference finally came to the heart of the problem—to a consideration of the harsh realities of the existing situation in Germany.

Several more days were to elapse, however, before the Council really came to grips with these realities. Discussions of procedure—of what document to discuss—again intervened to delay our work. However, on Monday, December 8, the procedural issues were resolved, and the Council began the consideration of the fundamental issues which eventually led to the adjournment of the session without agreement.

I shall endeavor to indicate briefly what those issues were without reciting the involved and prolonged discussions over individual items.

The general issue was simple. It was whether or not Germany was to continue divided or whether the Allies could agree to recreate a unified Germany. Unless this could be achieved, all other questions relating to Germany would remain academic.

What then were the particular obstacles to the achievement of German economic and political unity?

The United States Delegation considered that there were certain fundamental decisions which the four occupying powers should take if German unity was to be achieved. These were:

1. The elimination of the artificial zonal barriers to permit free movement of persons, ideas, and goods throughout the whole territory of Germany.

2. The relinquishment by the occupying powers of ownership of properties in Germany seized under the guise of reparations without Four Power agreement.

3. A currency reform involving the introduction of new and sound currency for all Germany.

4. A definite determination of the economic burdens which Germany would be called upon to bear in the future, that is the costs of occupation, repayment of sums advanced by the occupying powers, and reparations.

5. An over-all export-import plan for all of Germany.

When these basic measures have been put into effect by the occupying powers, then the establishment under proper safeguards of a provisional government for all Germany should be undertaken.

Reparations soon emerged as a key issue. For the benefit of those not fully familiar with past negotiations on this subject, I wish to explain that a definite agreement had been concluded two years ago at Potsdam that reparation payments would be made by the transfer of surplus capital assets, that is, factories, machinery, and assets abroad, and not by payments from time to time out of the daily output of German production. One reason for this decision was to avoid an issue that would continue through the years between Germany and the Allies and between the Allies themselves concerning her ability to pay and the actual value of payments which had been made in goods. Also, it was clearly evident that for many years Germany would be involved in a desperate struggle to build up sufficient foreign trade to pay for the food and other items on which she will be dependent from outside sources. The best example of this phase of the situation that I can give is the present necessity for Great Britain and the United States to pay out some 700 millions a year to provide the food and other items to prevent starvation and rather complete disintegration of that portion of Germany occupied by our forces.

In other words, reparations from current production—that is, exports of day-to-day German production with no return—could be made only if the countries at present supplying Germany—notably the United States—foot the bill. We put in and the Russians take out. This economic truth, however, is only one aspect of Soviet reparation claims. In the Eastern zone of Germany the Soviet Union has been taking reparations from current production and has also, under the guise of reparations, seized vast holdings and formed them into a gigantic trust embracing a substantial part of the industry of that zone. This has resulted in a type of monopolistic strangle hold over the economic and political life of Eastern Germany which makes that region little more than a dependent province of the Soviet Union. A very strong reason, in my opinion, for our failure to agree at London, was the Soviet determination not to relax in any way its hold on Eastern Germany. Acceptance of their claims for reparations from current production from the Western zones would extend that strangle hold over the future economic life of all Germany.

The Soviet position was nowhere more clearly indicated than by Mr. Molotov's categoric refusal to furnish the Council of Foreign Ministers with information concerning the reparations already taken from the Eastern zone or indeed any information at all concerning the situation there, until full agreements had been reached. In effect we were to tell them what has occurred in the Western zones, which we had already done, and they tell us nothing. That refusal to provide information absolutely essential for decisions as to the organization of German unity would by itself have made any agreement impossible. A remarkable illustration of the Soviet position in this matter was their carping criticism of the economic procedure in our zones, which we freely publish for the world to read, while virtually in the same breath blandly refusing to provide any data at all concerning their zone.

It finally became clear that we could make no progress at this time—that there was no apparent will to reach a settlement but only an interest in making more and more speeches intended for another audience. So I suggested that we adjourn. No real ground was lost or gained at the meeting, except that the outlines of the problems and the obstacles are much clearer. We cannot look forward to a unified Germany at this time. We must do the best we can in the area where our influence can be felt.

All must recognize that the difficulties to be overcome are immense. The problems concerned with the treaty settlements for Italy and the satellite countries were simple by comparison, since none of those countries were divided into zones of occupation and all of them had an existing form of government. Germany by contrast is subdivided into four pieces—four zones. No trace of national government remains.

There is another and I think even more fundamental reason for the frustration we have encountered in our endeavor to reach a realistic agreement for a peace settlement. In the war struggle Europe was in a large measure shattered. As a result a political vacuum was created, and until this vacuum has been filled by the restoration of a healthy European community, it does not appear possible that paper agreements can assure a lasting peace. Agreements between sovereign states are generally the reflection and not the cause of genuine settlements.

It is for this very reason, I think, that we encountered such complete opposition to almost every proposal the Western powers agreed upon. The Soviet Union has recognized the situation in its frank declaration of hostility and opposition to the European Recovery Program. The success of such a program would necessarily mean the establishment of a balance in which the sixteen Western nations, who have bound their hopes and efforts together, would be rehabilitated, strong in forms of government which guarantee true freedom, opportunity to the individual, and protection against the terror of governmental tyranny.

The issue is really clear-cut, and I fear there can be no settlement until the coming months demonstrate whether or not the civilization of Western Europe will prove vigorous enough to rise above the destructive effects of the war and restore a healthy society. Officials of the Soviet Union and leaders of the Communist Parties openly predict that this restoration will not take place. We on the other hand are confident in the rehabilitation of Western European civilization with its freedoms.

Now, until the result of this struggle becomes clearly apparent, there will continue to be a very real difficulty to resolve, even on paper, agreed terms for a treaty of peace. The situation must be stabilized. Western nations at the very least must be firmly established on a basis of government and freedoms that will preserve all that has been gained in the past centuries by these nations and all that their cooperation promises for the future.

# EUROPEAN RECOVERY PROGRAM [3]

## ARTHUR H. VANDENBERG [4]

Senator Arthur H. Vandenberg, Chairman of the Senate Foreign Relations Committee, opened the Senate debate on Monday, March 1, 1948, on the European Recovery Program (the Economic Recovery Act of 1948).

The bill called for $5.3 billion for aid to Europe for twelve months beginning April 1, 1948. The legislation was prepared as aid to "strengthen those who were resisting aggression and dictatorship." It was designed further to "fight economic chaos," to "sustain Western civilization," and to "take Western Europe completely off the American dole."

What, in brief, was the background of this legislation? (1) The Truman doctrine, enacted on March 12, 1947, proposed $400 million to strengthen economic, political, and military stability of Greece and Turkey.[5] The proposal was passed by Congress in May 1947. (2) On June 5, Secretary of State George C. Marshall, in a speech at Harvard, proposed the Marshall Plan for European Recovery. (3) On July 3, 1947, Russia boycotted the Marshall Plan and admonished her satellites to do so. (4) On September 22, sixteen Western nations approved the program. (5) On October 5 was launched the nine-nation Cominform (the successor to the Comintern) in opposition to the ERP. (6) On November 17, President Truman asked Congress for interim aid to Europe. (7) In November came Communist-inspired strikes in France and Italy, as a protest against the ERP. (8) On February 25, 1948, Russia took over Czechoslovakia. (9) Soon after, Russia signed a "non-aggression and mutual defense pact" with Finland, thus binding that country firmly to the Russian cause. (10) In February 1948, in Brussels, the representatives of Great Britain, France, and the Benelux countries (Belgium, the Netherlands, and Luxemburg) met to form an alliance against Russian expansion. Such was the situation when the Senate debate began.

Vandenberg's speech summarized clearly the background of the problem and analyzed the issues: how was "the gigantic trust" to be administered? what was the proper amount to be determined upon and administered? what factors, other than proper administration and adequate financing, were essential for the success of the plan?

[3] *Congressional Record.* 80th Congress, 2d session. 91:1981-6. March 1, 1948 (daily edition).
[4] For biographical note see Appendix.
[5] See *Representative American Speeches: 1946-1947.* p51-88.

The address is largely expository and non-dramatic in tone. It does reflect Vandenberg's ability in clear exposition and conciliatory argument to secure Senate endorsement.

At the end the Senators rose, applauded, and personally congratulated the speaker. The speech was one of the strongest of the many able Vandenberg debates in the Senate. The chief criticism came from Republicans, including majority leader Kenneth Wherry, of Nebraska, Joseph Ball, of Minnesota, George W. Malone, of Nebraska, and Robert A. Taft, of Ohio. Several amendments (e.g., the reduction of the proposed bill from 5.3 to 4 billions) were all voted down.

Senator Vandenberg became a masterful floor leader and defender of his bill. The Senate approved it on March 14, and the House (in an "omnibus measure" including aid to China) on March 31. Early in April the joint conference bill was approved. President Truman signed the bill and made law the "Foreign Assistance Act of 1948," calling it "America's answer to the challenge facing the free world." Paul G. Hoffman, President of the Studebaker Corporation, was quickly approved as Economic Cooperation Administrator in charge of the program.

Senators Vandenberg and Taft, through their speaking, continued to dominate the thinking of the Senate in the Eightieth Congress—Vandenberg in international policies and Taft in the domestic program.

Mr. President, with the unanimous approval of the Senate Foreign Relations Committee, I report the Economic Cooperation Act of 1948 in its perfected text. In the name of peace, stability, and freedom it deserves prompt passage. In the name of intelligent American self-interest it envisions a mighty undertaking worthy of our faith. It is an economic act—but economics usually control national survivals these days. The act itself asserts that "disruption following in the wake of war is not contained by national frontiers." It asserts that "the existing situation in Europe endangers the establishment of a lasting peace, the general welfare and national interest of the United States, and the attainment of the objectives of the United Nations."

Every Senator knows that these dangers are even greater than they were when those words were written only two short weeks ago. The fate of Czechoslovakia, where any semblance of democracy has just been gutted by subversive conquest, underscores this solemn thesis. The kindred fate of brave little Finland may be adding to the ominous score this very afternoon even while we debate an axiom, namely, that aggressive communism threatens all freedom and all security, whether in the Old World or in the New, when it puts free peoples anywhere in chains.

The act asserts sound doctrine when it says that it is "the policy of the people of the United States to sustain and strengthen principles of individual liberty, free institutions and genuine independence through assistance to those countries of Europe which participate in a joint recovery program based upon self-help and mutual cooperation." Mr. President, this act may well become a welcome beacon in the world's dark night, but if a beacon is to be lighted at all it had better be lighted before it is too late.

Nevertheless, Mr. President, the decision which here concerns the Senate is the kind that tries men's souls. I understand and share the anxieties involved. It would be a far happier circumstance if we could close our eyes to reality, comfortably retire within our bastions, and dream of an isolated and prosperous peace. But that which was once our luxury would now become our folly. This is too plain to be persuasively denied in a foreshortened, atomic world. We must take things as they are.

The greatest nation on earth either justifies or surrenders its leadership. We must choose. There are no blueprints to guarantee results. We are entirely surrounded by calculated risks. I profoundly believe that the pending program is the best of these risks. I have no quarrel with those who disagree, because we are dealing with imponderables. But I am bound to say to those who disagree that they have not escaped to safety by rejecting or subverting this plan. They have simply fled to other risks, and I fear far greater ones. For myself, I can only say that I prefer my choice of responsibilities.

This legislation, Mr. President, seeks peace and stability for free men in a free world. It seeks them by economic rather than by military means. It proposes to help our friends to help themselves in the pursuit of sound and successful liberty in the democratic pattern. The quest can mean as much to us as it does to them. It aims to preserve the victory against aggression and dictatorship which we thought we won in World War II. It strives to help stop World War III before it starts. It fights the economic chaos which would precipitate far-flung disintegration. It sustains Western civilization. It means to take Western Europe completely off the American dole at the end of the adventure.

It recognizes the grim truth—whether we like it or not—that American self-interest, national economy, and national security are inseverably linked with these objectives. It stops if changed conditions are no longer consistent with the national interest of the United States. It faces the naked facts of life.

Within the purview of this plan are 270 million people of the stock which has largely made America. These are 26 per cent of all the literates of the earth. Before the war they operated 68 per cent of all the ships that sailed the sea. They grew 27 per cent of all the world's cereals. They produced 37 per cent of the world's steel. They sold 24 per cent of the world's exports and bought 39 per cent of the world's imports. They are struggling, against great and ominous odds, to regain their feet. They must not be allowed to fall. The world—America emphatically included—needs them as both producers and consumers. Peace needs their healthy restoration to the continuing defense of those ideals by which free men live. This vast friendly segment of the earth must not collapse. The iron curtain must not come to the rims of the Atlantic either by aggression or by default.

I wish, Mr. President, swiftly to sketch the chain reaction of events responsible for the issue we here confront. It is a significant narrative which speaks for itself in behalf of the need and justification for this heroic adventure, the greatest ever initiated by any one nation for the sake of peaceful humanities. In the background, of course, is the war itself; the military defeat of the Axis; the utter prostration of postwar Europe amid the ashes of its victory; the resultant tragedy of far-flung human want and suffering; the paralysis of the peace that has not yet come; the rise of new aggression reaching out for ominous conquest amid distraught and disintegrating peoples. I do not here assess whatever mistakes in statesmanship may have helped precipitate or prolong these catastrophes. It is enough for the present consideration, that the tragedies occurred and that they still threaten the peace, stability, and security of this whole earth, the United States again emphatically included.

In the sanctuary of our relative good fortune where not one bomb fell during all those desperate days when the skies of Europe were raining death, we promptly and willingly went to the postwar aid of our prostrate friends. We literally leaped with them from one crisis to another. Bill after bill went through Congress for their relief, and billion after billion went from us to them. Two years of this went by. Often the efforts failed of the desired results—although, despite all debits, I hesitate to think what would have happened in the absence of the efforts. But it became clear that the process could not indefinitely go on, first, because Western Europe could not wait longer for real emancipation; second, because America could not longer afford to underwrite futility. We were both near the ends of our ropes.

Then came June 5, 1947. Secretary of State Marshall made a speech at Harvard. Just as at neighboring Concord in an earlier century, it proved to be "a shot heard round the world." At the moment it was just a few sentences in a quiet sequence. I quote:

It is already evident that before the United States Government can proceed much further in its effort to alleviate the situation and help the European world on its way to recovery, there must be some agreement among the countries of Europe as to the requirements of the situation and the part those countries themselves will take in order to give proper effect to whatever action might be undertaken by this Government. The initiative, I think, must come from Europe.

The role of this country should consist of friendly aid in the drafting of a European program and of later support of such a program so far as it may be practical for us to do so. The program should be a joint one, agreed to by a number, if not all, of the European nations.

Mr. President, the responsive effect in Europe was electric. History wrote with rushing pen. It was a new call to the colors— this time a peace call to mobilize for self-help and cooperation in quest of mutual survival. The British Bevin and the French Bidault promptly summoned a European conference. They consulted the Russian Molotov. He met with them in Paris on June 27. As usual, his demands were impossible; and, as usual, treacherous Moscow propaganda charged us with iniquitous American "imperialism," a charge shockingly echoed by some of our own citizens. The Soviets vetoed concerted action, but Bevin and Bidault went ahead. They invited twenty-two European nations— all of them—to meet in Paris. All Soviet-dominated countries sent their refusals, including Czechoslovakia, which, after a hasty summons to the Kremlin, withdrew its previous approval and

now finds itself forcefully communized against any further ex-
pressions of self-will. Sixteen nations accepted the invitation.
Here they are: Austria, Greece, Norway, Switzerland, Belgium,
Iceland, Portugal, Turkey, Denmark, Ireland, Sweden, United
Kingdom, France, Italy, Luxemburg, Netherlands.

They met on July 12 and organized the Committee of European Economic Cooperation known as CEEC. They met to co-
ordinate the independent nations of Europe in a self-help effort
to seek stability and preserve freedom in response to the dynamic
impulse of what was then called the Marshall Plan. They met
to plan hopeful cooperation that might justify American assistance. And they met bravely, Mr. President—"bravely" because
it was in virtual defiance of the Russian Bear, which promptly
showed its teeth.

Within four weeks Moscow dictated new reprisal agreements
and tighter affiliations with all her satellites, and quickly organized the Cominform, through which the Communists of nine
nations speak for the Communist world. The "iron curtain" took
on more "iron." The Cominform is a modern version of the
supposedly defunct Comintern, which was communism's prior
agent of world violence and revolution. It frankly calls upon
Communists everywhere to wreck the Marshall Plan and con-
demns it and us with a new intemperance of invective and dis-
tortion. It is indeed "cold war." It is pressure war against the
independent recovery of Western Europe. Obviously, it is also
aimed at us. It is a conspiracy to prevent the emergence of order
out of chaos, stability out of confusion, and Western freedom
out of hopelessness. Communists everywhere have responded.
The great sabotage is under way. Let me make it completely plain
that I do not suggest, even by the remotest inference, that all
opponents to the plan are Communists. I have already expressed
my complete respect for the honest opinions of citizens who
disagree. I simply point out, as part of the record, that while
every critic is not a Communist, every Communist is a critic, and
the orders from the Kremlin are to wreck the enterprise. Thus,
the postwar pattern continues in familiar and consistent form.

I said that the sixteen cooperating nations in CEEC acted
bravely, as I hope we, too, may do. I have in mind not only the

implications of the Cominform, but also such threatening statements as that by Mr. Molotov saying:

"The Soviet Government considers it necessary to caution the Governments of Great Britain and France against the consequences of such action."

Yet, Mr. President, there is nothing in this plan which threatens the Soviet police empire with any sort of consequence which she does not herself choose voluntarily to invite. It is not a plan against Eastern Europe, unless the independent survival of free peoples is on the blacklist. It is a plan for Western Europe. It is not external conquest. It is not dictation. It is internal recuperation by self-chosen methods. Eastern Europe was invited in. It was her own decision that keeps her out. It seems obvious that at least three of these countries behind the curtain would have joined if left to their own free wills. But, Mr. President, there are no free wills in police states.

East-west flow of trade in Europe is necessary to both. Its resumption will be profitable to both. There is nothing in this plan which retards this resumption, unless Moscow itself so elects. The healthy recuperation of Western Europe should facilitate this resumption for the good of all concerned, if we can have a peaceful world. All poisoned propaganda to the contrary notwithstanding, both at home and abroad, this is America's incentive and her dearest wish.

The honorable release of East-West tension would be the greatest boon of modern times. It can be released whenever there is mutual East-West fidelity to the objectives of World War II asserted by the united Allies on January 1, 1942, and whenever there is mutual East-West fidelity to the principles and purposes of the United Nations. It can be released whenever there is mutual East-West respect for the rights of free peoples to order their own lives. There is no consistent effort which the Government of the United States should withhold in pursuit of this objective. We must always be ready for any discussion to this end. Peace with justice is our utterly paramount concern. Any thought of another war is abhorrent to our souls. But peace and appeasement are not on speaking terms and they have not been since Munich, after World War I, and Yalta, in World War II.

But let me resume the narrative. The CEEC met for ten weeks in Paris, concluding on September 22. It has been cynically said that they met just to total up a bill to present to Uncle Sam. Nothing could be more cruel or further from the truth. They met to see what they could do to meet the Marshall self-help specifications, and they concluded mutual pledges of amazing portent and vitality. We did not dictate their ticket. They wrote it for themselves. They volunteered their pledges—to use all efforts to develop production up to agreed targets—to apply all necessary measures leading to the rapid achievement of internal financial monetary and economic stability—to cooperate in all possible steps to reduce barriers to the expansion of trade—to set up a joint organization to follow these objectives through and to insure them to the fullest possible extent. All these, and many other obligations, they offered to assume. It was a historic moment. Someday the United States of Europe may look back upon it as we do to the Annapolis Conference which preceded the Constitutional Convention at Philadelphia. It was a courageous and constructive answer to the United States. It offered the best chance for stable peace and for peaceful stability that there is on earth today—outside of a reinvigorated United Nations which it would immensely further. For myself, Mr. President, I assert the deep conviction that it is worth the wholehearted cooperation of the United States as the cheapest and most promising peace investment in our own self-interest that we face. What we can "afford to do" is one thing—and never to be minimized. But what we cannot afford not to do is just as vital in the estimates of prudent statesmanship.

I comment, in passing, that these were not idle words at Paris. Our friends meant exactly what they said. They have already begun to prove it. "Benelux" has already joined three of these countries in a customs union. Others are ready to come in. France has already performed major surgery on her currency. Italy and France have faced powerful Communist subversion and survived the test—a feat that might well have been impossible without our present and prospective economic aid. They, too, are negotiating a customs union. Bizonia in Germany is now well likely to become Trizonia in the spirit of new unity at the heart and core of European recovery. Britain's Bevin, backed by the united spokesmanship of his country, is calling for western union. These are new signs of the new times, Mr. President. If these trends are thwarted, if these hopes are dashed, I confess that I tremble for the consequences in this foreshortened world. This is not hysteria. It is simple candor. In my view, the approaching Senate roll calls are that important—to them and to us.

Now, Mr. President, make note of this: All these CEEC promises and pledges—importantly including, by the way, the acquisition of essential strategic materials for stock-piling in the United States—are to be written into agreements as a condition precedent to our cooperation. There will be specific bilateral contracts between the United States and each beneficiary country. There will be specific targets. There will be multilateral contracts in which all countries underwrite the common aim and the common cause. The obligations will be set down in black and white. This is no mere wishing well. For one example, in respect to the most vital commodity of all, coal production is pledged to go from 398 million tons in 1946 to 495 million tons in 1949 and 536 million tons in 1952.

Your Committee on Foreign Relations has made every possible effort to protect all these expectations. Indeed, this legislation which the Senate is asked to approve categorically asserts that

The continuity of assistance provided by the United States should at all times be dependent upon the continuity of cooperation among the countries involved.

The act categorically asserts that

The Administrator shall terminate assistance under this act to any participating country whenever he determines that such country is not adhering to its agreement or is diverting from the purposes of this act assistance provided thereunder.

No law can guarantee its own success. No man has a right dogmatically to say that any plan will succeed in these dangerous days of flux. But here is a warrant for maximum confidence that we do not indefinitely undertake a failure. All the more it makes the chance worth taking.

Now let me return to the narrative again. The CEEC summoned its best minds abroad to the council table. They had been warned by the Harvard speech that America expected a self-contained plan which could reasonably progress toward the restoration of economic independence and the end of American assistance. They had been warned that a successful recovery program must take the place of everlasting relief programs. They set to work to meet the challenge. At the end of ten weeks they produced the answer. It would take four and a quarter years of intensive self-help and cooperation, with progressively decreasing American assistance during this term of years. Their original estimate was that it might require an over-all total of 22.4 billions of American aid for Western Europe, including Western Germany. Chiefly by the deduction of capital-equipment items, this figure came down to 17 billions for four and a quarter years. In other words, this peace investment might cost one third as much in four and a quarter years as we appropriated for war in just one bill that passed the Senate in five minutes and without a roll call one June afternnoon in 1944. War has no bargains. I think peace has. I believe I am talking about one now.

I digress, however, to say that there is no 17 billion or any other comparable figure in this pending legislation. It was in the first executive draft that came to us months ago. I immediately asked for its deletion, and the State Department promptly acquiesced, because it could be no more than an educated guess of doubtful validity if we thus were to attempt to assess events and values so far in advance. Furthermore, it might be misconstrued abroad as a specific dollar commitment without their understanding that one American Congress cannot commit another. Yet the genius of the program, if we are to escape year-to-year relief, is sufficient continuity to encourage dependable long-range planning. We rightly demand continuity of performance from our friends as the price of continuity of aid. It is elementary and indispensable fair play, on the other hand, that continuity of aid similarly should follow continuity of satisfactory performance. It must be inherent and implicit in our purpose.

Otherwise, I repeat, this is merely one more stopgap, "rathole" operation.

Your Committee on Foreign Relations has met this situation, Mr. President, by familiar statutory advice. As is our standard practice when dealing with public projects overlapping into subsequent fiscal years, we have authorized to be appropriated from time to time for four and a half years such sums as may be necessary to carry out the provisions and accomplish the purposes of this act. But the only specific dollar authorization in the act is for one year, commencing next April. I shall discuss that later. Suffice it for the moment to point out that this has the effect of eliminating the necessity for subsequent annual authorizations. It thus simplifies the subsequent procedure. But it leaves each annual appropriation, as indeed it must, to the annual decision of the Appropriations Committees of the House and Senate and to the annual discretion of the Congress. The net of it is that the recovery program will pass in annual review. It will be tested annually for its promised accomplishments and for the continuity of its performance. It will be tested annually for its impact on our own economy. Each Congress is free to decide these subsequent issues for itself. But they will do so in the presence of the declared attitude and opinion of the Eightieth Congress, as expressed in this act, that the program, if successful, should carry through to whatever conclusion it proves to deserve. To withhold an expression of this purpose would be to repudiate our own thesis and to pitifully reduce this act to the status of just one more sterile dole. It would be to rob the act of all the cumulative values upon which we depend for net results and which can infinitely bless us all.

Now, Mr. President, let the narrative deal with equally significant events on this side of the ocean here at home. As soon as it became evident that CEEC intended to act upon Secretary Marshall's suggestion, the President began complementary studies at this end of the line. In my responsibility as chairman of the Foreign Relations Committee, I asked for his immediate appointment of an independent civilian group of seasoned and widely experienced citizens to survey the field and to report what America might wisely and safely do—I repeat those controlling words, "wisely" and "safely"—in connection with the contemplated program. As a result, such a group was named by the President on June 22, 1947, under the chairmanship of Secretary of Commerce Harriman, who was the only Government official on the panel. Its bipartisan membership was completely independent of the Government and its judgments were likewise. It had as fine and as representative a personnel as was ever gathered together to do an unselfish, patriotic job; and it labored with spectacular and unremitting zeal upon its complex task. Its ultimate report is one of the most comprehensive ever made in respect to a public problem. These credentials are important because, as a result, I think it is of paramount importance to us that this Harriman committee, despite occasional disagreement respecting details, came to the over-all conclusion that this recovery program not only is well within our American capacity but also that it is essential to the best welfare of the United States. This, remember, was the verdict of representative American citizenship. I do not know how any great problem in public policy could have been submitted to more competent audit. I commend this thought to prejudicial critics who do not and could not have comparable access to all the facts.

I quote one sentence from the Harriman committee's findings:

The committee is convinced that a sound program for Western European recovery should be formulated and adopted by the United States with the same boldness and determination, and the same confidence in the worthiness of the democratic cause, which characterized our action in World War II.

That is the target of private citizenship mobilized through the high spokesmanship of the Harriman committee.

I quote one other sentence:

The domestic consequences (of the fall of Western Europe to Communist dominion) are such as no American could easily tolerate.

Does that require any application? I think not. But it is a timely reminder that the Senate cannot contemplate its decision on this pending act with complete and comfortable detachment, as if there may be no price for us to pay if we reject or emasculate this plan. We have no such complacent option. There is an alternative price. I simply suggest, in passing, for example, that Secretary of Defense Forrestal and Army Secretary Royall testified to our committee that in the absence of some reasonable prospect for the stabilization of Western Europe they would find it necessary to urgently demand billions more for national military defense. That, however, is only a small part of what could be the alternative price in a Communist-dominated world. The Harriman committee says the total consequences could include, and I again quote the committee, the spokesmanship for the civilian population of this nation, "the immediate and sweeping limitation of our economic and political life, perhaps extending even to our form of government."

Which might be the alternative.

But let me again take up the narrative. In addition to the Harriman report, we have the survey by Secretary of the Interior Krug on Natural Resources and Foreign Aid. I quote one sentence:

The aggregate productive capacity of the United States appears ample.

In the same vein we had the so-called Nourse report, from the President's economic advisers. We also had the exhaustive studies of the executive departments through a large committee headed by able Under Secretary Lovett.

Now, Mr. President, I want to make it plain that all of this exploration dealt preponderantly with the most critical of all considerations, namely, the impact of this plan upon our own domestic economy. Nothing could be of more importance because we all agree that the maintenance of a sound and solvent United States is as indispensable to the hopes of the world as it is to us. It would be final blunder to jeopardize our stabilities at home. We shall not do so. I am glad to echo the warning of the Harriman report that "it is not wise to underestimate the steepness of the climb," and that "the aid which the United States gives will impose definite sacrifice on the United States." That is obvious. This is no happy picnic. Heavy postwar peace expenditures involve a burden, just as did the infinitely heavier expenditures of the war-that-was, or the expenditures of another war which we propose, with every resource at our command, to prevent. Any drain upon our commodities not in surplus also is a burden, although it is significant to note that the contemplated exports under this plan at its very peak are substantially less than our average exports for 1947. But all authorities agree that the plan can be managed to avoid serious interference with our domestic economy. They agree that it would not precipitate domestic controls which would not be required by the domestic situation alone. For example, there will be no competitive exports of meat under this plan for at least two years. There will be no exports of metal scrap. Petroleum products, by the explicit terms of the bill itself, must be purchased off-shore to the maximum practicable extent.

Sound administration of the act, Mr. President, will hold all these impacts to a minimum. The bill itself is explicit in these directives. In general terms it lays down the fundamental rule that "no assistance to the participating countries shall seriously impair the economic stability of the United States." In specific terms it lays down the injunction that

The Administrator must provide for procurement in such a way as to (1) minimize the drain upon the resources of the United States and the impact of such procurement upon the domestic economy, and (2) avoid impairing the vital need of the people of the United States.

The proponents of this measure, in a word, are not riding rainbows. They recognize the calculated risk. They think it is worth taking in our own enlightened self-interest. They prefer it to the alternative risk. But they proceed with prudence. They recognize the priority which self-interest assigns to the protection of our own domestic situation. We are not to be committed beyond this legitimate boundary. But they believe that we can do both jobs—at home and abroad—and that we cannot afford not to take the preferable chance. In a word, they believe in America.

Now, Mr. President, we come to the act itself, which is unanimously endorsed by the Senate Foreign Relations Committee after five weeks of public hearings and ten days of continuous executive sessions. I cannot speak too gratefully of the friendly patience and bipartisan unity with which my committee colleagues cooperated. If something of their spirit imbues those for whom this legislation is intended, the Economic Cooperation Administration, as it will be called, has hopeful augury.

We confronted many serious perplexities involving wide divergence of opinion in and out of Congress. Perhaps the greatest of these was the question how this gigantic trust should be administered. It is the universal opinion that the success of the enterprise is largely dependent upon the character of its management. It is the universal opinion that its overriding economic purpose requires the highest available type of seasoned business experience and the widest possible autonomous authority for those who patriotically assume these vast economic responsibilities. It is equally the universal opinion that the highest considerations of foreign policy are constantly involved and that, as I said upon a previous historic occasion, we cannot have two Secretaries of State at the same time.

To fit these conflicting specifications into common pattern was, indeed, a jig-saw puzzle. We invited the Brookings Institution of Washington, one of the most respected research laboratories in the country, to make an objective study of this enigma. I express our great obligation to the Brookings Institution for the masterly job it did. The provisions in the pending bill largely follow its recommendations. I am happy to say the result already enjoys well-nigh universal approval in and out of Congress.

We are creating the Economic Cooperation Administration. At its head will be an Administrator with Cabinet status. In him, under final Presidential control, is vested the responsibility for operating this enterprise. The Administrator and the Secretary of State will keep each other fully and currently informed. Whenever the Secretary of State believes that any action of the Administrator is inconsistent with the foreign policy objectives of the United States, he will consult with the Administrator and, if differences of view are not adjusted, the matter will be referred to the President for final decision. This is a paraphrase of the formula which has worked so well in the Atomic Energy Act involving somewhat similarly mixed functions.

Behind the Administrator, and his Deputy, will be the Public Advisory Board, headed by the Administrator, organized on a bipartisan basis, and consisting of not more than twelve members, to be appointed by the President and confirmed by the Senate, "selected from among citizens of broad and varied experience in matters affecting the public interest." Its functions are advisory. But its utility is profound.

Overseas a special economic mission will be established by the Administrator and under his direction in each participating country; and the chief of each such mission will cooperate with our Ambassador or Minister under a general rule of conduct reflecting the contacts set up for the Administrator and the Secretary of State to avoid inconsistent decisions by either. Meanwhile what might be called a roving ambassador will represent us in dealing with any European organization of participating countries as insistently envisioned by the act. The creation of this post underscores our firm conviction that the salvation of Western Europe lies in consolidated self-help and cooperation. Dollars alone will not save them. American assistance alone will not save them. All through the bill we bluntly assert these axioms. What they do for themselves will save them. What they do for themselves is the only possible vindication of our aid. But without a roving ambassador there would be no way for us to hold these governments to strict accountability for these relationships upon which they and we must depend for the final basic success of the undertaking.

To keep the House and Senate, here at home, in intimate touch with the evolution of all these plans, the bill creates the Joint Congressional Committee on Foreign Economic Cooperation—again borrowing this device of proved utility from the Atomic Energy Act. It will consist of seven Senators and seven Representatives. It will be bipartisan. It is already familiarly known as the watchdog committee. Little added definition is required. It will make continuous studies of what goes on. It will provide continuous and intimate congressional liaison with all these undertakings. In general sense it will represent the taxpayers of the United States. It will greatly simplify the subsequent annual responsibilities of Congress when, once each year during the life of this arrangement, it must determine in what degree yesterday's performance warrants tomorrow's continuing cooperation.

I omit further needless details. This is the picture and the pattern of administration. It gives every promise that previous errors in foreign aid will be avoided. It fixes and implements clear and specific responsibilities. It umpires in advance functional conflicts between business management on the one hand and foreign policy upon the other. It is our best possible promise of efficient and effective results in restabilizing a broken world.

Now, Mr. President, we come to the specific figure asked by the President for the first authorization under this bill. It was $6.8 billion for fifteen months from next April first. This was the result of rigorous screening by the executive authorities of the CEEC proposals for $8.4 billion and a realistic appraisal of domestic availabilities. It took full account of the Harriman, Krug, and Nourse reports. It was the composite judgment of diversified minds. Secretary Marshall said it was as near a precision figure as human judgments can foresee. Certainly it was sustained by the most complete studies and surveys I have ever seen in a congressional committee. It was further sustained by the independent investigation of the Harriman committee—composed, remember, of the best business brains available in our civilian life. The comparable Harriman figure was approximately the same. It was still further sustained by the head of the International Bank, who also examined the problem independently and concluded that the figure is a tight-fitting minimum. It was in no sense a stab in the dark. At the very least it is entitled to a presumption of relative dependability until more competent authority competently proves otherwise.

But I can fully understand, Mr. President, why this figure immediately became the subject of wide controversy. In the first place, there was a big gap between this figure and the President's budgetary estimate of actual cash disbursements for this purpose in the next fiscal year—a gap representing obligations and commitments which must be made in advance if our plans are to possess efficient continuity. In the second place, we have been overwhelmed with such a wealth and welter of supporting statistics that even our own experts—to say nothing of our committee members—have rivaled each other in their headaches. At such a moment it is dangerously easy to "lose sight of the forest for the trees." Busy pencils, playing with their decimals, can make objectivity impossible. The committee's unanimous recommendation escapes the horns of this dilemma by rooting itself in a few solid fundamentals which I commend to the common sense of my colleagues.

First. If this plan can succeed on the basis recommended by its authors, no well-wisher would allow it to fail at its inception through lack of original resources sufficient to its success. That would be "penny wisdom and pound foolishness." It could even be unwitting sabotage .

Second. Any estimate of these essential resources, in advance of experience with the plan, is problematical at best. In such circumstance we should start with figures which enjoy the preponderance of supporting evidence rather than to arbitrarily slice off what might be the difference between success and stillborn failure.

Third. Therefore prudence recommends that we launch the plan with figures which offer no alibi for failure; but on a timetable which permits us to review the figures at the earliest moment when experience will permit us to deal with the realities.

On the basis of these sanities, the Committee on Foreign Relations unanimously cut the duration of this first authorization from fifteen months to twelve and it reduced the figure from $6.8 billion to $5.3 billion. This latter figure accurately reflects the estimated expenditures and commitments for the first twelve months of the original work sheet for fifteen months. In other words, we have not undermined the resources for one year from April 1, 1948, which we are warned by the authors of this plan are essential to its success. We have not transferred from them to us the responsibility for a failure which might be charged to initial lack of funds. We have not impaired either the resources or the psychology upon which the plan depends. But we have made it imperative that the first task of the next Congress and the next administration next January shall be to resurvey this whole problem in the light of experience and reality; and thus we have reduced the first authorization by $1.5 billion.

Mr. President, I attach the greatest importance to this change in the timetable. By next New Year's we shall have had nine months' experience with this enterprise. We shall then know the efficiency of its all-important administrative management; and we shall have the benefit of the Administrator's advice. We shall also have the first-hand judgments of our own joint congressional watchdog committee. We shall know whether a good crop overseas has lightened the CEEC deficit. We shall know much more about the nature and extent—or perhaps even the suspension—of the sabotage campaigns of the wrecking crews. Most important of all, we shall know to what extent self-help and mutual cooperation in Western Europe are giving promise of the vitality upon which this plan inseverably rests. We shall know many things upon which today we can only speculate.

It seems to me that we have everything to gain and nothing to lose—assuming that we are entering upon this high adventure in good faith—by launching this hopeful enterprise full-steam-ahead; and reserving our seasoned and informed judgments for next January, as contemplated by the committee's recommendation, when we shall know whereof we speak instead of gambling now with unknown destiny. I beg of Senators to take this concept to their hearts. This is more than a problem of mathematics; it is a problem in peace, stability, and human freedoms. It may not work. I think it will. But if it fails, let the responsibility rest elsewhere. I say again—as I have said so many times before—these recommended figures are not sacred. But in the light of the powerful credentials they possess, unless the Appropriations Committee can strongly prove them wrong, let us give them the benefit of any doubts for the time being. Next January is not long to wait for the accounting with so much at stake.

One thing more about this figure of $5.3 billion. It goes for loans and grants. The division rests with the Administrator, counseled by his own board and by the National Advisory Council consisting of the highest officers of Government. The division will depend upon the beneficiary's ability to pay and upon the nature of the assistance. The loans will be serviced by the Export-Import Bank. It is roughly estimated that loans will represent from 20 per cent to 40 per cent of the grand total. Using the lower percentage in averaged application to the first year's authorization, its net cost to us is much nearer $4 billion than $5.3 billion. It could be—we may hope it will be—even lower in its net effect.

At this point I interject another vital fact. While it is impossible to establish accurate categories at the moment, it is expected that two or three of these sixteen countries in CEEC will be cooperators without any drain upon our dollar aid. They will pay their own way. It also is expected that three other countries will be exclusively on a temporary loan basis—without any grants. It is contemplated that only two countries will be exclusively on a basis of grants. The other eight countries will be on a variable scale of loans and grants. This is no loose giveaway. In every instance the plan is geared to hardpan economics.

I now speak of the method used to arrive at this figure. It involves so-called balance of payments. For each country this is the difference between national income from exports, foreign services, and foreign investments, on the one hand, and essential imports of goods and services, on the other hand. This is the balance of payments, and when the former are insufficient to pay for the latter, and there is no gold or convertible currency to make up the difference, any such deficit country is in jeopardy. Under normal exchange conditions, surplus exchange with one country can be balanced against an exchange deficit with others. But this situation does not exist today, and will not until foreign currencies and international exchange are restabilized. This is one of the long-range objectives of this plan—important to every trading nation on earth, our own emphatically included. Meanwhile, the immediate and indispensable objective is to overcome these deficits in Western Europe, including Western Germany.

Current calculations accordingly were made by the following process: First, estimating each country's import requirements; second, deducting therefrom each country's exports and earnings from foreign services and foreign investments and from any other sources; third, deducting available imports from other Western Hemisphere areas. This final figure, translated into dollars, represents the amount of support from us to permit these sixteen

European countries, plus Western Germany, to import from the Western Hemisphere the commodities essential to recovery. Import requirements of recipient countries were figured on a basis so close that they do not even restore full prewar living standards. In other words, the figures are down to bedrock.

Obviously, this brief description over-simplifies the process. There are many other factors influencing the net result. There are many imponderables, I say again and again. Only experience can demonstrate whether the realities will thrust upwards or push downwards the true evaluation. But this is generally accepted as the best measure of need. It was accepted by the Paris Conference, the executive departments, the Harriman committee, and the International Bank.

I do not undertake to demonstrate that the resultant twelve-month figure of $5.3 billion in the bill is precisely accurate. I am content to point out that it is little short of amazing how close together all these estimates, independently made, proved to be. I am content to point out that the timetable in this act, as we have reported it, permits the earliest possible congressional review in the presence of reality. I am content to urge that the burden of proof falls heavily upon those who would argue that, pending this early review, the preliminary figure is too large. I have no sympathy with any "take this or nothing" attitude. But I do prayerfully believe that adequacy is the essence of what we do; and surely we can all agree that success with $5.3 billion in the first instance is preferable to failure with something less. I remind the Senate further that, under the bill's new timetable, we can balance out even the next fiscal year by the appropriations for the fourth quarter. If facts, as we will know them next January, require readjustments, we can make them in the final quarter. Then we can put them up or down with some degree of justified assurance. When we try to adjust them today, we play with danger to the lifeline of the plan.

Many other features of the pending bill will develop with the debate. At the moment I refer, finally, to only two.

First. Local currencies must be deposited by each beneficiary country to offset the value of any aid not furnished on terms of payment. The beneficiary country and the United States will agree on the local expenditures of these local currency accumulations in behalf of the purposes of this act. Thus our grants will not become a budgetary windfall in the beneficiary country but will virtually become a revolving fund to do double duty in behalf of the act's objectives.

Second. The investment of private American capital, in approved reconstruction projects in the sixteen countries and Western Germany, is encouraged by our guaranty of the subsequent convertibility of profits or original investment into dollars. This obviates the hazard most likely to prevent private investment. At the same time it is a highly practical invitation to American private initiative to join in this great adventure on a free-enterprise basis.

Now, Mr. President, with apologies to my colleagues for the length of this intrusion upon their good nature, I conclude. With a few desultory comments, I am done.

First. This act does not include some of our other unavoidable international obligations. We shall have to deal at this session with China, Greece, Turkey, and Trieste, and with the occupied areas for which we are responsible as a legacy from the war. These things must be remembered as we proceed. We must deal with over-all considerations. Particularly we must faithfully remember the superlative importance of effective solidarity in the Western Hemisphere in unhappy, uncertain days like these. Mutually happy and healthy Pan American relationships are indispensable. They must be conserved. It ought to be entirely possible to substantially improve these economic relationships through the triangular trade that should be possible of development in connection with this European recovery plan.

Second. This act largely depends for its success upon the quality of its administration. The choice of the administrator and his associates is one of the most solemn responsibilities that has ever confronted a President of the United States. I beg of the President to search for the best and to be satisfied with nothing less. This act is a challenge to the best brains and to the best experience in the nation. They responded in the crises of war. I am sure they will respond in this crisis of peace. The cause is no less vital to our destiny.

Third. This act depends, again, for its success upon the prompt restoration of Western Germany to an effective place in the economy of Europe and the world. It must be decentralized. It must be demilitarized for keeps. But it must be restored to decent hope and productivity. The Western occupying powers must quit their indecision and put Germany wholesomely at work again without delay. The Ruhr alone could spell the difference between success and failure.

Fourth. This act depends also and equally upon the energy and devotion with which these Western European nations pursue the integration which they have volunteered to seek. Our dollars cannot substitute, I say again, for their own will to make common cause for the mutual defense of their own welfare. We do not presume to dictate the formula. But we relentlessly recommend the objective. Standing together these nations can face every vicissitude with hope. Standing apart they may face collapse and even conquest. By its own warning, the wrecking crew awaits.

Fifth. This act seeks and depends upon peace. Peace requires the economic stabilities which are here addressed. Peace also depends upon security against aggression. Security depends upon preparedness. Preparedness depends upon rival arms until, dependably there is a better way. The better way is an undivided United Nations which is made to work in its present or some other form. Regional arrangements under its charter can promote security. Unselfish mutual defense pacts, such as we have repeatedly offered, can promote security. Global disarmament—on a basis of rigid, instant, and conclusive discipline against bad faith—is the best security guarantee of all. We and the peace-loving sectors of the world must struggle on toward these ideals.

Sixth. The act has the amazingly unified support, according to their official voices before our committee, of practically all spokesmen in our own land for organized labor and capital and agriculture and industry, for veterans, for women's organizations, for American journalism and, by no means last, for the church. The friendly preponderance is overwhelming. I believe, Mr. President, that dynamic America is prepared to carry on.

Seventh. Whatever we are to do, Mr. President, let it be done without undue delay. Whatever our answer is to be, let it be made as swiftly as prudence will permit. The exposed frontiers of hazard move almost hourly to the west. Time is of the essence in this battle for peace, even as it is in the battles of a war. Nine months ago Czechoslovakia wanted to join Western Europe in this great enterprise for stability and peace. Remember that. Today Czechoslovakia joins only such enterprise as Moscow may direct.

There is only one voice left in the world, Mr. President, which is competent to hearten the determination of the other nations and other peoples in Western Europe to survive in their own choice of their own way of life. It is our voice. It is in part the Senate's voice. Surely we can all agree, whatever our shades of opinion, that the hour has struck for this voice to speak as soon as possible. I pray it speak for weal and not for woe.

The committee has rewritten the bill to consolidate the wisdom shed upon the problem from many sources. It is the final product of eight months of more intensive study by more devoted minds than I have ever known to concentrate upon any one objective in all my twenty years in Congress. It has its foes—some of whom compliment it by their transparent hatreds. But it has it friends—countless, prayerful friends not only at the hearthstones of America, but under many other flags. It is a plan for peace, stability, and freedom. As such, it involves the clear self-interest of the United States. It can be the turning point in history for a hundred years to come. If it fails, we have done our final best. If it succeeds, our children and our children's children will call us blessed. May God grant His benediction upon the ultimate event.

# PHILOSOPHY AND UNITED STATES
# FOREIGN POLICY [6]

## WALTER LIPPMANN [7]

Mr. Walter Lippmann gave this address at the College of William and Mary on December 5, 1947, before a Phi Beta Kappa group. The occasion was the celebration of the hundred and seventy-first anniversary of the creation and establishment of that organization. The celebration was held by the Alpha Chapter of the College, with a dinner and public meeting. New members were initiated; Mr. Lippmann's address followed.

Most addresses related to America's international policy proceed by analyzing specific problems and remedies. This speaker attempts to suggest a more catholic approach by formulation and examination of the underlying political philosophy. Superior speakers either state or imply basic assumptions behind whatever problem they discuss. Mr. Lippmann, in the role of historian and philosopher, has undertaken to describe such frame of reference.

His exposition has the merit not only of mature thought but of comparatively simple and direct expression. His style is that of the journalist whose daily syndicated column, "Today and Tomorrow," is published in almost two hundred newspapers. To clarify his philosophy, the speaker illustrated how it can be concretely applied to the Russian situation.

As of December 1947, Mr. Lippmann (as his daily column repeated) insisted upon (1) the United States' building up and maintaining an operational striking force capable "of delivering a sustained assault at long range"; (2) the passage of the Marshall Plan; (3) the strengthening of America's support of Italy against communistic domination; (4) the support of Italian claims to the trusteeship of the African colonies that were Italian before Mussolini; (5) the putting of Ruhr resources under an international statute; (6) a "positive rejection of the partition of Germany" and of a separate peace with Western Germany; (7) an attempt to secure a German government "which speaks for the whole of Germany"; (8) "a declaration that we regard all the European nations as members of one indivisible political and economic community." [8]

[6] *Congressional Record.* 80th Congress, 2d session. 93:A5203-4. December 18, 1947 (daily edition). Text and permission to reprint furnished through the courtesy of Mr. Lippmann.
[7] For biographical sketch see Appendix.
[8] *Des Moines Register.* December 6, 1947.

To what extent were these proposals of December 1947 actually carried out? The history of American-Russian relations since the Lippmann talk affords an interesting commentary on his point of view and the shift of events which realized only part of his program.

Mr. Lippmann continues to speak intermittently; he avoids radio broadcasting. He is nevertheless interesting and persuasive before an audience, even as he is one of the top columnists.[9]

I must suppose that it has occurred to many of you, as you looked at your program and saw the title of my address, that anyone who proposes to discuss philosophy and the foreign policy of the United States has chosen a rather wide and double-barreled subject. But I have been studying a list of the subjects which were debated here at William and Mary by the founding members of our society, and I find that tradition and historic precedents are with me. Phi Beta Kappa never shrank from the discussion of big subjects, or from questions on which the speaker of the day must not have been able to say the last word.

Thus, I find in Dr. Voorhees' *History of Phi Beta Kappa* that on April 22, 1780 the subject was: "Had William the Norman the right to invade England?" On May 21 the subject was: "Whether the execution of Charles the First was justifiable." On June 17 our revered founders had a debate on "Whether the rape of the Sabine women was just." On August 27 they asked themselves "Whether all our affections and principles are not in some manner deducible from self-love." And on September 12 "Whether polygamy is a dictate of nature or not."

So I feel I am in good company, and I may say that in coupling philosophy with the foreign policy of the United States, I did not mean to tease you or to mystify you. For if, as our society insists, philosophy is the guide to life, then in philosophy we ought to find the guide to the great difficulty which the American people have experienced—particularly in the past forty years—in forming a good and workable foreign policy. I have come to think that the root of our difficulty is to be found in our philosophy. And that is what I should like to talk about this evening.

[9] For further comment on Lippmann as a public speaker, and for examples of his speeches, see *Representative American Speeches: 1940-1941.* p292-309; *1943-1944.* p248-53; *1946-1947.* p103-11.

If we study the history of American foreign relations during the past forty years, we must be struck by an extraordinary paradox. During this period the United States has emerged from its long isolation. It has become one of the leading powers of the world. Not once but twice during this period the American people have had to face the awful issues of war and peace. Can it be said that during this momentous period we have ever succeeded in forming and agreeing on a foreign policy which foresaw correctly and enabled us to deal successfully with the actual course of events? The record is, I think, clear. We have won both wars. But on the crucial issues our diplomacy has thus far always miscarried. It has been unable to prevent war. It has been unable to avoid war. It has not prepared us for war. It has not been able to settle the wars when they have been fought and won.

At no critical phase in this epoch has the actual outcome conformed with our declarations and our expectations. Never has the country been able to achieve any of the principal objectives to which again and again it has been so solemnly and fervently committed.

Thus from 1914 to 1917 the country believed and hoped that it could avoid participation in the First World War. Yet it was compelled to participate. And when it did participate, it was unprepared because it had believed that it would not have to participate. During that war the country hoped and believed that by a victory it would achieve a lasting and democratic peace. The victory was attained. But the peace which had been promised was not achieved. After the First World War the country again decided to believe that if there were another war, it would be able to remain out of it. Again it did not prepare for war. Once again, it was unable to remain out of the war, when it came.

During the Second World War the country again decided to believe that with victory over the Germans there would begin an era in which all the victorious powers would agree and be harmonious and become unanimous on the terms and conditions of a just and durable peace. We have had the victory. But we have not been able to attain that peace.

Now, after two victorious world wars we find ourselves discussing the possibility of a third world war. And so we must ask ourselves whether we have become entangled in a degenerating cycle of wars that breed more wars, each more savage and more inconclusive than the last. It is a grim question. We must however face it, and I believe that we must answer it by saying that if our present estimates and calculations are no more correct than those on which we acted before, during and immediately after the first and the second world wars, then we shall be surprised and disappointed again. Once more we shall not know how to prevent war, nor how to prepare for it correctly, or how, assuming we win it, to make peace after it. And if a second world war leads to the third, if we cannot make a settlement of the war we have just won, what ground is there to suppose that we could settle a third world war so that it did not lead to a fourth?

Is it not true that in the twentieth century we have witnessed on the one hand the rise of the United States to preeminence among the nations, to a position of great leadership and immense responsibility in shaping the destiny of mankind? And on the other hand, is it not also true that the course of events during the American rise to preeminence is strewn with debris and wreckage of high and hopeful declarations of policy—Wilson's neutrality, Wilson's Fourteen Points, the Covenant of the League of Nations; with the Washington treaties of disarmament and the Kellogg Pact to outlaw war, with the Dawes plan, and the Young plan, and the Hoover moratorium to reconstruct the world after the First World War, with the Stimson doctrine to prevent aggression, with the Neutrality Act before the Second World War, with the quarantine speech of Franklin Roosevelt, and the Four Freedoms, and Mr. Hull's seventeen points, and the Atlantic Charter, and the Yalta declaration, and the so-called Truman Doctrine.

Must we not say that it would not have been necessary to improvise in rapid succession so many new plans and new formulae if any of them had worked out as, at the time they were announced, we hoped and believed they would?

When we reflect on this experience of repeated declarations and repeated disappointments, we must be struck by the contrast between our capacity as a people to develop national power and our ability to use it and to manage it successfully.

It is plain that our failures lie in the field of policy—that is to say, in deciding correctly when, where, how, and to what ends we shall exert the enormous power and influence which we are able to generate.

For it cannot be argued that the miscarriages of American diplomacy are due to the weakness of the American nation. Among the powers of the world the United States is the least vulnerable to invasion, to blockade or, with existing weapons, to decisive assault. The United States has the material resources, and it has the productive capacity to develop enormous offensive power in time of war. And in time of peace it produces a great export surplus—a surplus above and beyond a high standard of life at home—which renders it economically invulnerable in the outer world. Two great wars have proved the valor of American troops, the fortitude of the American people, and the military competence of American military commanders. Our institutions and our traditions are respected. And on the whole our participation in world affairs is welcomed by the great masses of mankind as promising liberty, justice, peace, and plenty.

It is, therefore, a reasonable conclusion, I submit, that we must seek the cause of our diplomatic failures in our own minds. We must look for the cause of trouble not in material circumstances but in our own habits of thought when we are dealing with foreign affairs and with the formation of American policy. Now, I believe that an inquiry will show—that in the period from Woodrow Wilson to President Truman our foreign policy has miscarried so regularly because there is interposed within our own minds, between the outer world and ourselves, a collection of stereotyped prejudices and sacred cows and wishful conceptions, which misrepresent the nature of things, which falsify our judgments of events, and which inhibit the formation of workable policies by which our available means can be devoted efficiently to realizable ends.

We have, I shall argue, brought along with us from our age of innocence, from the nineteenth century when we were isolated, and when we were sheltered from the rivalries of states and empires, an ideological picture of the world, a philosophical framework of preconceptions. We think this picture of the world is real and is noble. In fact it is imaginary and it is false. And because our philosophy of the nature of international life is imaginary and false, all our efforts to play an effective part in world affairs are frustrated.

What then is it in our philosophy which, instead of guiding us, misguides us continually? I think that the question can be answered. The point, as I have already indicated, where our declarations of policy have regularly miscarried is in avoiding war, in preparing for war, and in settling wars. We must ask ourselves whether there is here some common factor of error which confuses all of us on the issues of war and peace. I think there is. I think the error is a refusal to recognize, to admit, to take as the premise of our thinking, the fact that rivalry and strife and conflict among states, communities, and factions is the normal condition of mankind. The popular American philosophy of international life refuses to recognize this fact. It denies that in the world as it is the struggle for existence is fundamental and in the nature of things. This, I am convinced, is the philosophical error which prevents us from forming an effective foreign policy.

In the American ideology the struggle for existence, and the rivalry of nations for advantages, is held to be wrong, abnormal and transitory. Our foreign policy throughout this period has been dominated by the belief that the struggle does not exist, or that it can be avoided, or that it can be abolished. Because of this belief our aim has not been to regulate and to moderate and to compose the conflicts and the issues, to check and to balance the contending forces. Our aim has been either to abstain from the struggle, or to abolish the struggle immediately, or to conduct crusades against those nations who most actively continue the struggle.

Yet in the world as it actually is, the struggle is not abnormal, and it is perpetually renewed. Twice during this period we have sought to abstain from the struggle by declaring our neutrality. We have not been able to stay out of it. Twice we have conducted victorious crusades against the chief trouble-maker, believing what was soon disproved by events—that if he could be eliminated, we would then have eliminated all

troublemakers. Twice we have sought, by forming universal
societies like the League of Nations and the United Nations, to
abolish the struggle. They have not abolished the struggle. But
our efforts to use the universal society as if the struggle could
be abolished has wrecked the League of Nations and may yet
wreck the United Nations.

Our refusal to recognize the struggle for existence as the
normal state of mankind in international affairs has resulted in
the repeated miscarriage of American policies. Our efforts to
deal with events, as if they conformed or could be made to
conform with our ideological picture of what they ought to be,
has been rather like using a map of Utopia to find your way
around New York City.

The American refusal to recognize the struggle for existence
has in this century crystallized in a recognizable pattern of conduct—a neutrality which assumes that the struggle can be ignored
and avoided, in crusades that assume that by defeating the chief
troublemaker the struggle for existence will end, in the spon-
sorship of a universal society which assumes that the struggle
can be abolished.

Since 1914 American relations with the outer world have
oscillated among these three patterns of conduct. The great
debates within this country have turned upon them. But the
experience of these forty years shows conclusively, I think, that
if we insist on treating the conflict of states, communities, and
factions as abnormal, as exceptional, as transitory, we are unable
to form an efficient foreign policy. Our American ideology,
which we have brought over from a time when we did not have
to play a responsible part among the powers of the earth,
distorts our judgment when we deal with the problems of power.
It distorts our judgment when we determine our aims. It distorts our judgment when we have to calculate how a balance
can be struck between our aims and our power to realize them.

Yet in practical judgments—and diplomacy, when the stakes
are life and death, calls for very practical judgments—the criteria
are always relative. For there is no such thing as absolute power.
Whatever the wealth, the power and the prestige of a nation
may be, its means are always limited. The problem of the maker
of policy is to select objectives that are limited—not the best that

could be desired but the best that can be realized without committing the whole power and the whole wealth and the very existence of the nation.

But if we examine the issues of foreign policy as they are presented to our people, we find an overwhelming disposition to regard the choices before us, not as relative but as absolute. We are disposed to think that the issue is either this or that, either all or nothing, either isolationism or globalism, either total peace or total war, either one world or no world, either disarmament or absolute weapons, either pious resolutions or atomic bombs, either nonintervention or a crusade, either democracy or tyranny, either the abolition of war or wars of annihilation, either disarmament or military supremacy, either appeasement or unconditional surrender, either nonresistance or a strategy of annihilation.

There is no place in this ideological pattern of the world for the adoption of limited ends or limited means, for the use of checks and balances among contending forces, for the demarcation of spheres of influence and of power and of interest, for accommodation and compromise and adjustment, for the stabilization of the status quo, for the restoration of an equilibrium. Yet this is the field of diplomacy. These are the substance and the matter of an efficient diplomacy.

Our ideologists, however, condemn it as power politics and as appeasement. They would exclude it, they would outlaw it, and they would excommunicate those who discuss it. They insist on treating the rivalry of nations as something that could not exist among right-thinking men. They will not regulate the rivalries because they hold that the rivalries ought not to exist. So they are left with our three patterns of policy—to ignore the rivalries by proclaiming our neutrality, or to deny the rivalry and to believe it will disappear if the nations are members of a universal society, or to conduct crusades of annihilation against the lions who do not wish to lie down with the lambs.

You will have been asking yourselves how what I have been saying bears upon the subject which preoccupies us all so anxiously and so profoundly—upon our relations with the Soviet Union, which is today our great rival in the world, with which we are now engaged in a worldwide diplomatic conflict. You are entitled to ask the question, and I must try briefly to answer it by indicating what a true philosophy of international life can do to guide us.

The beginning of wisdom on the Russian question is, I believe, to recognize the historic fact that the division between Eastern and Western Europe, the rivalry between Russia and the nations of the West, did not begin with Marx, Lenin, and Stalin nor would it end if the Soviet regime were overthrown or defeated. The cultural and ideological division of Europe is as old as the division of Christendom between Rome and Byzantium. The imperial rivalry with Russia and the nations of the West, in Europe, in the Danube Valley, in the Balkans, in the Middle East, and in the Far East did not begin with the Communists and will not end with communism. It has been one of the great fields of diplomacy under the czars as it is under the Communists. Rivalry with Russia is a new problem for the United States of America. But the British Foreign Office has been preoccupied with it for a hundred and fifty years. We had better make up our minds that we shall now be preoccupied with it for a very long time to come.

That being the case, we must give up the notion that the choice is between one world, in which the Russians are our partners, and two worlds in which we must annihilate the Russians or they must annihilate us. I do not believe that we must either marry the Russians or we must fight them, that we must have either a perfect peace or a total war. I believe that the best policy is to recognize that the rivalry will remain, and not to expect it to disappear, and not to think it could be abolished by the United Nations and not to think it could be abolished by a victorious war—and having recognized that the rivalry is a permanent fact to use our whole power and influence to regulate it, to keep it within bounds, to establish spheres of influence which limit the rivalry, and a balance of power in the world which checks it.

I do not believe that we can settle the Russian problem once and for all. I do believe we have enough power and influence, if we use them efficiently, to bring about a settlement in this generation with Russia. But it will have to be a settlement which aims not at unanimity, not at ideological harmony, not at the abolition of all our differences and disagreements but at a truce in the cold war, a modus vivendi during which the nations can recover from the great war, at treaties which end in the withdrawal of the armies of occupation in Europe, and the restoration of Europe to the Europeans.

This will not be easy to achieve. It will require the pressure of power—which will offend those among us who do not like power politics. It will require political and economic compromises, which will offend those who regard all compromise as appeasement. But if a truce, and a modus vivendi, and a treaty are hard to achieve by power and by compromise, it is certain that without power on the one hand, and compromise on the other, nothing can be achieved.

If we will not or cannot use the classic procedure of diplomacy—which is always a combination of power and compromise—then the best we can look forward to is an era of disintegration in the civilized world, followed it may be by a war which once it began, would be savage, universal, and indecisive.

That must not happen. And it need not happen, if only our people will abjure their illusions about the nature of the world in which they have so recently become a leading power, and will permit and assist those who must form our policy, to go forward on the assumption that our aim is not to marry the Russians and then to live with them happily ever after, nor to fight them and let the whole world be devastated, but that our aim is to transact our necessary business with the Russians, at arm's length, coolly, shrewdly, without fear and without extravagant hope, and with as much justice as may be possible where there is as yet no agreement on first principles and where the rivals do not live in the same moral order.

# "NOT WAR, NOT PEACE" [10]

## JOHN FOSTER DULLES [11]

John Foster Dulles gave this speech before the Foreign Policy Association of New York at a luncheon at the Waldorf Astoria, on January 17, 1948. The address was also broadcast later that night over the Columbia Broadcasting System network.

Mr. Dulles had shortly before returned from the London meeting at which the Council of Foreign Ministers had failed to agree over peace treaties for Austria and Germany.[12]

Was Mr. Dulles historically accurate when he stated that for three years the United States had explored the way of peace "and that they [Soviet leaders] chose to call us enemy, not friend"?

The differences between Russia and the United States steadily developed after the Yalta Conference, February 4-12, 1945. There, the Big Three agreed on principles of peace and underwrote the United Nations. At the Potsdam Conference, July 17-August 6, 1945, there was talk—but not much else. In the Conference of Foreign Ministers in London, September 11-October 12, 1945, Russia blocked almost every effort toward framing peace treaties. (See Secretary of State Byrnes's speech of October 5, 1945, in which he indicted the Soviets as responsible for the lack of progress). In December 1945, another meeting of the Big Four was held in Moscow—to no avail. The meeting of the United Nations First Assembly, in London, January 10-February 15, 1946, further widened the breach. Almost every constructive proposal by Britain and the United States was stymied by the Soviets.[13]

The areas of friction included (1) Manchuria—Russian forces were still there, despite promises to leave, and were removing that country's industrial plants; (2) Iran—Russia announced that she would remain in Azerbaijan Province, Iran, despite the Big Three agreement for evacuation; (3) Central and Southeastern Europe—here Russia backed the Yugoslav demand for Trieste; refused to allow free elections in Bulgaria; demanded large reparations from Italy; blocked any satisfactory unified administration in Germany; promoted Communist penetration in France; dominated Poland, Rumania, and other countries behind the "iron curtain."

---

[10] By permission of Mr. John Foster Dulles. Text furnished by the author. See also *Vital Speeches*. 14:270-3. February 15, 1948.

[11] For biographical note see Appendix.

[12] See George C. Marshall's "Collapse of the London Big Four Conference," p15-23.

[13] See *Representative American Speeches: 1945-1946.* p45-60.

In February 1946, the United States began to take what was designated as a "firm American attitude toward Russia." In March 1946, the Security Council, meeting at Hunter College, supported the British and American view that Russia should get out of Iran. Gromyko left the conference for thirteen days, but the Soviets withdrew their forces and pressure in that oil-rich region. In April a Big Four Conference was held in Paris to write treaties—but without result. In June a deadlock developed in the United Nations over the problem of atomic energy control. Mr. Baruch proposed the United States offer to surrender the bomb under a system of international control not subject to big-power veto. Mr. Gromyko objected.[14] In September Henry Wallace delivered a speech criticizing Truman's strong stand against Russia and resigned on September 20, 1946.[15] In December 1946, the Foreign Ministers completed four minor peace treaties and, as the year ended, American hopes revived that the relations of Russia and United States might improve.

Early in 1947, however, optimism faded. In China, Communists were fighting the Nationalists. In Eastern Europe the Communist governments were consolidated through seizure of power. Russia was bringing pressure against Greece and Turkey. George C. Marshall became Secretary of State. In May 1947, the bill giving military aid to Greece and Turkey ($400 billion) passed Congress. The legislation was generally interpreted as representing a sharp break with Russia, a warning to her that the United States would resist further penetration in the Mediterranean.[16]

In March-April 1947, the Big Four met at Moscow and attempted to make a peace treaty for Germany. That session, like the previous one, failed. Secretary of State Marshall warned Russia that this country and Great Britain would dicker no longer and that henceforth we would build up a separate British-American Germany.[17] Mr. Dulles attended the conference and on April 29, 1947, gave a frank indictment of the Russian policy in Germany.

Then came Marshall's speech at Harvard on June 5—and the inception of the Marshall Plan. The European nations organized a Committee of European Economic Cooperation to "draw up a blueprint for reconstruction." Sixteen nations accepted the invitation to cooperate; at least eight rejected it. The Committee constructed a report outlining needs and estimating the five-year cost. When the General Assembly met in New York in September 1947, Andrei Vishinsky and other Soviets poured fourth bitter denunciations of "warmongering." The Americans replied.

In October the nine-nation Cominform was organized—officially announced as aiming to block the Marshall Plan. In both France and Italy came general strikes, Communist-inspired. Finally the London

[14] See *Representative American Speeches:1945-1946.* p120-31.
[15] See *Representative American Speeches: 1946-1947.* p33-42.
[16] For speeches on this topic by Truman, Vandenberg, and Pepper, see *Representative American Speeches: 1946-1947.* p43-89.
[17] See *Representative American Speeches:* 1946-1947. p89-102

Conference on treaties for Austria and Germany broke down. In December the French Communists were compelled to back down. President Truman submitted his $17 billion European Recovery Program to Congress.

Such was the state of affairs in the Soviet-United States controversy when John Foster Dulles spoke before the Foreign Policy Association.

Dulles has been prominently mentioned as a potential Secretary of State should the Republicans take office in January 1949.

He is no Churchillian orator, but has a high degree of platform competence. In his public discussions on international affairs he speaks with authority and the weight of much experience, information, and wise judgment.

The fifth session of the Council of Foreign Ministers ended a first phase of peacemaking. Across the Channel, Communists, under directions from Moscow, were making all-out efforts to sabotage French recovery. They lumped together the opposition parties as the "American Party," using the term as one of insult. Across the table, Mr. Molotov, facing Mr. Marshall, charged him with plotting to use Germany as a base for aggression. All who were present sensed the drama of the moment. Soviet policy, at the end of World War II, was that expressed by the Soviet slogan which emerged out of World War I, "Not war, not peace."

For nearly three years the United States had explored the way of peace. I myself have attended seven international conferences involving negotiations with the Soviet Union. I can testify, without reserve, that we had earnestly sought peace and had, indeed, expected it. We assumed the Soviet leaders would want to preserve the friendship which had developed when our peoples were comrades in arms. But that assumption proved wrong. Other motives were more potent.

The difficulty we encountered is that in Russia the members of the Communist Party believe fanatically that capitalistic nations are inherently imperialistic, aggressive and unfriendly. It is true that Stalin has occasionally said, for foreign consumption, that capitalistic and communistic societies could exist side by side in peace. But in Russia for thirty years the contrary has been taught. So Soviet leaders would find it very embarrassing today to treat America as Russia's friend.

Another difficulty is that if the United States were treated as a friend, that would cut the ground from under the despotic power of Soviet leaders. The Communist theory is that dictatorship will wither away as enemies disappear. So, in Russia, when men ask why dictatorship is so prolonged, they are told that the Soviet Union still has aggressive and powerful enemies. Today, only the United States is adequate to be a frightening enemy.

Also, competition with the United States seemed likely to pay big dividends in terms of increased Soviet power. The end of the Second World War left a vacuum. The Axis armies had overrun most of Europe and much of Asia and Africa. In the process, Great Britain, France and China had been gravely weakened. So, when Germany, Italy and Japan themselves collapsed, the United States and the Soviet Union were the only countries from which new power could flow. Of these two, only the Soviet Union was instantly ready. Its dynamic leaders knew what they wanted and they had a program for getting it. The United States seemed no obstacle. It apparently had no program beyond unconditional surrender, then relax.

So, when World War II came to its end, and Soviet leaders had to choose, they chose to call us enemy, not friend. We all know the fact, but we need also to know the reason why. Then we shall not be misled by those who say that friendship easily could be won. I do not say that our own policies and actions have in all respects been perfect. I do say that the causes of the present situation are not superficial, but profound and that those causes are predominantly to be found in the nature of Soviet dictatorship and the underlying philosophy of communism.

Though Soviet leaders chose "not peace," also it seems they choose "not war." In so doing, they hold to what has been basic Soviet foreign policy for thirty years.

It is not easy for American people to understand a policy of "not peace, not war." We think in terms of either peace or war. If there is not peace, then we think there is, or will be, war. But Soviet thinking is less simple. We need to understand it or else our own reactions may be misdirected.

I have repeatedly said that in my opinion Soviet leadership does not want to risk a major war. Nothing that has happened leads me to change that opinion. I do not hold it because of what Soviet leaders say. They would use any means which, they thought, would serve their ends. I rely on facts, not words.

The ultimate political fact in the Soviet Union is the supreme authority of the Soviet Communist Party. As Stalin has said: "Not a single important political question is decided by our Soviet without guiding directions from the Party." That fact has very important consequences, for the State and the Party have distinctive goals, and they have different instruments for getting to those goals.

The Soviet State has nationalistic goals. They reflect the fears and the ambitions of the Czars. As instruments of policy the State possesses great land armies, powerful for defense, but which, on the offense, do not have worldwide scope. The Soviet State lacks superiority in long-range weapons of sea and air.

The Party, on the other hand, has an international rather than a national outlook. It sees itself as the vanguard of the proletariat everywhere. It has the task of liquidating non-Communist governments wherever they may be found. But war has never been the preferred instrument of its policy. It has its own specialized weapons. It has developed, to a high degree, the techniques of propaganda and penetration, of smear and strike and sabotage. Its schools turn out agitators trained as specialists to operate in each capitalistic society. In this field they are supreme.

There are, of course, times when the Soviet Communist Party relies primarily on the State and its army. That was the case during the late World War and its immediate prelude and aftermath. By now, however, most of Russia's historic goals have been achieved. Some remain and may cause us concern. But the big, unattained goals are those of the Soviet Communist Party. These are far-flung goals and to achieve them the Party has means far superior to those of war.

In a duel where the Soviet has the choice of weapons, it will, of course, choose those in which it is superior. That is the more sure because only those weapons will enable it to reach its global ends. So if present Soviet policy is "not peace," equally it is "not war."

What should the United States policy be in the light of what Soviet policy is?

First of all, we can say without hesitation that United States policy will also be a policy of "not war." It is unthinkable that the United States should initiate a so-called "preventive" war. That is contrary to the nature of our democracy. Also, such a war would not, in fact, defend our free institutions. It would expose them to the utmost peril.

We can go further. If Soviet policy is a policy of "not war" then the United States should not itself assume that war is inevitable or even likely. Of course there is always some risk of war. Today that risk may be somewhat more than normal because "not peace" is a dangerous policy even if "not war" is also sought. It assumes that the other fellow has great self-control.

We need a strong military establishment and a backlog of citizenry with some rudiments of training, respect for discipline and recognition that continuing freedom calls for continuing sacrifice. But unless our self-control gives way and we ourselves increase the risk of war, the present risk is not great. Certainly it is not great enough to dominate our thinking when another risk is greater.

We are just emerging from a shooting war during which the President was in a literal sense the Commander-in-Chief and when all decisions had to be dominated by military considerations. Now we seem to be betwixt and between. There is not yet peace in the usual sense. In many areas, notably areas of occupation, there are compelling practical reasons why our army must be asked to play an important role. We have not civilian personnel adequate to do all that needs to be done. Also, Soviet propaganda constantly talks of war. That may be a plausible decoy. It may mislead us into concentrating on a threat which is not real and expose us to the damning charge that we are planning the war which all men dread.

Whatever be the Soviet purpose, their talk and gestures, combined with other causes, confuse us. Some think priority should still be given to military factors. Our government needs to make a choice and make it promptly, for we cannot afford divided counsel. The correct course seems clear. The first task is to win the struggle that is, not that which might be. The struggle that is, is a struggle to be fought with food and fuel and with creative ideas and lofty ideals. It is a desperate struggle and the outcome is doubtful. Therefore, we should use the tested peacetime way which, for generations, has made our nation supremely productive, both materially and spiritually. Military factors are not to be ignored, but in accordance with American tradition, let the military be an instrument of national policy, not itself the maker of that policy. That set-up will give us the best chance of winning the peace for which we yearn.

Peace requires that the free societies be so healthy that they will repel Communist penetration just as a healthy body repels malignant germs. That is the only way to prevent Communist dictatorships from so spreading that they will isolate us and eventually strangle us.

How can that need be met? A rich nation, like a rich man, is apt to think first that its money can save it. Speaking a year ago today, I said that no nation is so poor as a nation that has only dollars to give. We would, of course, have to provide money and goods. But the essential, I said, is that out of the physical vigor of our people and the intellectual stimulus of our free society should come the constructive ideas for which the whole world stands in wait.

During the last year such an idea was launched. It is, in essence, that the different nations of Europe should pool their economic resources to serve the welfare of them all. Secretary Marshall was the great spokesman for that idea, and it was at once endorsed by outstanding Republicans, as, for example, Governor Dewey and Senator Vandenberg. Sixteen nations of Europe have accepted the idea and have pledged themselves to make it real. From that beginning can come great results. I say "can come" for I dare not say "will come." I do not know, and I doubt that anyone can know. But the possibilities are there.

First are human beings. It is now clear that the people of Western Europe have not, in the main, been fooled by the Soviet propaganda which bombards them. They want to keep their own free institutions. They are prepared to struggle for them and will in fact, take big chances which are involved in that struggle if they have the food and fuel and clothing needed for physical and spiritual vigor and especially if they feel that a strong and loyal friend is standing at their side. Those of us who were in Europe this winter sensed, in the people, a new spirit.

Then, too, there are economic possibilities. These require that there be greater unity. Conditions today are unnecessarily bad. The nations of Western Europe are almost completely isolated from each other. Even internally, each of them is fragmentized. Farmers try to hold on to their produce unless they can immediately get goods in exchange. Few are interested in accumulating money when it is printed so fast that it seems to have little future value. So, barter takes the place of commerce, production lags and goods are withheld from consumption. These conditions automatically work for impoverishment. By changing them, there could be enrichment.

In Europe the leaders, public and private, see and say that Europe cannot be a vigorous and healthy economy without increased unity. I recalled to Prime Minister Attlee last month his earlier statement that "Europe must federate or perish," and he said he still believed that. President Auriol of France only last week said "Europe must unite itself if she wishes to recover and live." But also European leaders say that day-to-day problems are so urgent that it is very difficult for their governments to devise and carry through long-range projects. So, little has been done, and probably little will be done unless the United States supplies strong inducement and vigorous leadership.

We have the means for doing that. Thanks to labor, management and capital we have a productivity out of which we can provide powerful inducements. The point is that we should not allow our aid merely to subsidize what is, but use it as a lever to open up new productivity which excessive nationalism now represses.

In Germany we have a unique opportunity for leadership. There we ourselves are a Western European government. We can exercise a decisive influence in the Ruhr area which is the natural economic heart of Europe. If there is to be economic unity in Europe, that is the place to begin and it is a place where it lies within our power to begin. So far, however, German conditions conspicuously illustrate what ought not to be.

The Marshall Idea, if adopted and put to work, will have a great tonic effect. It will revive hope and increase physical vigor to sustain it. It can lead the way to increased unity. Also, of course, it will cost us something. No one can say how much.

Also, no results are guaranteed. It is not possible, even with 17 billion dollars, to buy peace. We shall have to make sustained, intelligent and friendly efforts, backed by money and goods. We shall have to pay in instalments, in amounts and over times that are unpredictable. In France, I saw Soviet sabotage destroy many economic calculations. Also, I saw a free people win a great victory and teach a lesson which will lighten everywhere the burden on free men. No one can foresee what the weather will be or what crops will be. No one can measure what new effort men will make when they are inspired by new hope or invigorated by a new economic climate. Thus there are bound to be great uncertainties. But there can be some certainties.

We can with certainty pick our goal.

We can know that that goal is one which can be reached.

We can know that it will be a major disaster if we do not reach that goal.

That much certainty is enough for our resolve. I do not ignore the necessity for diagnosis and planning and finding the effective, businesslike way to use available resources. But the resolve must be primary, the means secondary. If our resolution is clear, to ourselves and others, we will, I prophesy, achieve our goal more rapidly and more cheaply than could be calculated in advance.

Europe, of course, is not the only area where effort need be made. One idea is not enough. In the Far East, in Latin America, in Africa, and of course here at home, there are vast possibilities for creative action and opportunities to prove the worth of a free society. These opportunities we need to seize.

Acts will be decisive in this second phase of peacemaking on which we enter. No doubt there will be negotiations, through diplomatic channels, at special conferences and at the United Nations. It is important that talking relations should be preserved and there are still some areas where useful agreements can be made. But, for a time, deeds will carry more weight than words. As Secretary Marshall pointed out on his return from London, the free societies of the West must show that they have enough vigor to establish in fact an equilibrium with the East. It must be proved that Soviet leaders cannot indefinitely expand their power by trick devices of minority penetration and sabotage.

Once it is apparent that such means fail, they will be abandoned. Then a third phase of peacemaking can begin.

That third phase will not mark the end of struggle. But the struggle may then be at a more normal level, consistent with friendly intercourse. Proletariat dictatorship and Western democracy will probably still compete. But the tempo of that competition may be slowed down. It may take the form of each trying to show that it is better able to meet human needs. Such a state of affairs could be good for us and for the world. The Western powers have, perhaps, held unchallenged supremacy longer than was healthy. Competition is good, provided its methods are decent and tolerable. A competitive peace can be better than any we have known in modern times.

I do not predict that we will quickly, or even surely, get through to this happier new phase. There may be other intermediate phases that we know not of. But the known obstacle to peace is the confident belief of the Soviet Communist Party that their weapons of propaganda, penetration and sabotage will prevail. That obstacle must be cleared away. We must show that the free societies can generate forces for construction which will render impotent these Soviet methods of destruction.

As we have seen, that will be no easy task. Much depends on other people who, however, seem to be dependable. Much also depends on us. We must plan and act on a grand scale. We must do mighty deeds such as are usually inspired only by war itself. We must do that without generating a warlike spirit or striking a military posture which will, itself, make war more likely.

Men have never looked on peace as something that needs to be waged, as they wage war. War has had a near monopoly of moral fervor and the determination and courage and sacrifice it produces. It is that discrepancy in favor of war which must be changed. The world will never have lasting peace so long as men reserve for war the finest human qualities. Peace, no less than war, requires idealism and self-sacrifice and a righteous and dynamic faith. So it is that as we judge the Marshall Plan, so, too, that plan is judging us. The moral quality of our response, more than any ingredient of the plan, will determine whether this time we win the peace.

# ATOMIC ENERGY

## ATOMIC ENERGY—WHERE DO WE STAND TODAY? [1]

### DAVID E. LILIENTHAL [2]

David E. Lilienthal, chairman of the United States Atomic Energy Commission, gave this address before about 450 members of the Radio Executives Club, in the Grand Ballroom, Hotel Roosevelt, New York, on Thursday, February 5, 1948, at 1:30 P.M. The speech was broadcast on WNBC and WNYC, and was televised by NBC's station WNBT.

The address has structural and logical unity and progression—the student of speeches is advised to outline it. It states the thesis clearly and repeatedly—note the statement in the final paragraph but one. It adjusts to the immediate audience. It inserts illustrations and analysis to press home the point. The critical analyst will note other elements of good speech composition.

The Atomic Energy Commission, confirmed by a Senate vote on April 9, 1947, for the following year, was recommended in April 1948 for a five-year reappointment. The Senate struggle of 1947 over such appointments threatened to be repeated. Senator Taft, on April 24, announced that he would again oppose the appointment of Mr. Lilienthal. [3] In June the Senate extended for two years the terms of the members of this Commission.

The topic I have chosen to discuss, "Atomic Energy—Where Do We Stand Today?" may give you the impression that I intend to tell you how many atomic bombs this country has, and where they are; or the progress in use of atomic energy for the treatment of disease; or how the new super-cyclotron has split and shattered the nucleus of such a common substance as lead.

But I have something quite different in mind. I shall talk with you chiefly about people. For people are the most im-

[1] Text and permission to reprint supplied by the United States Atomic Energy Commission, Washington 25, D. C.
[2] For biographical note see Appendix.
[3] For addresses and background information, and for further comment on David Lilienthal as a speaker, see *Representative American Speeches: 1946-47.* p113-43, 150-2.

portant fact about atomic energy. What goes on in people's minds—and in their hearts—is even more important in determining the fateful future than what goes on in atomic energy laboratories and vast production centers.

The theme of what I shall say to you is this: The people must know; the people as a whole must come to understand the essentials of this new world into the outer reaches of which science has brought us so suddenly. We must not, we dare not, enter upon this new era of human life if the very facts that set our time off from any that preceded it are, in their essentials, not widely known. For men generally to be in the dark as to the nature of the fundamental structure and forces of the atom— and of the evil and the great good this knowledge can bring— would be for us to live in a world in which we are, in elementary knowledge, quite blind and unseeing. It would be almost as if we did not know that fire is hot, that water is wet; as if we did not know there are seasons and gravity and magnetism and electricity.

I am persuaded that the people are increasingly determined to find out, to learn about these things. Some of the obstructions in their path are being exposed as myths. For example the widely circulated piece of nonsense that atomic science in its entirety is a military secret is about exploded. The well-cultivated fiction that atomic energy is a bomb and nothing else, that it has no humanitarian and practical uses—this too is being understood for what it is, a bit of pure moonshine. The myth that the essentials are too technical, are "over people's heads" is giving way to the truth.

The mischievous notion that people are such utter dopes that they are not and cannot be made interested in the atom— though every cell of their bodies and everything they eat and touch is made up of atoms—this notion does persist, but it is taking a beating in those communities where the people are setting out to find out about what makes the physical world tick.

What is happening in the country, at the grass-roots, is an encouraging and heartening story. The people, in their home towns and neighborhoods, in their churches, and schools, in their service clubs and farm organizations and local professional societies, the people are on their way.

They have, it is true, made only a beginning, and there are difficulties to be overcome. Some of these difficulties in creating wider interest and understanding the radio industry (with the press, the periodicals and the films) could help mightily to overcome. You of the radio, if you are willing to pitch in with your great skill and your vast facilities—you can give a great and perhaps decisive impetus to this effort by the people to understand the atomic world.

I said that the important thing about atomic energy is people, what goes on in people's minds, how well the people understand the broad outlines of this "knowledge so new" to man that with it "he can become a new man." I do not mean any special kind of people—scientists or generals or public officials. By people I certainly do not mean leaders only. No, when I speak of what goes on in people's minds about atomic energy I simply mean people as they come, as you find them up and down the country, the people in the drug stores and art galleries and churches and bars and banks and union halls, the people who go to the ball games and horse shows, the people, in short, who listen by the tens of millions to the radio programs for which you are responsible.

For me to discuss people and what people think is appropriate before a radio industry audience. For people are your business, you who own and manage the radio industry, you who get in the revenue and direct the programs and analyze the news and do all the other things that have persuaded the families of this country to put in their homes more radio sets by far than there are in all the rest of the world put together. It is your business and your responsibility to know what it is that will hold the interest of millions upon millions of people, from hour to hour and day to day; and not only to entertain—a very important function indeed—but to inform, to stimulate and to inspire.

The energy within the atom has been released and put to use. This event, dreamed of, speculated about for centuries, has actually taken place, and on a large dramatic scale. Something has happened that has quite fundamentally changed the world. The river of time has abruptly altered its course. You and I and all men now alive have actually seen this happen. In the drama now unfolding there is no one—not a single one of us—who is a mere spectator, no one who is just listening in. There is no one who can turn a knob and tune himself out; no one who can just pick up and leave if he is bored, or horrified, or is more interested in his private affairs. You and I are all in this, we are all players, participants in that future chain of events that these epochal discoveries have set off. The world looks the same. Radio City and Fifth Avenue and all the familiar sights of our world look the same. But they are not the same. They are not the same, because of this culmination of new knowledge about Nature and matter and about force and destruction that we call "atomic energy."

Now I began by saying that it is of great importance what people in our country and elsewhere think about atomic energy. But it is wrong to assume, off hand, that this is self-evident. Actually, what difference does it make? What does it matter what the people think about this admittedly startling series of scientific discoveries about the fundamentals of life? In the case of other great discoveries and events, it didn't make a great deal of difference, one way or the other. It is a notorious fact that on very few occasions did people understand the significance of great events at the time they occurred, nor for a long time thereafter, for that matter.

There is a classic story about this very thing. Some forty-odd years ago there were two young fellows who ran a bicycle repair shop in Dayton, Ohio. Gadgets interested them. They read in the paper that a fellow by the name of Otto Lilienthal had broken his neck trying to fly by jumping off hills in a pair of wings. This gave the bicycle boys a harebrained idea. They thought that if they mounted a motor on a pair of wings they could make the darned thing fly. They took their contraption to the sand dunes of the North Carolina coast. One day their sister in Dayton got a telegram reading: "First sustained flight today. Fifty-nine seconds. Very happy. Home by Christmas. Signed Orville and Wilbur." She rushed to the local newspaper office with this great news. The next day in the Personals column there appeared the following headline:

## POPULAR LOCAL BICYCLE MERCHANTS
## EXPECTED HOME FOR HOLIDAYS

As I say, in the past other great changes have taken place and have not been well understood, most of them have not even been widely known, at the time. The voyage of Columbus marked a sharp turn in events, affecting every human life from that time forward. But apparently Columbus himself did not understand what he had found. The discovery of fire, the invention of the wheel, of gunpowder, of steam as a source of energy, Faraday's discovery of electro-magnetic induction (or electricity, as we say), the discovery by Hertz of radio wave propagation—what people thought about these events at the time was mighty little, and what they thought was largely wrong. Then why should we expect atomic energy to follow any different course? Why can't we go about our business and not fret about understanding atomic energy in its essentials, what with all the other things there are to understand—from just how a zipper works, or how to meet the crisis when it doesn't work, to the facts about the Marshall Plan? Isn't it enough if the scientists and engineers know what they are doing, and keep at it? As for the rest of mankind, well, suppose we do ignore the whole thing, or miss the point; suppose we do think that the real news is that those up-and-coming Wright boys will be home for Christmas, or that a new route to India has been found rather than a new world. If it didn't matter what people thought before what is there about this particular discovery that makes it different?

The answer is found in the circumstances that set off this discovery and its effects on human life from any that have gone before. The first and most important circumstance is *time*. There was no long time interval between the *discovery* of the controlled release of the fantastic energies within the atom, and the large-scale *application* of that knowledge. The very first atomic bomb, though just the beginning, became almost overnight the most successful and potent weapon of all time. It was almost as if the Wright brothers in their first attempt at Kitty Hawk had flown smack across the Atlantic Ocean, or as if Marconi instead of tinkering with a spark gap started off the first crack out of the box with a 1948 television network complete with coaxial cable links.

The second circumstance that sets the event of atomic energy off from all previous new beginnings by man is this: the very first application of this knowledge was in the form of a weapon, but a weapon so utterly revolutionary and devastating that it shook all existing ideas of warfare and international relations. Even before it had been improved—and on top of a mesa in the mountains of New Mexico we are improving it—the very first product at once affected the lives of every being on the globe, and almost every institution to which men have somehow adjusted themselves and grown accustomed, including the idea of nations, and of balance of power, and of how wars may be prevented, fought and begun.

There is a third circumstance about atomic energy that makes it different not only in degree but I rather think in kind, among the great ideas and events of history. Atomic energy presents the two-sidedness of knowledge—good and evil—in the most dramatic way possible. Indeed it may be said to symbolize the two-sidedness of knowledge, and the choice men must make. It is difficult to recall any discovery or any idea in all of mankind's history in which the choice between the beneficial uses of knowledge and the destructive uses of the same knowledge is presented on such a heroic scale, and with such unmistakable clarity.

The development of our knowledge of this fundamental force for the improvement of the lot of men everywhere holds out promise of benefits that stir the imagination. And these are not merely remote hopes. This same knowledge that has put a cloud of fear and uncertainty over the future, is the means of searching out some of life's most baffling secrets. In laboratories and hospitals quite near us today they are aiding dramatically in research that may uncover the cause of dread diseases and aid in their cure, and in the alleviation of human suffering. Benefits to the health of millions, increased food and better nutrition and vast new sources of energy—these we may look forward to with confidence as a consequence of knowledge of the atom. And it was this knowledge that made the Bomb.

Now of course almost all knowledge has such a two-sided aspect; all knowledge can be used for good or for evil. The closest modern parallel is probably radio itself. Radio has been used and is being used to develop and strengthen freedom, and all that is good and humane and creative. But radio was also used to inflame the minds and poison the hearts of the German people, and thereby to crush European civilization. \ Atomic energy, the new-found land of the atom, is beyond our ordinary human experience.| There is little now to which we who are laymen can immediately relate this extraordinary phenomenon. But given time—a generation or so—gradually to get used to the idea, we would come to understand it, and make good sense of it.

But we were not given time. We do not have time today. That is the crux of the matter. You recall the circumstances. Radio broadcasts around the globe told mankind that a single bomb had destroyed an entire city. That single bomb had the power of 40 million pounds of TNT. There followed a most remarkable horror build-up. The effect—though this was not the purpose—was to make the mysterious and the horrible even more mysterious and even more horrible. We were to be frightened into our salvation. We were told that we must have world government and have it at once—within a definite and implacable time schedule of a few years—or we were "goners." Our own special vulnerability to atomic warfare was told and retold in a way that was correct but fearsome in the extreme. Maps of the New York City were published showing in detail just what ghastly horrors would occur if an atomic bomb no more powerful than those already used was dropped in the Hudson River or above the Roosevelt Hotel—accounts that were scientifically correct, but harrowing. We were reminded that these bombs need not be dropped by air armadas, that could be intercepted, but might be smuggled in, in parts, or easily concealed in the cargo of a tramp steamer moving innocently up the Hudson or into the Golden Gate. Such bombs, we were told, could poison the air and all plant life, and used in numbers render areas of the earth uninhabitable for decades.

Nothing quite like the effect of this upon the human mind has happened before, in the case of a new idea or discovery; certainly not on such a scale. And the most important factor has been *time*. There has simply not been an adequate or decent interval of time between the advent of the discovery and its application in a manner that affects most of our institutions. Usually we've had a generation or even a century or two to adjust ourselves to the new and incomprehensible. This jump has been the biggest one we have ever been called upon to make, in our thinking. For example, after fifty years of continuous development the destructive power of explosives was about doubled. Atomic energy multiplied the power of the highest explosive previously known not by two times but by seventeen million times —and this occurred virtually overnight. Similarly as to the release of energies for peaceful uses. In the atomic furnace at Oak Ridge the energy we are releasing from the splitting of the fissionable atoms of a pound of uranium is greater than from the burning of a pound of coal, but greater by tens of millions of times.

These are all big jumps for the human mind to adjust to overnight.

And then to top all the difficulties, this new discovery comes at a time of bitterness and unhappiness in the world, and a state of international distrust such as has rarely existed before in time of peace. I certainly need not labor this fact. We shall need good steady judgment and cool heads in the coming years. Public thinking that is dominated by great fear, by fantasy, or by indifference to one of the central facts of our century provides a sorry foundation for the strains we may find it necessary to withstand, and the hard decisions and courses of action that may inhere in this extraordinary situation.

Anyone experienced in human affairs recognizes fear as a dangerous state of mind. To those who have given little thought to such matters, it might have seemed a good idea to scare the world into being good, or at least sensible. But fear is brother to panic. Fear is an unreliable ally, it can never be depended upon to produce good. One result of intense fear may be panic, but another is likely to be fantasy, a dream-world. For men can stand great fear only so long. The sturdier ones look around for something specific they can do to overcome the cause of their fear. But most people unable long to endure fear, turn to unreality. Things that are disturbing just don't exist. Other more pleasant objects are substituted. People who insist upon talking about unpleasant facts, and after a while facts of any kind, are condemned or avoided.

If not fear, then what? Our answer is: understanding, comprehension, knowledge. Now this is a big order. But it is by no means an impossible one. Even the fact that there is not as much time for understanding to develop among people generally, even this time factor does not present impossible difficulties. For we have today some offsetting advantages. Never before in man's whole history did we have at hand such magic to aid in the communication of ideas and of information: the radio and television; our newspapers and magazines, both now at a peak of quality, usefulness and reliability unequaled in our history; the motion pictures with their infinite potentialities; our amazing network of formal educational agencies—schools in every hamlet, colleges and universities by the thousands, with the greatest enrollment of men and women in higher education ever known; the churches, and lay churchmen's organizations; the thousands of local societies and service clubs and forums and libraries in every town and city. What forces for stimulating understanding we have in such as these!

The radio is a medium so new, so pervasive, so potentially helpful in this crisis that it is nothing less than providential that it should be ready at this hour when the world needs desperately to shorten the time necessary for the dissemination of knowledge and understanding. Here is this great instrument, manned by a corps of talent capable not only of entertaining and stimulating but of finding ways as yet undiscovered—but discoverable—of inspiring man's interest and aiding his comprehension of knowledge that holds our common destiny. The magnificent performance of radio during the war in promoting public understanding and individual action essential to the winning of that war shows clearly that the radio industry can do an heroic job in the public interest. Your industry is in a sense trustee of a natural resource—the broadcast frequencies. This, in the public mind, makes it all the more reasonable to expect and to demand that radio play an important part in the task of stimulating interest in and communicating facts about a subject so vital to all men everywhere.

You are the people by and large who decide just what it is your fellow countrymen will have a chance to learn over the air. The tens of millions of homes of this country can receive broadcasts about atomic energy only if you choose to transmit them—and this is quite a responsibility: it is not a responsibility that is remote and vague, and I'm not going to exhort you about it. But it is my duty simply to say to you that public knowledge and understanding of atomic energy involves your own security, your own profits, your own future. There is nothing remote or academic about this. This theme I have chosen to discuss with you is not sensational. No big headlines in it. It can't compete with colorful talk about "push-button warfare" or spies or crystal-ball stuff about atomic pie in the sky by and by. It is not a spectacular theme, and it is part of my job and that of my colleagues *not* to be spectacular.

But can the atom be made interesting? Many people think so—interesting and in many aspects deeply heartening and hopeful, and dramatic too. What is in people's minds today, about atomic energy is important. But what *may be in their minds next year* at this time, or two or three years hence, when tensions may have increased, when steady judgment may be essential, depends upon what we do in the meantime. What may be in people's minds a year or two hence depends largely on leadership in each community; it depends upon how successful the press, the radio and education generally will be in inspiring people to think about atomic energy, and to appreciate the force of the facts about it.

As people become more and more convinced that they must know about this new "critter," the atom, and what it holds for evil and for good, this is going to happen: people are going to become less patient with explanations that informing the public is not part of the business of radio or the press or the periodicals. This may be especially resented in the case of radio, since it is an industry that in this country makes use of a natural resource of the whole people. People will become particularly impatient— impatient is a weaker word than I think might be justified— they will be particularly impatient as more and more of them come to understand the following fact—at least I believe it to be a fact—*that the principal and perhaps the only solid hope for preventing the use of atomic energy for destruction on a scale that has not yet been disclosed is for peoples everywhere to come to understand the atomic world; and to understand thereby the opportunities that lie before us to put this knowledge to uses beneficent and humane.*

A vacuum of knowledge about the atom will be filled; of that we may be sure. As time goes on it may be filled by utter indifference. This would be tragic and disastrous for a people to whom some of our well-intentioned compatriots orate sweet-nothings about peace being had if we wish for it hard enough. Or that vacuum of lack of knowledge may be filled by deep un-reasoning fear and panic. The vacuum may be filled by fantasy, by illusions. Neither panic nor fantasy provides the basis for a world of peace and security. But whether the vacuum is filled by indifference, or panic or wishful nonsense—the vacuum of public knowledge *will be filled.*

If people have knowledge and understand they may or may not be happier as individuals. But the country will be safer. The peace of the world will be more secure. We will be less likely to be taken in by sweet talk, or scared by shadows, or stumble—or be pushed—without knowing what we are doing, into some desperate finality. An informed and understanding people will take the facts as they come, not reject them because some of them may not be pretty. We will, with familiarity with this subject, set out to live with the facts of life, begin to take them into our thinking, into our everyday vocabulary. We will then begin to form common-sense judgments, not only as in-dividuals, but as neighborhoods, as communities, as a people. There are no supermen, no all-wise to solve these problems for us. There is no substitute, no good substitute, for the common-sense judgment of a whole people.

# KING OF ENERGIES [4]

## WILLIAM WESLEY WAYMACK [5]

W. W. Waymack, member of the United States Atomic Energy Commission, gave this commencement address at Montana State University, Missoula, at the fiftieth commencement, June 9, 1947. More than three hundred undergraduate and graduate degrees were granted. The honorary degree of Doctor of Science was conferred on Robert C. Guthrie, Montana, 1929, "in recognition of his outstanding achievements in the field of electronics, and specifically, his contributions to the development of radar as a weapon of our armed services during World War II." President James A. McCain introduced the speaker.

The Senate, two months previously, had confirmed Mr. Waymack to the Commission. The speaker's prestige thus gave added significance to his remarks. The address indicates interesting audience adaptation, organizational skill, concrete treatment of the points. The speaker's long experience in newspaper work was reflected in the compositional effectiveness. Although on this occasion Waymack followed his manuscript, he has much ability in extemporization. [6]

Twelve months after Mr. Waymack spoke, the future of atomic energy control was still clouded. In January 1946, the United Nations General Assembly had set up an Atomic Energy Commission for the purpose of working out international control. After June 1946, the Commission held more than one hundred meetings. In March 1948, the Commission finally decided against further talks as futile.

The position of the United States was that atomic weapons should be outlawed *after* international controls and safeguards had been put into operation. The Soviet counterproposal was that atomic weapons should be prohibited and the American bombs destroyed *before* the establishment of any controls. Although most of the Commission supported the position of the United States, it finally became evident that no reconciliation of the different positions was possible at that time.

Meanwhile, under the United States Atomic Energy Commission, the stock-piling of bombs continued, as did further experimentation in the Far Pacific.

---

[4] Text and permission to reprint furnished through the courtesy of W. W. Waymack.
[5] For biographical note see Appendix.
[6] For further comment on Mr. Waymack, see *Representative American Speeches: 1939-1940.* p155-60.

I shall speak not as a public official but as a fellow American, a fellow denizen of the planet.

What I say will of course be determined by my own experiences, including observations, which condition my capacity to understand.

Either because they have broadened me, or perchance thickened, some of my more recent experiences, particularly two, have contributed a good deal to the firmness of my views, fortifying rather than altering them. The two that I have in mind, compressed within a year and a half, are an inter-allied mission to Greece which took me into the area and atmosphere of a great civilization of the past and my involvement in our national management of atomic energy, which I suspect to have some relation to the civilization of the future.

My uncertainty always, in a situation like this, as to whether one should talk to the graduating class, to the assembled faculty, to the trustees of the University, to the audience in general, or, ignoring all these, to the voters—that uncertainty I resolved by choosing the graduating class.

Finally, since I really do consider this a serious kind of occasion, and since all the evidence that I know about suggests that we are living in a rather serious time, I intend to be serious.

For that I do not feel it is necessary to apologize. This is hardly an occasion when you should want primarily to be entertained. You men and women of the graduating class are, I believe, as intelligent as you will ever be. I refer to you as men and women because not until long hence will you wistfully delight in calling yourselves boys and girls. All that you lack for judgment-forming now is not at all thinking capacity, but merely years filled with experiences. Years filled with experiences, unfortunately, can mean the formation of successive shells around your thinking capacity, your intelligence, rather than a sharpening and a freezing of that capacity.

If I have envy, as I suppose I do, for the energy reserves of youth, I also have respect for the brains of youth. I happen to be involved in an operation (it has been referred to as Operation Migraine) in which we of the top authority, the Commission, average fifty-one years, and have been identified as "Old Crocks."

We wince as we wonder how long it will be before someone complimentarily refers to us as "spry." We are deliberately building an organization of young men to enable us to deal with new problems of great complexity and of immeasurable importance to all our people. The average age of our dozen most responsible staff chiefs, including the general manager of America's whole vast atomic energy enterprise, is thirty-nine.

We are doing this, as I said, deliberately, because we think that young men can think. And I, for one, am well satisfied with at least that part of our approach.

I hope that will appear to be evidence that I am not flattering you and not consciously fooling myself when I ask you to follow me for a while, or intelligently to refuse to follow me as I go along, in an attempt to get at some fundamentals as to problems and as to answers in the world in which we live.

I intend to talk about people, of whom we here are a tiny part. But first I shall ask you to make with me a quick excursion into the physical universe, because I think that what we shall find there has some relevance. Man can hardly be dissociated from the universe.

First, let us look outward. We, thanks to our minds and to such products of our minds as giant telescopes, can do that, though we live altogether within incredibly thin layers—a few miles, up and down, on the surface of this little planet, a quite narrow range of radiation that to us means sight, a very narrow range of vibration that for us constitutes sound, a very narrow range of temperature beyond which, either way, is death. We can nevertheless look outward, using "look" in the figurative sense.

We discover (of course we do not literally see) first our little solar system, then the great galaxy of which it is a part, then the vast universe of galaxies. And in it all we see the process of aging and being born. We see also, taking our solar system as the most comprehensible example, symmetry, the appearance of design, law, balance of forces, unity. The more we learn the more there is unity, based on equilibrium of forces.

Let us turn now and look inward, into the atom, of which all matter, animate and inanimate, is made up. Only very recently have we been able to do that. And there, too, we discover order, symmetry, design, law, balance of opposite forces, unity. The more we learn the more there is of unity based on equilibrium of opposing forces.

Having finished that brief digression, which I regard merely as background, let us shift now to people. I say people instead of mankind, meaning the same thing, because I find it easier to recognize myself as part of people. What we are talking about is millions of humans much more like us, meeting here in Missoula today, than unlike us, billions of others who have preceded, possibly billions who will yet come.

Now please don't ever let leak to my top-flight scientific friends, least of all to Dr. Bacher, my colleague on the Commission, what I am now going to do. I am going to use some terms rather loosely. It takes temerity to do that. For often when I say "energy" I am told that I mean "force," and also vice versa. If I happen to say "energy" and that is correct, I sometimes learn through a very gentle and courteous process, that I am confusing two fundamental kinds of energy, kinetic and potential.

I count on you to be good fellows and keep the secret; and I count on you the more confidently to do that, inasmuch as I myself have heard quite a number of commencement addresses, and recall little that I heard in any of them.

The words that with perhaps reckless looseness I shall try to apply to people are words like "properties" and "constants." Scientists, seeking fuller understanding in the field of atomic energy, as in others, must have such knowledge. How does a substance behave under these conditions, and these, and these? What are the dependable basic facts about atoms (or the parts of atoms) of one element of another? What, therefore, is predictable? Exactly what is the degree of probability with respect to this happening or that? The degree of probability is quite vital. The first nuclear chain reaction, under the stands of Stagg Field at the University of Chicago, was a trumph of calculated probabilities. The atomic bomb also was.

Recognizing that people are not atoms, are there, with respect to people, properties, constants, degrees of probability that have any meaning?

All we can do is to look at the record, to see if we can discern the urges and aspirations that are deepest, that are never really relinquished, and that point the way. My own device for today, adopted as a method of doing this, is the device of making three different approaches in turn, with the idea that they will be found to merge in the end.

Let us take a look swiftly at the long record of people.

Primitive people, we know, lived in caves or elsewhere, in small tight clusters. The line of development from them until now is clear. Our next stage was the tribe or clan, beginning as a grouping of "families," involving more elaborate forms of custom and organization, but involving very small numbers and very small areas. Thence evolution was into the walled community, the city-state (our Babylons, our Thebeses, eventually our Athens and others). The city-states became city-ruled empires, illustrated by Rome. Then finally came the nation-state, combining cities, principalities and lesser units of various designation. The nation-states tended to become nation-dominated empires. A newer form is what could be called the federal state, of which the United States of America and the Union of Soviet Republics are in different ways examples, and of which the British Empire by a reverse process of "devolution" has become another example. And today, indeed, for the last thirty years, people have been at the stage of trying to organize worldwide.

In short, with all the reverses, explosions and disintegrations, the course of people's development has been resistlessly toward extending law and order over ever larger areas, over ever larger populations; and now it is recognized everywhere, regardless of all controversy over the "how" of it, that it has to be carried over the whole of our little planet.

Let us note that in the Middle Ages, in a time of fragmentation, the goal was still sought through church overlordship.

Let us note, too, that whatever the motives of the great conquerors, the Alexanders and Napoleons and even the Tojos and the Hitlers, they put their appeals on the basis of larger stabilities, which is a goal of people.

Also we must recognize that modern communications, steamship and railroads and airplanes and all—have only accelerated the trend along an already clear direction; they are not the cause.

And now, when organization of people has reached the stage
of great concentrations just short of world stability, the conflict
inherent in separation, the destructiveness of war, has become
more appalling.  Given the stage of organization and concentration of today, given the present development in the "industrial
age," war is inevitably "total."  Distinction between combatant
and noncombatant is inevitably gone.  War must be directed at
productive capacity.

War cannot longer be a test of strength between "champions,"
or between small armed forces, followed by a negotiated compromise peace; war has to be fought by whole peoples, to unconditional surrender, enforced by ruthless devastation.  The old
axiom that a defense is invariably found for every weapon of
offense has ceased to have meaning.  For, while "defenses" for
rifle, machine gun, tank and airplane certainly have been evolved,
the upward curve of destructiveness of war itself has become
almost vertical.  Many cities of Europe are rubble, and cities of
Japan are hardly even that.  The political institutions in defeated
countries and even in some of the victor countries are practically
rubble, too.  And there is the atomic bomb; there also is the
V-2 rocket.

This is merely to say that the pressure on *people* toward
"unity or else" is greater than ever.

My point is that progress for unity is a "constant" of people,
never permanently abandoned, a principle guiding evolution.

*But*—when unity is pursued directly, exclusively and in that
sense logically, it inevitably collapses.  The conquerors always
fail.  That is not because the principle is wrong but because something else is wanted, something equally indispensable.

Let us therefore, as our second approach, take another look
at the record, compressing very drastically.

Organizing into larger unities has been slow, difficult, accompanied by innumerable setbacks.  Even the most primitive people,
in the smallest organization, have had to be held together by
customs, taboos, divine sanctions, and what not else.  There was
resistance to *being held*.  Something even in the grunting savage
made him not want to be held.  When this began to be articulated in language nobody can say.  But certainly some thousands
of years ago it was being articulated in language very under-

standable today. People were always individuals as well as social creatures. People long ago translated the negative recoil from individual suppression into the affirmative Principle of Freedom. The Athenians were great expressers of it, but relatively late expressers of it. The Principle was defeated again and again, but it never died, and yesterday—I mean about a century and a half ago—it was reexpressed, and magnificently, in theory; it became the great dynamic of the Western world; and in America more dramatically than anywhere else, this Principle of Freedom became accommodated to the Principle of Unity and our Republic was on its way.

The Principle of Freedom therefore is also a "constant" among people. They *will not* surrender it. Not permanently.

But recognizing these things would be valueless unless we also recognized the fact that the Principles of Unity and of Freedom are opposites. If the pursuit of Unity directly and exclusively leads to tyranny, which will not be borne, the pursuit of Freedom, directly and exclusively, leads with perfect logic to Anarchy, which cannot be tolerated.

Just as in the physical universe, so in the relations of people to people, of you to me and of others to us, in the social order of an American village or in the social order of the world, Unity balanced by Freedom is the basic condition of stability. The nucleus of a stable atom is like that; the nucleus of a stable society, of people in the group, is like that.

But there is yet a third indispensable ingredient, essential to making a go of Unity limited by Freedom and Freedom limited by Unity. If we were to take another look at the record of people, making a third approach, we should discover that the third principle, the glue that holds the other two together when they are held together, is the Principle of Morality. The reaching out of people for justice, as at any stage they have comprehended justice, has been just as continuous, just as irrepressible, just as truly a "constant" as either of the other urges. People want to be just. They may argue or even slaughter each other because of differences as to what is justice. But people are preponderantly benevolent. They do not prefer to hurt their neighbors. The normal person approves fairness, wants other persons

to have justice, is willing to make some sacrifice personally to
that end. Put it to the test yourselves. You are people. You
are, I may add, mostly or all Europeans, conditioned somewhat
but not fundamentally altered by the especially favorable American environment. Do you recognize, within yourself, that Principle of Morality? If you do, do you assume that you are altogether peculiar?

Now I suggest to you, not because I think you doubt it but
because I think it profoundly important that you recognize why
you do not doubt it—I suggest to you that the system, the complex system which we call Democracy, is the only system that
takes account of all three of these Principles. Essentially the
American experiment is an attempt to maintain unity, with the
maximum of individual freedom, through the progressive real-
ization of justice for people. That is the practical meaning of
the great liberal philosophy, which we Americans did not invent, but which we have been trying to exemplify. The mechanisms of our "Democracy" are means for continuously doing it.

I repeat, with the emphasis of deep conviction, that it is not
enough to have faith in and to repeat the slogans of Democracy,
but that it is imperative to understand what the democratic faith
is and why it is valid.

I also want to say that even in placid times, about which you
can know little, each generation has to do its own capturing of
meanings, has to understand the fundamental values, has to make
the best of systems work. Forefathers cannot do that. The
necessity of understanding deeply, of seeing problems whole instead of piecemeal, of continuously and intelligently applying
the Principles of Unity, Freedom and Morality in the light of
new conditions and of new realizations of need, is even more
imperative in a time not of placidity but of dislocation and
change.

Your generation comes on in the midst—and apparently
midst means midst—of one of the great critical periods of
human experience. There cannot be and is not even the superficial illusion of placidity. This period began, or began to manifest itself, in 1914. Clearly since then a new world has been
in process of being born. Obviously the capacity of people to

make work the values and systems that mean so much is in test. It is a period of shock, change, adjustment, invention, unforeseeables.

And it is in such a period, complex and troubled indeed, that there has also come one of the greatest discoveries, one of the most portentous advances of knowledge, in the whole record of people.

Suddenly and altogether unexpectedly, as far as all but a very few of people were concerned, we have had to begin to face the fact of the tapping of atomic energy. If already we were moving into a New World, the contours of which were undiscernible, certainly this opens up vaguely outlined but vast possibilities. Already this great fact has had tremendous effects, as yet inadequately comprehended, from which other effects will flow, most of them unpredictable.

As a weapon, the release of nuclear energy by the splitting of atomic nuclei of uranium 235 and plutonium has altered all concepts of warfare. It is revolution in that field.

Already the potency of this weapon has radically affected the bases of international relationships. Because of it, the American Government has officially adopted and is pressing resolutely upon other governments proposals for permanent international control of atomic energy by measures which would invade "national sovereignty," including our own, far more drastically than we should otherwise conceivably have proposed. That is change, of an astounding order.

Already, in order to control this new thing in the interest of our national defense and security, and in the general interest of all our people on the side of peaceful developments, we have been forced to invent and to start to use new governmental mechanisms that superficially seem to fly in the face of many of our major articles of faith, but which actually represent an attempt to apply our basic ideas and values to a new force so great in its potentials that it could not otherwise be dealt with. Under the Atomic Energy Act of 1948 we have government monopoly in this field from raw materials to finished products, much of the operation surrounded by necessary secrecy, and with many stern departures from customary American practice all along the line.

That this raises problems, very difficult ones, of democratic capacity surely needs no emphasis.

What the release of atomic energy can do in the future is unquestionably enormous. It is important to distinguish between what has so far been accomplished and what is of the future. For instance, intercontinental push-button war, which contemplates combining the atomic explosive with improvements of long-range missiles, probably traveling at speeds beyond that of sound—this may be of the future, but it is not of the present.

Likewise, with respect to the use of atomic energy as "power" to propel ships or drive the machinery of huge factories—that also is not yet. No informed person, I think, doubts that this can come and will. When one reflects upon the magnitude of the energy that we call atomic, in comparison with the several forms of energy that we have made use of heretofore (the energy released by altering molecules) one's imagination is tried. The comparison can be put in any number of ways. This one will do. If all the atoms in a pound of uranium were split, the energy released would be greater than the energy released by "burning" a pound of coal—greater by three million times.

After the splitting or fission of the atom, the energy still untapped within that atom is 99.92 per cent of the whole.

Atomic energy as "power" will come; *but* the technical and engineering problems yet to be solved before large-scale power production is an economic reality is going to take years.

More important, I shall guess, than turning wheels with atomic energy will be the gains in appliable knowledge by use of the great new tool of research that our atomic energy program has given us. It is possible to produce in our atomic furnaces, and we are now producing, artificially radioactive tracer atoms in relatively large quantities and at a reduction in price of (in one typical case) from $1,000,000 to $50 a unit. These tracer atoms can easily be followed through many of the most mysterious processes of life.

Actually, radiation of various kinds can be introduced to selected parts of the body (into thyroid tissues, for instance) for that kind of treatment of some disease. There are curative possibilities; though again I stress that in this we also are at the beginning, and must not talk of miraculous cures of all forms of cancer "just around the corner."

Aside from any direct curative possibilities, what will (and I do not say "may") be learned in time about the fundamental processes of the living cell is bound to be of great value to human well-being.

But the easily produceable "tagged atoms," of many kinds for many uses, can be and already are beginning to be applied in fields almost as wide as the economic activities of man. I shall mention only one phase of it, the application to agriculture.

The whole livestock industry is obviously within the range. And all plant production, indeed the whole field of botany, from soil and soil needs to fertilizers and their efficiency, and beyond, is opened up to the researchers as in no other way it could be. In dozens of universities and laboratories the pursuit of such knowledge, potentially of enormous economic value, is already in progress. The same new tool is equally applicable to the more effective combating of plant blights, insect destroyers, and competitive vegetation—weeds. Finally, through the tool of study and analysis that we now have, that very fundamental process of all life, vegetable and animal, photosynthesis—a process by which green leaves, under the influence of the sun's radiation, create from water and air the carbohydrate compounds—may cease to be a secret. It is this process which provides nutrition for all animal life, including man. Some exciting progress already has been made in precisely this area of study.

And we are only in the beginning. If this is to be the atomic age, we have stepped through the door, that only.

The Congress of the United States has said:

The effective use of atomic energy for civilian purposes upon the social, economic and political structures of today cannot now be determined. . . . It is reasonable to anticipate, however, that tapping this new source of energy will cause profound changes in our present way of life.

We have of necessity embarked upon some of those dangers, without knowing what they will ultimately be, relying on adaptations of the democratic process to see that they are eventually good.

Our people could not possibly be ready for this. There cannot possibly be reality in the democratic process unless education of the people advances very fast indeed. If decisions are left to be made by others, if they are left to be made by guess or by uninformed prejudices and emotions, the risks seem to me appalling. Despite the efforts of the atomic scientists, who foresaw the tremendous educational need even before the mushroom of Hiroshima, despite the efforts of other groups, I think I see—and how could it be otherwise?—a very urgent need still. There is much of confusion, much, I fear, of fear, and some disturbing indicators of a tendency of people to retreat mentally from a subject which seems too difficult and too awesome for them to comprehend. I am concerned about the danger to democracy of the self-sealing mind, sealed in a defense reaction not to keep something in but to keep something out.

Nothing, I think we can safely say, is so terrifying as the Unknown—in other words, as Ignorance.

Primitive people built up grotesque superstitions to account for nature's hazards. It was in part a manifestation of the inner drive to find explanations, to answer the question "why." It was also practically always a retreat to fatalism. It exaggerated fear commonly, and translated it into paralysis.

It is knowledge and knowledge only that brings things within the possibility of sane appraisal.

It is possible, quite possible, for literate ordinary people to cut through the barriers of strange words, like isotope and neutron, and to understand the essentials of the physical discovery that has been made. It is possible for them to know what the content of the American Government's program for control of this energy internationally is and why it is that, and to comprehend also the nature and meaning and reasons for our own American law under which atomic energy is now being controlled and under which it is intended to nourish its development. This is *not* beyond *people*. If it were, democracy would be finished.

There are energies of bouncing molecules, with which we warm our houses, drive our cars, propel our airplanes.

There are the staggeringly greater energies within the atom, part of which we know how to release and use.

But King of Energies is that one with which these were released; it is the one by which we may command the others and not be commanded by them.

The energy of the human intelligence, adequately informed, is the reliance.

Let us remember that the new discovery was not an accident, not a miracle, not (except in terms of some accelerations) a response to war necessity. It was a natural and inevitable product of the conclusion that individual men have a right to think, to seek truth, and to communicate. That conclusion is the very essence of the liberal philosophy, of the democratic way. It is not, therefore, a new question, a new challenge, that the atomic age presents us, but a suddenly-appearing new form of the challenge that our basic American philosophy has always faced—are we worthy, in brains, in knowledge and in spirit, of the faith on which our institutions are founded?

Today, for you, is Commencement—in the true sense of a beginning, not an end.

It interests me to reflect that the event, if not the ceremony, is being widely shared, and not alone by other university graduating classes but by millions upon millions of people, be they aware of it or not, in every land of earth.

For all have moved into a world that they know not, rich in potential, adventurous in proportion, challenging to courage, great in demands upon knowledge.

Commencement—you, and I, and the others—it is a considerable company, I think.

# LABOR AND THE COST OF LIVING

## LEWIS CONTEMPT CASE [1]

### T. ALAN GOLDSBOROUGH [2]

Associate Justice T. Alan Goldsborough, of the United States District Court in the District of Columbia, gave this verdict of civil and criminal contempt against John L. Lewis and the United Mine Workers of America, in the District of Columbia court, on April 19, 1948. He held that the defendants had refused to obey a court order to end a strike.

In November 1946, when the government was operating the coal mines under wartime powers, Mr. Lewis proclaimed that the contract was canceled. The miners stopped work. The Government obtained a court injunction against the strike. Mr. Lewis defied the court order. Federal Judge Goldsborough found him guilty of contempt, fined him $10,000 and the union $3,500,000. In March 1947 the Supreme Court upheld the conviction under the Government's power to enjoin its own employees and fined Mr. Lewis $10,000 and the union $700,000.

In July 1947 the United Mine Workers and mine operators signed a contract to include a union welfare fund financed by operators' contributions of ten cents a ton on all coal mined. Three trustees were appointed (Lewis, one mineowner, and a "neutral") to work out details of the fund. On March 12, 1948, Mr. Lewis informed the miners that the contract had been "dishonored" by the operators' refusal to agree to pension plans. Three days later most of the miners began their "strike." Lewis rejected administration mediation offers.

On March 23 President Truman ordered federal intervention under the Taft-Hartley law, which would include hearings and a report, an eighty-day injunction against the strike, and finally, if no settlement occurred, a resumption of the strike.

On March 29 Lewis testified that the stoppage was voluntary and not a "strike" ordered by him. On April 3 the Federal Court ordered the United Mine Workers to send the miners back to work, issued an injunction against the stoppage, and directed the resumption of collective bargaining. The strike continued.

The UMW petitioned the Court to set aside the injunction; the Government petitioned the Federal Court to find Lewis and his union

[1] The text is from the *New York Times*. p20. April 20, 1948. Reprinted by permission of Justice T. Alan Goldsborough.
[2] For biographical note see Appendix.

guilty of contempt for defying the order to end the "strike." The unionist argument before the Court was that the work stoppage was a spontaneous action by individuals. Any interference with these individual rights would be a violation of the Thirteenth Amendment. The Government argument was that Mr. Lewis was using subterfuge in denying that he could be enjoined.

In the midst of this legal battle, on April 10, Senator Styles Bridges suddenly became the third member of the trusteeship to settle the issue of the fund. Speaker of the House Joseph Martin, of Massachusetts, was the go-between to call the trustees together and to get an agreement. He announced that an agreement had been reached whereby miners over sixty-two, employed for a suitable term of years, would be retired on $100 per month. Mr. Lewis straightway notified his miners to this effect. Later the strike was gradually ended.

On April 20 the Court passed sentence and fined Lewis $20,000 and the UMW $1,400,000.

The Federal Court decision in favor of the Government argument was based upon a definition of what constitutes a "strike" in this case. The judge also based his decision upon his interpretation of a union's responsibility as contrasted with an individual's freedom to quit work.

The issues, argument, and evidence in this trial made the case of considerable significance. Students of debate will find interest in reviewing Justice Goldsborough's decision.

Gentlemen, the matter before the Court this morning is the verdict of the Court on the contempt proceedings which were tried in this Court last week, and concluded, I believe, on Thursday morning.

This controversy arose upon the question of pensions to miners. The United Mine Workers of America and its president, Mr. Lewis, desired that the miners who had been employed for twenty years and were sixty years old should have a pension of $100 a month, regardless of whether or not they were presently employed.

The Court, of course, thinks that that was a worthy objective and if that was the matter before the Court it would receive very sympathetic consideration. But that is not the matter before the Court. The matter before the Court is whether or not the defendants refused to obey a lawful order of this Court.

Under an act passed in 1947 which is commonly known as the Taft-Hartley Act, the President, if he is advised that a cessation of work or a strike imperils the national health or safety, should appoint a board of inquiry; they shall pass upon the facts after investigation, make no recommendations and report the situation as they understand it, to him.

On March 23, I think, the President appointed such a board. The board reported to him on March 31 that a cessation of work in the bituminous mines was in process, or that the cessation of work in the bituminous mines which was then in process did imperil the national health and safety.

During the course of that inquiry one of the witnesses subpoenaed to testify before the board was the individual defendant, John L. Lewis, president of the United Mine Workers. He failed to comply with the subpoena and then an order was served on him which he obeyed, and his testimony was a part of the material which the Board of Inquiry had and upon which they based their conclusion.

On April 3, the President, acting under the provisions of the Taft-Hartley Act, directed the Attorney General to file a complaint for an injunction against the United Mines Workers prohibiting the strike, and on the evening of April 3 this Court issued a preliminary restraining order ordering that the strike cease until the merits of the controversy could be decided in the injunction proceedings.

In other words, in the simplest sort of language, they ordered that the status quo be resumed, that is, that the miners go back to work and that then the Court would ascertain, after full judicial investigation, whether or not the national health and safety was imperiled by the walkout. If it was not, the Court would allow the miners to stay out, or go out.

On the other hand, if it was, they would have to go back into the mines.

Now, of course, in order for an injunction to be effective there would have to be a strike. The United Mine Workers and their president claim that there was no strike. He defends on certain constitutional grounds, but claims that the miners left the mines entirely of their own volition and without any instructions from him, direct or indirect. Now, that is a matter which has to be sifted in this inquiry. Obviously, if as a matter of fact no strike was called, while the restraining order should have been obeyed, yet the penalty for its disobedience would very naturally be very slight; it would be very small.

On February 2 the president of the United Mine Workers wrote the following letter to all signatories to the National Bituminous Coal Wage Agreement of 1947. That agreement was made, as I remember it, early last fall.

The National Bituminous Coal Wage Agreement of 1947 required, among other things, the designation of a pension fund (out of the United Mine Workers of America Welfare and Retirement Fund) "to be used for providing for pensions, or annuities, for the members of the United Mines Workers of America, or their families or dependents and such other persons as may be properly included as beneficiaries thereunder."

On this date, seven months after the effective date of the agreement, your representative trustee, Mr. Ezra Van Horn of Cleveland, Ohio, continues (as he has consistently continued) to thwart the fulfillment of that contractual obligation. It now constitutes an outstanding unresolved dispute, national in scope and character, affecting the integrity of the contract and impeding its fulfillment.

Now, what follows is what the Court thinks is a very significant sentence:

The United Mine Workers of America, therefore, now advise you as a signatory to the agreement that it reserves the right at will to take any independent action necessary to the enforcement of the contract.

Signed, John L. Lewis, president, United Mine Workers of America.

On March 12 a letter was written to the officers and members of all the local unions in all bituminous districts in the United States, by Mr. Lewis, signed as trustee, United Mine Workers of America, Welfare and Retirement Fund, and also as president of the United Mines Workers of America. It is a long letter. The Court doesn't think it is necessary to read all the letter. But the following statement is made at its conclusion:

The winter is now gone. This office proposes to go forward in requiring the coal operators to honor their agreement. Your ears will soon be assailed by their outcries and wails of anguish. To relieve themselves, they need only to comply with the provisions of the agreement, which they solemnly executed in this office on July 8, 1947.

Please discuss this matter in your local unions so that our membership may be fully advised. You will later hear more from this office on this subject.

That letter, dated March 12, and which I suppose went out at that time, was received on March 13, maybe some time a little later, on the fourteenth, was followed immediately on the fifteenth, I think it was, by a walkout of some three hundred fifty to four hundred fifty thousand miners in the bituminous coal mines, 87 per cent of whom, according to testimony here, were members of the United Mine Workers union.

The preliminary restraining order was served on the United Mine Workers of America on April 5. On April 7, after waiting two days, the Government filed a petition for a rule to show cause why the United Mine Workers of America should not be held in contempt. On the same day the United Mines Workers of America filed a motion to dismiss the preliminary restraining order.

On last Monday, at ten o'clock—maybe five minutes to ten; approximately ten o'clock—the United Mine Workers of America filed their answer to the petition of the Government asking that they be held in contempt.

Now, the answer was based, practically speaking, on two grounds. The answer claims that the First, the Fifth, and the Thirteenth Amendments of the Constitution were violated by the issuance of the restraining order.

The First Amendment is an amendment which permits any expression of speech, that is, any legitimate expression of speech.

The Fifth Amendment provides for due process of law.

The Thirteenth Amendment prohibits involuntary servitude.

I presume the theory of the claim that the restraining order was in violation of the Fifth Amendment is that it was issued without a hearing, and it is evidently, or admittedly, claimed, although it was not argued, that it was mandatory in character, and therefore should not have been issued without a hearing.

It appears on the surface, and only on the surface, to be mandatory in character, that is, in the nature of a mandamus. Certainly a preliminary restraining order would have been legal if irreparable injury had been demonstrated by the petitioner, if it had been prayed for prior to the walkout.

It is an emergency legal measure and there is just as much reason for its issuance after the walkout as before. What it did was to state facts and attach affidavits which were sufficient to indicate that irreparable injury would happen to the country if the strike was allowed to continue, just as it would have said, if it had been issued prior to the strike, that irreparable injury would be the outcome if a walkout occurred.

So that as a matter of fact, legalistically speaking and practically speaking, it was simply an order to return to the status quo, return to the position that the parties were in until the Court could determine in the injunction proceedings whether or not the peace and security of the country were imperiled by the walkout.

So much for the objection on constitutional grounds as to the Fifth Amendment. As to the First Amendment, providing for liberty of speech, it has never been held by any court that an injunction to prevent a strike was a deprivation of the liberty of speech, nor has it ever been held, in so far as the Thirteenth Amendment is concerned, that an injunction preventing a strike constituted involuntary servitude, or an injunction which ordered a strike to cease, involved involuntary servitude.

But the defendants' contention is this: That the First and the Thirteenth Amendments were violated because, as a matter of fact, no strike was called, no strike existed. These men, it is contended, did, as individuals, what they had a right to do, work or not to work, and they decided not to work.

Now, we have to consider the validity of that claim objectively. If a nod or a wink or a code was used in place of the word "strike," there was just as much a strike called as if the word "strike" had been used. Now let us see.

In the letter of February 2 to the signatories to the National Bituminous Coal Agreement the following words were used:

The United Mine Workers of America therefore now advises you, as a signatory to the agreement, that it reserves the right at will to take any independent action necessary to the enforcement of the contract.

What independent action could be taken by them, except strike?

Now in the letter of March 12 they say:

The winter is now gone; this office proposes to go forward in requiring the coal operators to honor their agreement.

Go forward in what way? Any other way except strike?

Your ears will soon be assailed by their outcries and wails of anguish. To relieve themselves they need only to comply with the provisions of the agreement which they solemnly executed in this office on July 8, 1947.

Now, does that constitute a nod, or a wink, or the use of a code in order to call a strike? Is there any other reasonable interpretation?

And then this Court believes that there is a principle of law which, as far as I know, no court has ever been called upon to announce, because this use of a code in order for a union to avoid responsibility is a new thing. It is a new method of endeavoring to avoid responsibility.

Now, the Court thinks the principle is this: That as long as a union is functioning as a union it must be held responsible for the mass action of its members. It is perfectly obvious, not only in objective reasoning, but because of experience, that men don't act collectively without leadership. The idea of suggesting that from 250,000 to 350,000 men would all get the same idea at once, independently of leadership, and walk out of the mines, is, of course, simply ridiculous.

So that, in general, this Court announces a principle of law. The Court has no means of knowing whether higher courts will adopt the principle or not, but the Court has no doubt about its soundness, not any—that a union that is functioning must be held responsible for the mass action of its members.

You can't preserve a union any other way. And the unions are the only thing which labor has to give it comparable bargaining power with capital. It is the only thing which the employee has to give him equal or comparable bargaining power with his employer.

So that the rule of law which I have announced is the only rule which will preserve the unions, because if the plan is adopted throughout the country of trying to use a wink, a nod, a code, instead of the word "strike," and if that sort of a maneuver is recognized as valid by the courts, then you will have among the unions lawlessness, chaos and ultimate anarchy. And then the unions will have to be socialized. In other words, they will have to be destroyed.

So that when the Court thinks that the union must be held responsible, as long as it is functioning, for the mass action of its members, the Court is announcing a principle for the salvation of the unions themselves and their preservation and the only rule that will save them from destruction.

Of course if a union comes in and says "We have lost our hold on our members; they have gone; John Smith has executed a coup; he has taken them away from us," and if they can show the Court by legitimate testimony that that is true, of course they are not guilty of contempt. But that is not the situation here.

The union and its president make no such claim. They don't contend for one instant that this union isn't operating and functioning as a union and that its members are not controlled from headquarters.

And so the Court has no difficulty in reaching a conclusion.

The Court thinks that the following telegrams, issued by the union, who had disregarded the temporary restraining order from April 5 to April 12, are also significant.

The first telegram is as follows, and it was issued prior to the meeting of the Court on last Monday. This is a wire sent to all district presidents and International Board members, bituminous districts of the United Mine Workers of America of the United States:

This message is for your official information and for immediate transmission to all members of the union. The trustee vacancy in the 1947 welfare fund has now been filled by the selection of the honorable H. Styles Bridges, who has accepted the appointment. An early resolution of the question at issue may now be expected. Your voluntary cessation of work should now be terminated and your protest ended.

It is the belief of the International Union and your officers that the production of coal should be resumed forthwith. It is to your best interests and those of our union and the public welfare that this should be done. Therefore you are now definitely advised that you should return to your usual employment immediately upon receipt of this telegram. This message is sent on behalf of the International Union as well as in my official capacity as president.

Then later in the morning this telegram was sent to all bituminous local unions, United Mine Workers of America:

Pensions granted. The agreement is now honored.

You will notice, and it is in the evidence, that in the letter of March 12, which preceded what the Court now holds to have been a strike, the coal operators are charged with dishonoring their agreement. And in a telegram of April 12 the statement is made: "The agreement is now honored."

The miners walk out when told "the agreement is dishonored," and they go back when they are told "the agreement is honored."

Now, can that be anything else except a code, taken in connection with the other statements of what has happened objectively that the Court has made?

The Court thinks, gentlemen, that there is no difficulty about deciding that the evidence, beyond all reasonable doubt—practically beyond all doubt—is sufficient to show that a strike was called, and, of course, is sufficient to show that the defendants are guilty of criminal contempt.

Of course, they are obviously guilty of civil contempt in a technical manner. Civil contempt is usually used to reimburse someone who suffered by the strike, or by the violation of an injunction.

Of course, in this case what any fine imposed for civil contempt would do would be to transfer money from the United Mine Workers to the United States Treasury. It would transfer a medium of exchange from one class to the whole people. But it would not salvage in any manner or to any extent the damage which the strike has caused. And so the Court doesn't particularly emphasize the civil aspects.

Now this, of course, is a tremendously important matter. The Court naturally has felt a tremendous responsibility resting upon the Court. What the Court does, or will do, in assessing punishment, or what the Court has done in holding these defendants guilty, is a matter which is being watched by every lawless element not only in this country but in the world.

It is also being watched by all decent people to ascertain whether or not the courts have power to protect citizens of this country in their normal way of life. The Court doesn't think this matter can be viewed from the standpoint of expediency.

The Court thinks it should be acted upon as any other case is acted upon.

The Court also thinks it is not all-wise.

This action was instituted by the President of the United States, I mean it originated with him, and every individual in this country, including the miners, including the unions, has a stake in its proper determination and in the penalties imposed in the regular course.

So that the Court is not going to pronounce sentence this morning. The Court is going to pronounce sentence tomorrow morning at ten o'clock, and the Court asks the Government, tomorrow morning at ten o'clock, to give the Court its recommendation. And of course, if the defendants also want to make any statement, any recommendation, they will also be permitted to do it.

But the Government has access, possibly, to practical information that the Court doesn't have access to, which may be perfectly legitimate for them to consider in making their recommendation.

But in closing, the Court is firmly convinced—firmly convinced—that this situation has got beyond the bound of expediency. The issue has to be met. The Court will take a recess until 11:15.

# THE AMERICAN STANDARD OF LIVING: HOW CAN IT BEST BE IMPROVED? [3]

## ROBERT A. TAFT AND WALTER P. REUTHER [4]

Senator Robert A. Taft, of Ohio, and Mr. Walter P. Reuther, president of the United Automobile Workers of the Congress of Industrial Organizations, broadcast this debate on the *People's Platform* on Sunday, April 11, 1948, over the Columbia Broadcasting System, from station WTOP in Washington from 12:30 to 1:30 P.M.

The debate is an interesting presentation of the contrasted approaches to the problem of how to elevate the American standard of living. Taft in this dialog most ably expounds the managerial concept and philosophy of private enterprise. According to Taft, full recognition should be given to management in enterprise. Capital should be provided with sufficient net income and incentive to maintain and expand industry. Thus jobs would be provided for all. As the industry prospers, so will wages rise and so will the general elevation of standards of living result. The government, to be sure, should curb monopoly, but it should preserve competition. Government control of credit and tax policies should keep the business cycle in equilibrium and so guarantee stability in living costs.

Reuther, on the other hand, argues that the present government legislative political policies favor big business. Such a program, argues Reuther, has resulted in undue profits and relatively little or no advance in labor's standard of living. The argument between these two able debaters, therefore, resolves itself into questions of definition of the machinery of programs now operating and questions of fact concerning the effect of these programs upon profits, industrial expansion, wages, and consumer spending and saving abilities.

The student of debate will brief the respective positions, examine the chief lines of argument, the organization of the total affirmative and negative cases, the issues, the supporting data, the refutatory devices and skills, the personalities of the respective debaters as revealed through their methods of statement and reply, and the more definitely persuasive features. (Each speaker was undoubtedly attempting to consolidate his own constituency and win the large body of "undecided" listeners.)

[3] Text and permission to reprint furnished by the Columbia Broadcasting System. See also *Congressional Record*. 80th Congress, 2d session. 94:A2514-18. April 20, 1948 (daily edition).
[4] For biographical notes see Appendix.

The state of the nation as of April 1948, concerning the labor-management issue, is clearly revealed in this debate. The argument should be read with full understanding of the immediate background. A crippling coal strike, for example, was in progress, automobile workers were negotiating for wage increases, and Taft was campaigning in the Nebraska Republican primary and was soon to compete with Stassen in a similar campaign in Ohio. Railroad, meat-packing, and other strikes were under way or about to start soon after this debate was given.

Each speaker had repeatedly demonstrated his ability as a public speaker and debater.

The first broadcast of the *People's Platform* was on July 20, 1938, with four participants, one of them a New York City housewife and another a grocer from Connecticut. Dr. Lyman Bryson started the series and was chairman for several years.

COOKE: Senator Taft and Mr. Reuther, what can we do now to get more of the good things of life for us all?

ANNOUNCER: From Washington, Columbia presents the *People's Platform* with Dwight Cooke. This broadcast marks the anniversary of the five hundredth program on Columbia's *People's Platform*. For almost ten years, the *People's Platform* has brought to its microphone prominent and well-informed guests to present in spontaneous discussions their opposing views on the vital issues of our time. Today, another timely debate as Republican presidential candidate, Senator Robert A. Taft, of Ohio, and labor leader, Walter P. Reuther, president of the United Auto Workers, CIO, join Chairman Dwight Cooke to discuss the question: "How Can the American Standard of Living Best Be Improved?" We hear first from Mr. Cooke.

COOKE: On this five hundredth broadcast, it's a pleasure to see sitting around the table with me two Americans who represent important and powerful sections of thought about our future, a presidential candidate and the president of the largest labor union in the United States of America.

Gentlemen, if you're both willing, let's jump right past how incredibly better the American standard of living is than any enjoyed by any other people in the history of the world. It's typical of Americans, I hope, that we don't sit back on our over-stuffed laurels. So, Senator Taft, what should we do to raise our standard of living and to realize even better the potential in the American way?

TAFT: Well, first, Mr. Cooke, of course, the standard of living of any people depends on production. The more commodities and products of all kinds that are produced, the more things people have to eat, to wear, to use; homes to occupy. The greater the productivity of each workman on the average, that is, the more he has to enjoy and the higher his standard of living. The best way to increase his production is to give him better tools with which to work, better plants and machinery. There can be no doubt that the great improvement which has occurred in this country in the past century is due to improvements in the tools of labor, therefore, the first answer to your question is—encourage people in corporations to save and invest their money in productive enterprise. Second—keep the markets free from monopoly; keep collective bargaining free and equal. Competition is the best regulator of the distribution of the money after you get it and of incentive rewards. Third—run government spending and tax policies and government control of credit to keep the economic machinery running at full speed and, thus, prevent depressions, which can reduce the standard of living more than anything else. Fourth—reduce government expenditures and taxation, particularly for armament when possible so our production of civilian goods can be increased instead of military goods.

COOKE: Mr. Reuther, what do you add to Mr. Taft's suggestions here—production and competition and the role of the government?

REUTHER: Well, we've got to do more than just expand production. Our basic job in America is to achieve a balance between purchasing power and productive power. We've got to get the purchasing power in the hands of the American people, the workers in the city and the farmers on the farm, so that they can buy back the goods that we turn out in the factories and on the farms. In 1929, and the years before that, we had production, but, under Mr. Hoover we got in an awful jam because 36,000 families at the top of our economic pyramid had more income in 1929 and '30 than 12 million families at the bottom of the pyramid. That meant that the few on top had more than they needed while millions on the bottom didn't have enough. This production part of the problem is only half of the problem. The other half, and the more important half at the moment, is distribution, purchasing power. At the moment, prices are too high and profits are too high and purchasing power in the hands of the people—workers, farmers, white collar groups—is too low and, unfortunately, Mr. Cooke, most everything Congress has done the past six or eight months has moved in the direction of giving more to the people who already have too much and taking away from the people who need more. Take the tax bill just as an example. The tax bill just passed by Mr. Taft and his group in Congress gives a man with four in the family, with a $2,500 income, a $69 tax reduction, but gives a man with $250,000 income a $34,700 tax reduction. This means more yachts and less bread and butter for the people.

TAFT: Well, Mr. Cooke, as far as the tax bill is concerned, we took a hundred per cent of the taxes off seven million people and, of course, we took $69 off, but he wasn't paying very much more than that. The percentage of increase given to . . . the reduction given is a far higher percentage in all the lower income groups. According to Mr. Reuther, he doesn't want to give the top people anything. Of course, they were paying. If a man who was paying a hundred thousand dollars gets a 5 per cent reduction that's more than any man can get who pays less than $5,000. But . . . Mr. Reuther's whole thesis is wrong. The reason prices are going up today is that there is too much purchasing power. More purchasing power because of savings and other circumstances than we can get our production up to, consequently, the natural economic demand and supply has forced prices up. We may get to a point where we need more purchasing power, but we're not there yet.

REUTHER: Well, let's get back to this tax question now. Senator Taft, people can't eat percentages, they need bread and butter. You gave in your tax bill a worker with four in the family with a $2,500 income—you gave him a 3 per cent increase in his purchasing power than he had last year and you give a fellow who makes $250,000, with four in the family, a 59 per cent increase in the purchasing power he has.

TAFT: As you say, Mr. Reuther, these percentages don't mean anything. A man with $2,500 and four in the family before this paid about a hundred dollars. Now, he gets the $69 reduction and pays about thirty, according to your own figures.

REUTHER: Well, why not give him more and take more away from the fellow who gets $250,000 because he can live on what he gets after he pays a high tax.

TAFT: Of course, your theory would simply exempt the 25 million people altogether, no taxes, put all the taxes on the people who save money, and accumulated it, the very savings that are necessary, too, if you ever want to invest in new plants and give people new jobs. Of course not! I mean, you can go on the principle of taking a hundred per cent of all profits. You can go on the principle and take a hundred per cent of all incomes over $5,000. The trouble is that that kind of a theory would simply get you back to a straight socialist plan in which nobody saves any money any more.

REUTHER: Senator Taft, that's the same kind of economic theory that we practiced under Harding and under Coolidge and under Hoover. That's the Hoover-Taft economic theory. And what happened under that theory? America went down the road until the purchasing power became so low and the productive power so out of balance that we got into the worst economic jam in the history of the world. Mr. Hoover used to talk about prosperity being just around the corner and we waited and we waited because the American people were behind the eightball and we never got around the corner and we didn't get around the corner till we started to pump purchasing power into our economy and, if we practice your kind of economics, the Hoover-Taft economics, we'll go right back to another depression because you've got to balance purchasing power with productive power.

TAFT: Mr. Reuther, you're simply advancing the socialistic theory that nobody ouught to be allowed to save anything. How about talking about the present instead of the past. The purchasing power theory was the theory of the New Deal. It was absolutely wrong and pumped purchasing power for ten years and at the end of that time you had 10 million people still un-

employed. The whole theory that you want more consumer purchasing power—what happens to the product, to the money that
goes in? A certain amount of it has to be saved. In fact, the
whole future of the increased cost of living depends upon somebody saving it; whether it's corporations, whether it's individuals, you want people to spend every cent they get; to give the
money to people who spend it entirely for consumers' goods and
you will have exactly what happened, a depression will continue
indefinitely in the United States. Prosperity here depends upon
a large percentage of our products, of our proceeds of our wealth,
being invested in new tools, new investments, and it takes about
six or seven thousand dollars to create one good, new job at
good wages today.

REUTHER: Senator Taft, the difference between you and me
is—I'm not opposed to people saving excepting I want the little
fellow to be able to save. You want the corporations to do all
the saving. You want the people who've already got too much
to go on saving and getting more and more and more. The basis
of—

TAFT: No! no! no! I don't care who saves.

REUTHER: Just give me a minute! This is not a Senate
filibuster! Give me a minute, please! The trouble with America
is that the people that you're supporting, economically and politically, are the people who've already got too many things and
want them to have a monopoly not only on the good things of
life, but also a monopoly on the right to save. I want the little
fellow, not only to be able to buy enough food for his kids, to
give them a decent home, to give them proper clothing, decent
medical care, and educational opportunity—I want them to be
able to do that and still have a little bit left over.

COOKE: I want to make a [point] if I may here, gentlemen,
in terms of the central point each of you have made. On the one
hand, the question of the necessity of increased production, and
Senator Taft's point that there is more than enough money and
more than enough purchasing power now to buy what we pro-

duce now, and, on the other hand, Mr. Reuther's point that we need considerably more purchasing power now. How are you going to put the two together?

TAFT: Well, let me analyze Mr. Reuther's argument. He's got two things. First—he talks about more consumer's purchasing power to buy the things that are made. That's a fair point. I don't think it's material today, but certainly we have to keep consuming purchasing power in balance with saving. We don't want to get too much saving and we don't want to get too much consumer purchasing power. His other point is just the plain socialistic point that he doesn't like present distribution of wealth and he wants to distribute it in a different way. Both people will spend the money. I agree with him! I think the more you can distribute equally the income of this country among different people the better; but, you can take all the corporation profits, for instance, that he's talking about and add it to income and it'll add about ten or twelve per cent to the average income and, of course, half the corporations will close up and there won't be any jobs and you'll decrease the income again.

REUTHER: Well, let's look at two phases of the problem that Senator Taft has raised. He's raised, first of all, the profit question and, then, the question of competition. Let's take up the question of competition first. Senator Taft has been saying repeatedly in the past couple of years that free enterprise and . . . under competition will bring down prices and that's all a very lovely theory, but in practice, because American monopoly controls the basic industries in this country, free enterprise and a free market is just a myth. Now, I—[Interruption]

REUTHER: Now, just a moment! On February 21, I was testifying before the Senate Committee and Senator Taft said at that time that prices were just about ready to come down. That was February 1947, more than a year ago, and after that date they continued to go up more than 10 per cent. Now, here's what happened since they smashed price control. Price control ended in November '46 and from November '46 to January '48 production only increased 2 per cent. Prices went up 17 per cent and profits of 1,500 manufacturing corporations, according to the report of the National City Bank, went up 54 per cent more in 1947 than in 1946. Now, let's talk about competition for a second. What happened?

COOKE: Let's let Mr. Taft talk for a minute about your first question there on profits.

REUTHER: Yes, of course!

TAFT: I agree with Mr. Reuther that there is some monopoly and that monopoly ought to be gone after and prevented. Of course, he says you can't prevent it, so he wants a socialistic plan by which the government, in effect, shall run all industry, shall certainly regulate all prices and wages, and I prefer to say (and I believe very strongly) that competition can be enforced and that competition is bound to bring prices down. These profits will take care of themselves in time. As a matter of fact, the President's report points out that the profits up to date have been well used. They've been reinvested. They've been . . . the principal savings invested in the expansion of plants. I think it can go on too long. I think, as a steady diet, the present profits are much too high, but competition will bring them down. Just to go back to the years '32, '33, and '34 where for over five years there were no net corporation profits and look what happened to employment. Look at the number—ten, fifteen million people out of work because there were no corporation profits.

REUTHER: Senator Taft, you see, it's a very convenient excuse. Every time you start talking about helping the little fellow you conveniently put a socialist tag on it. That's what Mr. Hoover did when—

TAFT: Now, look, suppose, Mr. Reuther you talk . . . you get rid of the demogoguery and all this political stuff and talk economics.

REUTHER: I'm going to talk economics! I'm trying to say that every time someone proposes helping the little fellow in the world, whether it's the worker or the small farmer, you get out a socialist tag, but when the RFC gives billions in help to bail out big corporations, subsidizes the railroads and the ship-ping interest, that's of course, a good American practice. I say what I'm advocating is no more socialistic than these other things excepting it's an attempt for the people of America to try to have their government help the little fellow instead of the big corporation. Now, getting back to this compensation—

TAFT: Mr. Reuther, I want to help the little fellow! Now, let's just settle that problem. How do you want to help the little fellow? I want to help the little fellow and I say that the only way you'll help the little fellow is to improve the plants, the machinery, that he has; to increase the production in the United States, not by a lot of government bureau regulations. It's never helped the little fellow yet and never will.

COOKE: All right, gentlemen! Since you both agreed you want to help the little fellow, let's examine three specific areas and see what kinds of action each of you recommends so as to help the little fellow; first of all, in the area of government is Senator Taft, who just started. What do you want the govern-ment to do in here, Mr. Reuther?

REUTHER: First of all, I think the government's got to take positive action with respect to price control. It's got to roll back the prices of basic commodities and take that rollback out of the profits of American industries, because those profits are scandalously high and they can afford to give up some of those profits in the way either of a wage increase or a price decrease. Secondly, I think the government's got to break certain serious material bottlenecks in order to release the productive power of the American economy. The steel situation is very critical. We need about 10 million more tons of steel production. In Detroit, we've been suffering up there with a shortage of gas. Two hun-dred thousand workers were on the streets for three weeks and we're threatened with another shortage. We need 40 thousand tons of steel to get a new pipeline into Detroit, to get gas in there. The government's got to get into these things. I say, let free enterprise do all it can, but where free enterprise puts their selfish interests, private corporations, above the welfare of the people, the government, as the democratic agency of all the people, has to move in to protect the public welfare and I say in this case the government has not done that. It's strengthened monopoly. It's made possible for people who've got too much already to get more at the expense of the great mass of people.

COOKE: All right! Now, Mr. Taft, would you [discuss] Mr. Reuther's points and then go on to your own?

TAFT: Well, in the first place, you could take all the corporation profits and distribute them back in prices and you get a 10 per cent reduction on prices. You'd close up half the corporations in the country; you'd throw millions of people out of jobs; you'd interfere with the whole operation of the economic machine; competition will bring down the profits, but the total profits (that's the point that I'm trying to make), the total profits are only, I think, about 12 per cent of the . . . kind of the wages the people get. That's an immaterial factor. What can the government do? The government, I think, can put its own house in order, can reduce the taxes and the government spending, because that simply adds to the prices, in the long run those prices are . . . those taxes are passed right on to the consumer. The government, I think, is interested in seeing that the saving and spending is in balance, that agricultural production is in balance with industrial production, that wages are in balance with prices, but wages have increased more than prices in the last seven years and the actual condition under the government operation has been that today the actual net income of workmen in the United States has increased about 42 per cent over what it was in '39 according to the per capita disposable income, in real income, and is allowing for the higher prices, and has gone up from $838 a person to $1,190 a person in '47.

COOKE: And how about the whole area of price controls in this situation, Senator Taft?

TAFT: Well, price controls, in my opinion—nobody can do it right. The thing is bound to break down in time of peace. If it is successful in holding prices down, it discourages people from going ahead with new plants and new investment and more production.

REUTHER: You see, that's the whole point! Senator Taft keeps talking about price control discouraging production. In the shoe industry let's talk about specific industries—shoes are things that all the people need. After Senator Taft and Congress destroyed price control, the shoe industry had its highest monthly production in July of 1946. Now, assuming that Senator Taft is correct—having gotten finally rid of price control, production should go soaring and ultimately prices have to come dropping down. What happened? Since July '46, the shoe industry has averaged 16 per cent less production per month and prices have gone up 50 per cent. Let's look at the cotton goods industry. Their production was the highest in November '46. It has come down 12 per cent and prices have gone up 23 per cent. Now, why? Because here you've got monopoly control where these monopoly groups arbitrarily decide at what level of production they're going to operate, based upon how they can get the highest prices and the greatest profits. . . . If your theory is correct—that having eliminated price control, production will go soaring and prices will come tumbling down—then how do you account for the fact that in the shoe industry and the cotton goods industry they have cut production and increased prices since you abolished price control?

TAFT: Well, in the first place, I deny the facts! The second place, the price control, when we had price control of shoes and cotton goods, nobody could buy a white shirt, nobody could buy the shoes they wanted, you couln't get any of the things you wanted. Today, you can buy anything you want in shoes, or white shirts if you've got the money. If you've got the money, and wages have increased 102 per cent where the cost of living —shoes and cotton goods—have only gone up 70 per cent. The better workman is better off today than he was eight years ago. Now, I think he ought to be still better off. Surely, I think the way to do that is to get this cost down and, if the government is permitting the monopoly to go on, then the government is highly to be condemned. I can assure you, Mr. Reuther, if there's one thing that I think is absolutely essential to the whole theory of free enterprise, it is free competition and I am willing to go the limit in seeing that that competition is produced, and what happened is that there's been this high, very high, purchasing power. Wages outran prices. I am glad to see high wages, but they outran prices so that they produced a demand—inevitably, a larger demand than a supply is going to raise prices. The whole condition will come to an end within a very reasonable time, I think.

COOKE: You've both now come into the area of what business should do about this problem. You want business to reduce prices and—

REUTHER: I want business, Mr. Cooke, I want business to take 29 billion dollars in profits, which they made in 1947, which was an all-time record. They had 17.5 billion dollars left over after they paid their taxes. I want them to give some of that money back to the people in the form of purchasing power either by reducing prices or by holding prices and increasing wages. Industry, last year, according to the National City Bank, the manufacturing industries, made 17 per cent net return on its investment. In the auto industry, for example, the automobile industry—eight companies—made 38 per cent return on their investment in one year, in '47, and after they paid their taxes they still made 22.2 per cent and I say that that's a scandalous profit and the American people are entitled to participate in that wealth either in lower prices—and I would prefer lower prices to wage increases—and if prices are not rolled back, then wage increases are justified.

TAFT: Well, now, in the first place, the corporation net profits in '47 were about 17 billion dollars. Wages were 128 billion dollars, so that actually that's about 13 per cent. If you take half of it away, or take it all away, you're not going to have many corporations continue in business at all and give jobs. I think profits are too high, but also profits go up and down. For five years in the thirties there wasn't a single dollar of profits for corporations and many of them closed up and we had ten, fifteen million dollars unemployed. Those profits will come down as far as that's concerned.

REUTHER: When will they come down, Senator Taft? Let me show you what—

TAFT: I don't know when they'll come down! They'll come down just as fast as the competition brings them down and in many fields they're coming down—

REUTHER: Do you challenge, Senator Taft, the figures which I gave on the shoe industry and the cotton goods industry and both sets of figures come from the Federal Reserve Board report, the most authentic governmental report in this field? These are facts that nobody can dispute.

TAFT: Now, the point is that everybody is getting shoes, everybody is getting all the shirts they want. They have more income than enough to buy them. Of course, the prices, I think, should still come down. I think profits should come down.

REUTHER: You ought to try living on a worker's family income and feed and clothe and shoe a lot of kids and—

TAFT:—And I want to steadily increase that income, Mr. Reuther, and . . . in the last eight years the net condition of all workers on the average has increased 40 per cent. If we can do another 40 per cent in the next eight years, I would—no one would be more pleased than I and that's the purpose of our policy.

COOKE: All right! You've made clear, Mr. Reuther and Mr. Taft, you've made clear where you think business should act here and how you think it should act. Now, let's finish this and talk about what labor and labor unions should do. Mr. Taft, let's give you the first shot here.

TAFT: Well, I think labor unions should—I have no criticism of labor unions. I think they're entitled to get the wage that is justified in the industry in which they are in return equal to the productivity of the things they're producing in that industry.

I'm in favor of higher wages. . . . I don't think you can lay down a flat rule, but there isn't any doubt that in many industries wage-earners are entitled to more and ought to get more in accordance, certainly, with the . . . cost of living, but, rather, in accordance with the increased productivity. That's the best guide.

REUTHER: I've always taken the position that labor has to make progress with the community and not at the expense of the community and that's why two years ago we advocated that we wanted to get wage increases out of the profits of these corporations and not out of the consumers' pockets because we are not fighting for more dollars, Mr. Cooke. We're fighting for more purchasing power and, if we give a wage increase on one hand and it's taken away by higher price increases on the other hand, we've made no progress. We've merely accelerated the speed of the economic merry-go-round. Our basic fight is for purchasing power—dollars that will buy things. The farmer needs those purchasing-power dollars, the city worker needs them, and so we're trying to make progress not at the expense of the community and our neighbors; we're trying to make progress with them, because we know that the only way we can solve the problems in a democratic society is for all the people to be pulling together, to try to make progress together.

TAFT: Now, on that statement, Mr. Cooke, I agree 100 per cent with Mr. Reuther and we can close at least in an agreement.

COOKE: Well, I'd like to interrupt here a minute, gentlemen, if I may give you a back-handed compliment, important as the things are which you are saying today, there's something even more important here, I think. The fact that you've said these things here, the fact that two responsible Americans, a leading presidential candidate, and a leading labor spokesman, are willing to face each other and defend your convictions here on the *People's Platform,* honestly, directly, and without any scripts, though with plenty of figures, I must say—it's out of such stuff that real freedom of speech is built and it would be best for all of us if we had more Americans of your caliber willing to be this frank and honest with your fellow-citizens. Now, how about a quick summing up of the points, you've made. Mr. Taft.

TAFT: Well, my statement is still the same. The government is interested in keeping a balance between these different economic factors. People can't have a higher standard of living than the goods that will be produced. The big thing is to produce the goods. The best way to do that is to see that there's enough saving whether it's through corporate profits or through individual savings, to put money into machinery and plants that will increase productivity and increase production. That's the big way in which we can improve the condition of all the people and particularly of the people on the lower income levels.

COOKE: Mr. Reuther!

REUTHER: Mr. Cooke, I think that fundamentally our problem is not only to expand production but to expand purchasing power to balance that expanded productive power. I think that the fundamental difference between Mr. Taft and me is that he thinks you can build prosperity from the top down and I take the position you've got to build it from the bottom up.

TAFT: I never said anything of the kind, Mr. Reuther! . . .

REUTHER: You've got to broaden the purchasing power base of the American people. If you try to build prosperity from the top down, it gets top-heavy and it topples over just as it did in 1929. I want to build it this time on a solid basis. The American people fought a war not to go back to something. They fought a war to go forward to something better and finer than they ever had before.

COOKE: Well, thank you, gentlemen! I have to go forward with a bit of closing here. We could go forward for another hour, as Mr. Taft has just indicated. As we finish this five hundredth program, I want to take a second to thank my colleagues on the *People's Platform*. . . . With their help, I think it's safe to promise you all many more forceful and stimulating debates here on the *People's Platform*. Thank you, gentlemen, for joining me today.

# COST OF LIVING AND INFLATION [5]

## HELEN GAHAGAN DOUGLAS [6]

Congresswoman Helen Gahagan Douglas gave this speech before the House of Representatives, on Wednesday, April 28, 1948. It was near the end of a busy day in which the lower house had debated and passed the oleomargarine tax repeal bill. Under a previous order of the House, Mrs. Douglas was recognized for sixty minutes to discuss inflation and to offer a bill for its control.

In the domestic field Congress during 1947 had spent its energies mainly on passing the Taft-Hartley bill to deal with labor unions and on attempting to reduce income taxes.

With regard to prices, an "inconclusive running battle" was carried on. Between July 1946 and October 1947, after controls were abandoned, the consumers' price index rose 23 per cent, food costs rose 40 per cent, and clothing 19 per cent. Congress passed, on June 3, 1947, a rent bill permitting a 15 per cent "voluntary" increase.

President Truman called Congress into extra session on November 17, 1947, and proposed a ten-point program to deal with prices. The most important request was for a return to wartime wage and price ceilings. Congress, on December 19, 1947, passed a Republican anti-inflation bill providing for "voluntary" curbs.

In 1948 the consumer price index continued to rise, as Mrs. Douglas indicates in her speech. (See the tabulation she refers to as of March 15, 1948.) Congress, nevertheless, passed the Republican Housing and Rent Act of 1948 which threatened "the consumer with further inroads on his rent dollar." Congress, moreover, in 1948, over Truman's veto, passed an income tax reduction bill. It was a bill that "in every respect was inflationary." Congress, also, passed the Marshall Plan bill for economic aid to Europe and China. Thus the country was committed to further inflation—unless drastic anti-inflation legislation should be enacted. In a presidential campaign year, there was little prospect that any effective action in this direction would be taken.

Mrs. Douglas' argument is closely reasoned and filled with concrete evidence. She moreover buttressed her argument with sustaining documents, including the President's ten-point program.

Her case was developed much as any intercollegiate affirmative argument would be. She analyzed in detail the need for action, the

[5] From the *Congressional Record*. 80th Congress, 2d session. 94:5134-42. April 28, 1948 (daily edition).
[6] For biographical note see Appendix.

results of the inflationary trend, the weaknesses of the panaceas attempted, and the advantages of her plan as suggested by the bill she sponsored.    Her argumentative style, although personal and lively, avoided mere rhetoric.

This speaker is highly effective in voice and platform speaking. Her considerable experience on the stage obviously contributed to her clear diction and ability to project her voice to an audience.    Notable was her address before the Democratic National Convention at Chicago, on July 20, 1944.    There she demonstrated her ability to transcend routine debate and to produce genuine eloquence.

Mr. Speaker, last Monday, I was by unanimous consent granted official leave to go shopping for America's housewife because it is quite as important for the members of this body to know what is going on in the grocery stores of America as in our munitions plants.

I now wish to report my findings, and have brought with me in this market basket the results of my study.

Mr. Speaker, whether or not this Congress is making sound economic policies depends on whether the housewife is able to obtain what she needs in this basket without going into debt and mortgaging the economic future of her family.

Can the housewife today balance her own budget?

This is the major issue.    It is not a partisan one.

Are all Republicans so rich that they can afford a 25 per cent increase in the cost of living?

I do not believe it.

Are all Republican tenants so rich they can afford to have their rent doubled?

I do not believe it.

Do all Republicans approve of pursuing reckless economic policies which invite economic collapse?

I do not believe it.

Economic collapse would cost us the confidence of people all over the world in our system of free enterprise.    Do all Republicans dare that risk in this hour?

I do not believe it.

The Russians have predicted economic collapse for the United States, and are banking on such a development.    But if there were no people in Russia tomorrow, communism would still be a challenge to democracy and would still seek its gains among the ruins of economic collapse.

Are all Republicans unaware of this?

I do not believe it.

Surely, all clear-thinking people are aware that economic collapse would mean that we could no longer give leadership to other nations in their struggle for freedom.

A sound and stable American economy is essential if we ourselves are not to promote the spread of communism and if we are to maintain and preserve free democratic processes in the world.

A year ago I made a similar report to this House on the status of the American housewife's grocery basket.

I come again today with the same basket but with different price marks. The reason why the price of this basket of groceries is greater than it was a year ago is the business of this House.

It would be easy to speak at great length about the Republican opposition in the House to price control—about the reasons why the cost of living has risen; why the budgets of most housewives in the United States are out of balance. But the world situation today is so acute and the problem of inflation is so much a part of the chance for world peace that partisan politics has no more place in our discussion of this critical issue than it would in answering a four-alarm fire.

In view of the facts that I have in this basket and of our common knowledge of what the world will lose if this Congress adjourns without having reenacted the control measures necessary to halt inflation here and around the world, I plead, Mr. Speaker, for the statesmanship that is needed.

I plead that the majority forget that we have a Republican Congress and a Democratic President who has asked for the reenactment of measures necessary to secure a stable economy.

I plead that we face the economic facts in this basket with an open mind.

Mr. Speaker, a little over a year ago I reported to the House on what had happened to the cost of living in the first year of decontrol when we were asked to let prices seek their natural level in the open market.  Remember the decontrol that the NAM promised would bring goods for everybody at prices they could afford to pay and a better tomorrow?

I reported on the NAM's "better tomorrow" last year and found it far short of the promises made.  We were told then that the NAM "tomorrow" had not had enough time to dawn.  Well, now we have given them another year, and where are prices?

They have changed again, Mr. Speaker, and again for the worse.  The enemies of price control and rent control in June 1946, and ever since—even in the face of the steadily mounting cost of living—must in the name of common sense reconsider their opposition.

As the elections draw closer, prudence should dictate the protection of all the people, regardless of the pressures from the special interests.

The sudden action on Capitol Hill—on the north slope—in the field of housing may be a good omen.  I pray that it is—for the people's sake—for they must have relief.

The market basket of groceries that I brought onto the floor of the House last year contained essential items in the everyday life of our people.  Today I bring the same evidences of economic facts with which every housewife in America is daily confronted—bread, milk, flour, eggs, fats, meat, soap.

These items were again purchased in the shadow of the Capitol—at the lowest-priced chain store in Washington.

I reported last year that in the nine months between June 1946, when price control was done to death, and March 1947, the prices of these basic items had increased 50 per cent.  After nine months of NAM-sponsored decontrol the housewife had to pay $15 for the same amount of food she could get for $10 under OPA.

Let us see what another year of the NAM's "better tomorrow" has brought.  The same items I used as exhibit A last year in the same lowest-priced grocery store I find now—April 26, 1948—cost $16.23 instead of the $15.02 of a year ago, and the $10.08 of predecontrol 1946.  And this despite the headlined temporary price dip in some foods in February of this year.

Mr. Speaker, for the convenience of the members I ask unanimous consent to include at this point in the *Record* the comparative price table for nineteen specific grocery commodities. . . .

These are the items in the housewife's basket that I priced a year ago and priced again yesterday. I want to just show you here what the difference is.

Here was a pound of butter. Under OPA it cost you 65 cents. Last year it cost you 82 cents, and it cost 93 cents today in the lowest-priced store in Washington.

Two quarts of Lucerne milk cost 29 cents under OPA, 34 cents last year, and 38 cents today.

A dozen eggs cost 53 cents under OPA, 69 cents last year, and 65 cents today. That is a seasonal drop, Mr. Speaker.

Three pounds of of round steak cost $1.35 under OPA, $2.07 last year, and $2.76 today.

Two pounds of Maxwell House coffee cost 60 cents under OPA, 98 cents last year, and $1.06 today in the cheapest-priced store in Washington.

Two loaves of Wright's bread cost 22 cents under OPA, 20 cents last year, and 24 cents this year.

Margarine. We have been talking a lot about it today. Everybody thinks they have done so much for the housewife in passing this bill. I will tell you, Mr. Speaker, that we have done practically nothing for the housewife. If the members think they have changed the facts represented in this basket, they are greatly mistaken. If the effort put forth to pass the margarine bill was expended as a sop to the housewife, the members have another guess coming.

Well, let us take margarine, the cheapest margarine. There are different grades of margarine you know. The cheapest grade of margarine cost 18 cents under OPA, and 40 cents today in the cheapest-priced store.

But suppose a housewife does not live near one of the cheapest-priced stores? With the shortage of housing a family lives wherever they can find a roof. If you live near a high-priced store, if you are buying flour, then maybe you do not pay 89 cents for ten pounds of flour, you pay 95 cents. Maybe you do not pay $2.76 for three pounds of round steak, but you pay $2.94; and so it goes.

Mr. Speaker, I hope I can have this chart set up outside for the convenience of the members, so that they can study these figures next week.

The increase in these basic household food items which every housewife must have, is now not 50 per cent as it was a year ago, but 61 per cent over the prices charged when price control was killed—an increase of 11 per cent in the last year.

In no case, despite all the promises of the opponents of price control, is the price of any of these basic articles lower than the June 1946 prices. In all cases, prices have gone up tremendously—in some cases, over 200 per cent since 1946.

This list does not contain luxuries, but the essential items in every family's grocery budget—bread, milk, flour, eggs, fats, soap, and meat—and I mean so-called cheap cuts of meat.

I am talking about ground round steak, hamburger, sausage —greasy, and pork chops—mostly fat. I am not talking about lamb chops, steak, roast beef, and leg of lamb.

These typical American dishes are today prohibitive for most American families.

Remember that the Bureau of the Census showed that in 1946 two out of every three nonfarm families had total family incomes of less than $3,500 a year, and two out of every five less than $2,500 a year.

Round steak at 92 cents a pound, lamb chops at 98 cents a pound, roast beef at 85 cents a pound, leg of lamb at almost $5 a leg are not on the grocery list of these American families.

Under OPA our economy permitted the average family to buy chicken on Sunday and roast beef on Thursday. The low income family had as much opportunity to buy the better cuts of meat as the high income family. As a matter of fact, more opportunity, because they generally have more children and therefore had more points.

During the war, whether or not the housewife could buy beef depended upon how she apportioned her points. Now it depends upon whether or not she has enough money—and she has not. . . .

Mr. Speaker, the facts and figures I have given you show us clearly where we are headed. A very interesting independent survey of the current financial position and plans of consumers, made for the Board of Governors of the Federal Reserve Board in July 1947 by the University of Michigan shows that the people are already aware of these facts and figures. The conclusions of that survey were published in the Federal Reserve Bulletin for October 1947 and are in its usual objective style.

Taking it out of Federal Reservese, Mr. Speaker, and putting it in plain American, people are eating up their savings and going broke.

We are willing to appropriate billions of dollars to stop communism elsewhere, but we do nothing to stop the conditions which will breed it here. There is apparently no willingness to stop the rising cost of living and bring it down to the point where $1 will buy 100 cents worth of consumers' goods, and not 60 cents worth, as it does now.

Family life will face a crisis if this disastrous inflation continues. Anxiety and strain over the problem of how to make ends meet; over where to find a place to live, with houses being sold from under renters who cannot afford to pay the exorbitant prices asked; over illness unattended because doctors cannot be paid, cannot be safely overlooked. It is this kind of strain that drives people to all sorts of panaceas, including communism.

The first line of defense in a democracy is a people well-fed, well-housed, and well-clothed.

Last year, Mr. Speaker, I placed my market basket and its problems squarely in the lap of the Republican Party where it belonged, but the record of the past year has proved that the American housewife's market basket has not fared well there.

Not only has the majority failed to forward any measure of its own to combat inflation, but it has placed measure after measure proposed by the President or introduced by members of this body in the dungeons of its committees where they never see the light of day.

I, myself, have sought, time after time, to present measures that would aid in the fight against inflation. Among these are:

H. R. 1750—1947—a bill to continue a sound rent-control program.

House Resolution 236—1947—a resolution to discharge from its committee dungeon the long-range housing bill.

H. R. 4726—1948—the only noninflation tax bill to provide a democratic cost-of-living credit straight across the board for every federal taxpayer compensated by the reimposition of the excess-profits tax.

H. R. 5823—1948—a bill to continue a sound rent-control program.

To date I have not introduced a price-control bill believing that such a bill should and would come in face of steadily mounting prices from the majority side of the House.

What has the Republican leadership in this Congress done to protect the housewife's budget?

It presented and passed in the Congress three programs.

First.  Hatched up and passed in the special session a voluntary allocation bill.  I am not going to waste any time on that. The Democrats were never for it and the Republicans have probably forgotten about it.  If they have not, everybody else has.  Indeed, no one ever took it seriously in the first place.

Second.  Passed a second rent bill to further decontrol rents and therefore increase the cost of living.

Third.  Passed a tax bill which provided an increase in the take-home pay, after taxes, for those with an income of $3,000 of 3.2 per cent; for those with an income of $25,000 an increase of 18.5 per cent; for those with an income of $250,000 an increase of 58.4 per cent.  It was a tax bill that in every respect was inflationary.

Mr. Speaker, excuses, party slogans, trumped-up charges, whipping boys, accusations are not going to be accepted by the housewives of America, whether they be Democratic or Republican.  They want action.

It is late—yes, but it will never be earlier.

The housewife cannot feed her family on speeches and declarations of Americanism.  She knows that this Congress has done nothing to protect her budget.  She knows that this Congress has done nothing to halt rising prices. Every day she is reminded of this fact when she pays the grocery clerk for the food in her basket.

Congress must get at the root of the problem. I am therefore introducing this afternoon an anti-inflation, price-control, and allocation measure. It has already been introduced on the other side of the Capitol and is the only bill which has been introduced to date which faces squarely the facts as represented in this basket. It provides an answer to the lessons we have learned from the market basket.

I warn this Congress that it had better pay attention to these lessons. The market basket is a yardstick of the effectiveness of the economic measure we take in this Congress. There is an atomic bomb in this basket, which if allowed to go off can lose for us the peace man must have.

I say again, take heed of the recent warnings of President Truman, his Council of Economic Advisers, and Marriner Eccles of the new waves of inflation that this basket will soon reflect. If we are going to avoid another and final spiral that will throw us into economic collapse, some measure such as this proposal that I now introduce must be passed before we adjourn for the conventions. . . .

The bill I am introducing would provide an immediate price freeze at the January level of this year. It covers everything.

Luxury items and those items not in short supply can be taken out from under price control as the situation warrants.

It would go behind present prices and break some of the production bottlenecks which result in shortages and higher prices.

It would provide an orderly system of allocation of scarce materials so that the productive machinery of the United States can get out of its present tangle in which basic industries are unable fully to produce for lack of necessary materials.

It would provide for the allocating of steel, aluminum, lead, copper, and other vital materials just as we today control the use of tin, in order to insure maximum production where it counts. We must expand our basic industries. We must produce more, as well as hold down the prices of the things we produce if we are to lick inflation.

Our current fuel shortage, which is the most serious threat to our production, is due primarily to the lack of equipment for oil and gas wells, the lack of transportation facilities, such as pipeline pipe and hopper cars, and the lack of power-generating equipment. These shortages are threatening all of our basic industries and our European Recovery Program.

The vital fuel bottleneck cannot be broken unless steel is available for these purposes. We have been told this clearly, again and again, in connection with the hearings on the European Recovery Program. The Krug, Nourse, and Harriman reports clearly indicated that the allocation of steel would be needed. And in the special session the President himself made it clear that these powers to allocate scarce materials must be available if we are to maintain our own production and to provide the goods needed abroad.

The West has a power shortage which cannot be broken unless steel is available for generators and turbines.

Detroit has a natural-gas shortage. Its plants were shut down last winter for over two weeks and 200,000 people were thrown out of work. This will happen next winter and the winter after that unless pipe made of steel is available to bring fuel to these plants.

We must assure our industry the materials it needs to maintain a high level of production and employment; allocation of materials is necessary if essential production abroad is to be assured.

The bill I am introducing will also place a necessary restraint on inflationary expansion of bank credit. These provisions are identical with the measures proposed by the Federal Reserve Board last November.

The bill also provides for an economic stabilization coordinator and an anti-inflationary advisory board with representatives of business management, labor, and agriculture serving on it.

This bill does not restore the balance between wages, prices, and profits which today are hopelessly out of line.

It does not provide a rollback in prices.

This bill does not provide for freezing wages. These are still to be determined by collective bargaining.

I should like to say at this point that were Congress willing to roll back prices so as to restore the balance which existed between wages, prices, and profits in the middle of June 1946, before price controls were effectively terminated, I would support a provision for the control of wages as well as prices in this emergency. . . .

I am hoping that we will have a strong expression of public opinion on this matter so that we can in the months that remain between now and November do something to bring a balance between prices, profits, and wages.

Is it hopeless to introduce a price control bill at this late date? Is it hopeless to expect that this Republican-led Congress will now take steps that they have steadfastly opposed?

Mr. Speaker, there are six months left before November. Are the Republicans in this Congress prepared to meet America's housewife at the polls, having left unsolved the economic problems represented in this basket?

Is the Republican housewife indifferent to the shortcomings of Congress as they are reflected in this basket?

I do not believe it.

Mr. Speaker, this Congress, in its farsightedness and understanding, has passed the ERP bill.

This Congress has just voted for an expanded Air Force.

Mr. Speaker, unless we initiate the necessary controls, our ERP program and our contemplated defense program are going to increase our inflation until we go bust. In that process the people of America are going to be forced to accept a lower standard of living month by month and year by year. Is that what this Congress wants? I do not believe it.

# NATIONAL DEFENSE

## EMERGENCY PROGRAM FOR
## NATIONAL PREPAREDNESS [1]

### HARRY S. TRUMAN [2]

President Harry S. Truman gave this speech in the House of Representatives before a joint session of Congress, shortly after 12:30 P.M. on Wednesday, March 17, 1948.

The Cabinet members and Supreme Court Justices were in front of Speaker Martin's dais. The diplomatic galleries were full with the exception of the representatives of Russia and her Iron Curtain allies.

Two days before, the President's secretary had announced, out of a clear sky, that the President would report to Congress concerning the international situation.

What events allegedly accompanied the crisis? The Communists had taken over Czechoslovakia. Stalin was demanding a mutual assistance treaty with Finland—and so threatening to bring that country completely within the Iron Curtain. Italian Communists were active and were reported by the American Embassy in Rome as having a good chance of winning the elections of April 18. The civil war in Greece continued to flare up with the rebels' cause actively promoted and supported by communistic Albania and Bulgaria. The Palestinian territory, tentatively divided between the Jews and Arabs, with the prospective withdrawal of Britain, had developed into active civil war, with worse to come. In Brussels, Belgium, France, Great Britain, Luxemburg, and Holland were drawing up a fifty-year political and military pact of defense against Russia. In Paris, sixteen nations were meeting to discuss the implementation of the European Recovery Program (assuming that Congress would enact that legislation).

Mr. Truman had spent several days working on the speech. Secretary of State George C. Marshall, Secretary of Defense James V. Forrestal, and Secretary of Commerce W. Averell Harriman were closeted with the President. But the address was apparently largely the work of the speaker himself.

Mr. Truman's delivery was more effective than that of his previous presentations. He had a more lively sense of communication and full appreciation of the content of his discourse. It sounded less like a paper perfunctorily read. Applause was at a minimum. "The President

[1] *Congressional Record.* 80th Congress, 2d session. 94:3082-5. March 17, 1948 (daily edition). Text furnished by the President's secretary.
[2] For biographical note see Appendix.

read carefully but rapidly from his prepared text, occasionally stressing a point with an abbreviated gesture of the hand or finger. Only occasionally did he look up from the text before him and his stance was unaltered throughout the address." [3]   At the end the Democrats were demonstrative in their support of the speech. The Republicans were largely noncommittal.

The national reaction to the speech was mixed. Congress was ready to endorse the ERP and perhaps a limited draft. Universal military training was still vigorously opposed. (That bill had been pigeonholed for almost a year by the House Rules Committee.)

The chief domestic criticism was that the speaker had not let the public in on the real reason for his drastic "solution." Great Britain and the other Western European democracies hailed the address with enthusiasm. The Moscow radio denounced it as "saber rattling".

The speech received a Hooper rating of 33.4. About 17.6 million adult listeners, according to the C. E. Hooper Audience Measuring Form, listened—"the largest audience to hear the President speak since his V-E Day broadcast."

Later in the day, Mr. Truman flew to New York and, with several million others, reviewed the St. Patrick's Day parade. He then spoke at a dinner of the Friendly Sons of St. Patrick. Here he supplemented his congressional address. He summarized his recommendation to Congress, insisted that his policy had been to protect the United Nations, argued that his aims were to avert war, justified his program as backing the Brussels agreement "signed a few hours ago," and stated the issue as "tyranny versus freedom." The student of Truman's address to Congress on March 17 should also examine this later speech.

Mr. President, Mr. Speaker, Members of the Congress:  I am here today to report to you on the critical nature of the situation in Europe, and to recommend action for your consideration.

Rapid changes are taking place in Europe which affect our foreign policy and our national security. There is an increasing threat to nations which are striving to maintain a form of government which grants freedom to its citizens. The United States is deeply concerned with the survival of freedom in those nations. It is of vital importance that we act now, in order to preserve the conditions under which we can achieve lasting peace based on freedom and justice.

The achievement of such a peace has been the great goal of this nation.

Almost three years have elapsed since the end of the greatest of all wars, but peace and stability have not returned to the

[3] *New York Times.*  p3.  March 18, 1948.

world. We were well aware that the end of the fighting would not automatically settle the problems arising out of the war. The establishment of peace after the fighting is over has always been a difficult task. And even if all the Allies of World War II were united in their desire to establish a just and honorable peace, there would still be great difficulties in the way of achieving that goal.

But the situation in the world today is not primarily the result of the natural difficulties which follow a great war. It is chiefly due to the fact that one nation has not only refused to cooperate in the establishment of a just and honorable peace, but—even worse—has actively sought to prevent it.

The Congress is familiar with the course of events.

You know of the sincere and patient attempts of the democratic nations to find a secure basis for peace through negotiation and agreement. Conference after conference has been held in different parts of the world. We have tried to settle the questions arising out of the war on a basis which would permit the establishment of a just peace. You know the obstacles we have encountered. But the record stands as a monument to the good faith and integrity of the democratic nations of the world. The agreements we did obtain, imperfect though they were, could have furnished the basis for a just peace—if they had been kept.

But they were not kept. They have been persistently ignored and violated by one nation.

The Congress is also familiar with the developments concerning the United Nations. Most of the countries of the world have joined together in the United Nations in an attempt to build a world order based on law and not on force. Most of the members support the United Nations earnestly and honestly, and seek to make it stronger and more effective.

One nation, however, has persistently obstructed the work of the United Nations by constant abuse of the veto. That nation has vetoed twenty-one proposals for action in a little over two years.

But that is not all. Since the close of hostilities, the Soviet Union and its agents have destroyed the independence and democratic character of a whole series of nations in Eastern and Central Europe. It is this ruthless course of action, and the clear design to extend it to the remaining free nations of Europe, that have brought about the critical situation in Europe today.

The tragic death of the Republic of Czechoslovakia has sent a shock throughout the civilized world. Now pressure is being brought to bear on Finland, to the hazard of the entire Scandinavian peninsula. Greece is under direct military attack from rebels actively supported by her Communist-dominated neighbors. In Italy, a determined and aggressive effort is being made by a Communist minority to take control of that country. The methods vary, but the pattern is all too clear.

Faced with this growing menace, there have been encouraging signs that the free nations of Europe are drawing closer together for their economic well-being and for the common defense of their liberties.

In the economic field, the movement for mutual self-help to restore conditions essential to the preservation of free institutions is well under way. In Paris, the sixteen nations which are cooperating in the European Recovery Program are meeting again to establish a joint organization to work for the economic restoration of Western Europe.

The United States has strongly supported the efforts of these nations to repair the devastation of war and restore a sound world economy. In presenting this program to the Congress last December, I emphasized the necessity for speedy action. Every event in Europe since that day has underlined the great urgency for the prompt adoption of this measure.

The Soviet Union and its satellites were invited to cooperate in the European Recovery Program. They rejected the invitation. More than that, they have declared their violent hostility to the program and are aggressively attempting to wreck it. They see in it a major obstacle to their designs to subjugate the free community of Europe. They do not want the United States to help Europe. They do not even want the sixteen cooperating countries to help themselves.

While economic recovery in Europe is essential, measures for economic rehabilitation alone are not enough. The free nations of Europe realize that economic recovery, if it is to succeed, must be afforded some measure of protection against internal and external aggression. The movement toward economic cooperation has been followed by a movement toward common self-protection in the face of the growing menace to their freedom.

At the very moment I am addressing you, five nations of the European community, in Brussels, are signing a fifty-year agreement for economic cooperation and common defense against aggression.

This action has great significance, for this agreement was not imposed by the decree of a more powerful neighbor. It was the free choice of independent governments representing the will of their people, and acting within the terms of the Charter of the United Nations.

Its significance goes far beyond the actual terms of the agreement itself. It is a notable step in the direction of unity in Europe for the protection and preservation of its civilization. This development deserves our full support. I am confident that the United States will, by appropriate means, extend to the free nations the support which the situation requires. I am sure that the determination of the free countries of Europe to protect themselves will be matched by an equal determination on our part to help them to do so.

The recent developments in Europe present this nation with fundamental issues of vital importance. I believe that we have reached a point at which the position of the United States should be made unmistakably clear.

The principles and purposes expressed in the Charter of the United Nations continue to represent our hope for the eventual establishment of the rule of law in international affairs. The Charter constitutes the basic expression of the code of international ethics to which this country is dedicated. We cannot, however, close our eyes to the harsh fact that through obstruction and even defiance on the part of one nation, this great dream has not yet become a full reality.

It is necessary, therefore, that we take additional measures to supplement the work of the United Nations and to support its aims. There are times in world history when it is far wiser to act than to hesitate. There is some risk involved in action—there always is. But there is far more risk in failure to act. For if we act wisely now, we shall strengthen the powerful forces for freedom, justice, and peace which are represented by the United Nations and the free nations of the world.

I regard it as my duty, therefore, to recommend to the Congress those measures which, in my judgment, are best calculated to give support to the free and democratic nations of Europe and to improve the solid foundation of our own national strength.

First, I recommend that the Congress speedily complete its action on the European Recovery Program. That program is the foundation of our policy of assistance to the free nations of Europe. Prompt passage of that program is the most telling contribution we can now make toward peace.

The decisive action which the Senate has taken without regard to partisan political consideration is a striking example of the effective working of democracy.

Time is now of critical importance. I am encouraged by the information which has come to me concerning the plans for expeditious action by the House of Representatives. I hope that no single day will be needlessly lost.

Second, I recommend prompt enactment of universal training legislation.

Until the free nations of Europe have regained their strength, and so long as communism threatens the very existence of democracy, the United States must remain strong enough to support those countries of Europe which are threatened with Communist control and police-state rule.

I believe that we have learned the importance of maintaining military strength as a means of preventing war. We have found that a sound military system is necessary in time of peace if we are to remain at peace. Aggressors in the past, relying on our apparent lack of military force, have unwisely precipitated war. Although they have been led to destruction by their misconception of our strength, we have paid a terrible price for our unpreparedness.

Universal training is the only feasible means by which the civilian components of our armed forces can be built up to the strength required if we are to be prepared for emergencies. Our ability to mobilize large numbers of trained men in time of emergency could forestall future conflict and, together with other measures of national policy, could restore stability to the world.

The adoption of universal training by the United States at this time would unmistakable evidence to all the world of our determination to back the will to peace with the strength for peace. I am convinced that the decision of the American people, expressed through the Congress, to adopt universal training would be of first importance in giving courage to every free government in the world.

Third, I recommend the temporary reenactment of selective service legislation in order to maintain our armed forces at their authorized strength.

Our armed forces lack the necessary men to maintain their authorized strength. They have been unable to maintain their authorized strength through voluntary enlistments, even though such strength has been reduced to the very minimum necessary to meet our obligations abroad and is far below the minimum which should always be available in the continental United States.

We cannot meet our international responsibilities unless we maintain our armed forces. It is of vital importance, for example, that we keep our occupation forces in Germany until the peace is secure in Europe.

There is no conflict between the requirements of selective service for the regular forces and universal training for the reserve components. Selective service is necessary until the solid foundation of universal training can be established. Selective service can then be terminated and the regular forces may then be maintained on a voluntary basis.

The recommendations I have made represent the most urgent steps toward securing the peace and preventing war.

We must be ready to take every wise and necessary step to carry out this great purpose. This will require assistance to other nations. It will require an adequate and balanced military strength. We must be prepared to pay the price of peace, or assuredly we shall pay the price of war.

We in the United States remain determined to seek, by every possible means, a just and honorable basis for the settlement of international issues. We shall continue to give our strong allegiance to the United Nations as the principal means for international security based on law, not on force. We shall remain ready and anxious to join with all nations—I repeat, with all nations—in every possible effort to reach international understanding and agreement.

The door has never been closed, nor will it ever be closed, to the Soviet Union or any other nation which will genuinely cooperate in preserving the peace. At the same time, we must not be confused about the central issue which confronts the world today.

The time has come when the free men and women of the world must face the threat to their liberty squarely and courageously.

The United States has a tremendous responsibility to act according to the measure of our power for good in the world. We have learned that we must earn the peace we seek just as we earned victory in war, not by wishful thinking but by realistic effort.

At no time in our history has unity among our people been so vital as it is at the present time. Unity of purpose, unity of effort and unity of spirit are essential to accomplish the task before us.

Each of us here in this chamber today has a special responsibility. The world situation is too critical, and the responsibilities of this country are too vast, to permit party struggles to weaken our influence for maintaining peace.

The American people have the right to assume that political considerations will not affect our working together. They have the right to assume that we will join hands, wholeheartedly and without reservation, in our efforts to preserve peace in the world.

With God's help we shall succeed.

# THE POLITICAL CAMPAIGNS

## "I SHALL RUN IN 1948" [1]

### HENRY A. WALLACE [2]

Henry A. Wallace gave this speech, announcing his candidacy for the presidency on an independent ticket, in Chicago, over the Mutual Broadcasting Network (but *not* over Chicago station WGN), on Monday, December 29, 1947.

The announcement had been anticipated since December 15, when the Progressive Citizens of America strongly urged the ex-Secretary of Commerce to run.

Mr. Wallace flew from New York to Chicago, closeted himself in the Drake Hotel, and completed his address. Almost certainly he composed it without collaborators. On Monday he conferred with the Progressive Citizens of America committee and others from some eighteen states.

Why had Wallace set in motion a "third party" with himself as leader? Presumably because he was convinced that the Truman foreign policy was leading to war. Allegedly, also, Truman's dismissal of Wallace as Secretary of Commerce in 1946, in the issue of Byrnes versus Wallace,[3] was a factor. Wallace was supposedly ready to wreck the Democratic party, if necessary, to displace Truman. Allegedly, too, Mr. Wallace was disappointed because Roosevelt had sidestepped him in favor of Truman, as the vice presidential running mate, in 1944. But for that turn of fate, the ex-cabinet member would now be in the White House. Still another motive ascribed to Wallace, according to some commentators, was that he was setting out to build up his own following with a view to capturing the Democratic nomination in 1952.

Whatever these motives, the independent party spokesman was listened to over many stations during his Chicago broadcast. His subsequent radio and other campaign speeches also drew considerable audiences. As the political activities of 1948 started, the stock of Wallace rose higher and higher. As of May 1, 1948, his estimated following among the voters was more than five million.

[1] Text furnished by the National Wallace for President Committee, New York City, through the courtesy of C. B. Baldwin, Campaign Manager.
[2] For biographical note see Appendix.
[3] See *Representative American Speeches: 1946-1947*, p33-42, for Mr. Wallace's speech that led to his dismissal; see also the comment on that speech.

What of the address? Like many other campaign appeals, it was punctuated with personal pronouns (at least thirty *I's*, as well as a number of *we's*); personal experiences; direct discourse (e.g., "Henry Wallace, we'll welcome your support but we will not change our policies"); exhortation to his listeners to "stand upright, as men"; appeal to the basic drives of security, idealism, brotherhood, peace, hatred of Wall Street, hatred of militarism, love of fair play (e.g., toward Russia); and ethical proof (his own American ancestry) and assumption of logical propositions rather than proof of them.

Wallace was a seasoned speaker, government official, and campaigner. He had been editor of *Wallace's Farmer,* Secretary of Agriculture under Roosevelt (1933-1940), Vice President (1940-1944), Secretary of Commerce under Truman (1944-1946), and editor of the *New Republic* (1946-December 1947). During these years he had campaigned and lectured continually.

He had made progress in the art of oral composition and platform appeal. His specific influence, however, rested more fully on his ideas and political prominence than on his oratorical skill. He was no Bryan, Beveridge, or Borah. In extempore utterance before large outdoor audiences, he was unimpressive. In most of his campaign speeches he relied more on appeal than on close reasoning and mustering of concrete facts.

What of the effects of the Chicago speech? Several million voters set about to support him. Most of them came from the left wing of the Democratic party. His chief strength was derived from the Progressive Citizens of America, the American Labor party, and the Communist party. All signs pointed to the defeat of the Democratic party in November 1948, unless his candidacy was abandoned.

For the past fifteen months I have traveled up and down, and back and forth across this country. I have talked with half a million people in public meetings and with thousands in private gatherings. I have been working for, and I shall continue to work for, peace and security in America, grounded on a foundation of world peace and security.

Everywhere in the United States today, among farmers, workers, small business men and professional men and women, I find confusion, uncertainty and fear. The people do not ask, "Will there be another war?"—but "When will the war come?"

Everywhere I find that people are spending so much for food and rent that they cannot afford their customary services from the doctor and dentist. They do not ask, "Will there be another depression?"—but "When will the real depression start?"

Peace and abundance mean so much to me that I have said at a dozen press conferences and in many speeches when asked about a third party, "If the Democratic party continues to be a party of war and depression, I will see to it that the people have a chance to vote for prosperity and peace." To those who have come to me asking the conditions of my adherence to the present Democratic administration, I have said, "Let the administration repudiate universal military training and rid itself of the Wall Street-military team that is leading us toward war."

I have insisted that the Democratic administration curb the ever growing power and profits of monopoly and take concrete steps to preserve the living standards of the American people. I have demanded that the Democratic administration cease its attacks on the civil liberties of Americans. In speeches in the North and in the South at non-segregated meetings, I have stated the simple truth that segregation and discrimination of any kind or character have no place in America.

My terms to the Democratic high command have been well known. By their actions and finally by their words, they have said—"Henry Wallace, we welcome your support but we will not change our policies."

In answering me, the Democratic leadership also gave its answer to millions of Americans who demand the right to vote for peace and prosperity. Thus, the leadership of the Democratic party would deprive the American people of their rightful opportunity to choose between progress and reaction in 1948. So far as the Republican party is concerned, there is no hope—as Geoge Norris, Fiorello La Guardia and Wendell Willkie long ago found out.

When the old parties rot, the people have a right to be heard through a new party. They asserted that right when the Democratic party was founded under Jefferson in the struggle against the Federalist party of war and privilege of his time. They won it again when the Republican party was organized in Lincoln's day. The people must again have an opportunity to speak out with their votes in 1948.

The lukewarm liberals sitting on two chairs say, "Why throw away your vote?" I say a vote for a new party in 1948 will be the most valuable vote you have ever cast, or ever will cast. The bigger the peace vote in 1948, the more definitely the world will know that the United States is not behind the bipartisan reactionary war policy which is dividing the world into two armed camps and making inevitable the day when American soldiers will be lying in their Arctic suits in the Russian snow.

There is no real fight between a Truman and a Republican. Both stand for a policy which opens the door to war in our lifetime and makes war certain for our children.

Stop saying, "I don't like it but I am going to vote for the lesser of two evils."

Rather than accept either evil, come out boldly, stand upright as men and say so loudly all the world can hear—"We are voting peace and security for ourselves and our children's children. The peace of a full life; the security of full production. We are fighting for old-fashioned Americanism at the polls in 1948. We are fighting for freedom of speech and freedom of assembly. We are fighting to end racial discrimination. We are fighting for lower prices. We are fighting for free labor unions, for jobs, and for homes in which we can decently live."

We have just passed through the holiday season when every radio and every church proclaimed the joyous tidings of peace. Every year at this time the hearts of the American people swell with genuine good will toward all mankind. We are a kindly, well-meaning people. But the holiday season soon passes and one of the first items on the agenda of the new Congress is universal military training. I say the first political objective of progressives is the defeat of this bill, which would deliver our eighteen-year-olds over to the army and cost the nation two billion dollars a year. Universal military training is the first decisive step on the road to fascism. We shall fight it to the limit, and all Congressmen who vote for it.

The American people read of the fantastic appropriations that are being made for military adventures in Greece, Turkey, China—and billions for armaments here at home. Slowly it dawns on us that these newspaper headlines have stepped into our everyday lives at the grocery store when we pay $1 for butter, 95 cents for eggs, and 90 cents for meat.

We suddenly realize that we can't have all the people of the world getting ready for the next war without paying for it in our daily lives with less food, clothing and housing. War preparations create record profits for big business but only false prosperity for the people—their purchasing power shrinks as prices rise, their needs go unfilled, and they are burdened with new debts. Yet, corporation profits are over three times what they were in 1939, but every family is paying for our war policy at the grocery store.

A new party must stand for a positive peace program for abundance and security, not scarcity and war. We can prevent depression and war if we only organize for peace in the same comprehensive way we organize for war.

I personally was for the humanitarian aspects of the Marshall Plan long before it was announced. Because I saw the postwar need of helping human beings I was accused of wanting a quart of milk for every Hottentot. I pushed for help for Greece against the opposition of the administration eight months before the Truman Doctrine was announced.

But I have fought and shall continue to fight programs which give guns to people when they want plows. I fight the Truman Doctrine and the Marshall Plan as applied because they divide Europe into two warring camps. Those whom we buy politically with our food will soon desert us. They will pay us in the base coin of temporary gratitude and then turn to hate us because our policies are destroying their freedom.

We are restoring Western Europe and Germany through United States agencies rather than United Nations agencies because we want to hem Russia in. We are acting in the same way as France and England after the last war and the end result will be the same—confusion, depression and war.

It just doesn't need to happen. The cost of organizing for peace, prosperity and progress is infinitely less than the cost of organizing for war.

We who believe this will be called "Russian tools" and "Communists." Let the fearmongers not distort and becloud the issues by name-calling. We are not for Russia and we are not for communism, but we recognize Hitlerite methods when we see them in our own land and we denounce the men who engage in such name-calling as enemies of the human race who would rather have World War III than put forth a genuine effort to bring about a peaceful settlement of differences.

One thing I want to make clear to both Russia and the United States—peace requires real understanding between our peoples. Russia has as much to gain from peace as the United States, and just as we here fight against the spreaders of hate and falsehood against Russia, the Russian leaders can make a great contribution by restraining those extremists who try to widen the gap between our two great countries.

I insist that the United States be fully secure until there is real peace between the United States and Russia and until there is an international police force stronger than the military establishment of any nation including Russia and the United States. I am utterly against any kind of imperialism or expansionism whether sponsored by Britain, Russia, or the United States, and I call on Russia as well as the United States to look at all our differences objectively and free from that prejudice which the hatemongers have engendered on both sides. What the world needs is a UN Disarmament Conference to rid humanity for all time of the threat, not only of atomic bombs, but also of all other methods of mass destruction.

It happens that all of my mother's and three fourths of my father's ancestors came to this country before the American Revolution. I love the Americanism I was taught to respect in the public schools of Iowa half a century ago. That Americanism was betrayed after World War I by forces which found their origin in monopoly capitalism, yellow journalism and racial bigotry. Today there is a greater menace than ever before. We are losing friends, destroying basic liberties, and making enemies at a time when the cost of failure is complete destruction.

That failure can be met and overcome only by a new political alignment in America which requires the organization of a new political party.

To that end I announce tonight that I shall run as an independent candidate for President of the United States in 1948.

Thousands of people all over the United States have asked me to engage in this great fight. The people are on the march.

I hope that you who are listening to me tonight will lead the forces of peace, progress and prosperity in your communities and throughout our country.

Will you let me know that you have come out fighting against the powers of evil?

We have assembled a Gideon's Army—small in number, powerful in conviction, ready for action. We have said with Gideon, "Let those who are fearful and trembling depart." For every fearful one who leaves, there will be a thousand to take his place. A just cause is worth a hundred armies. We face the future unfettered by any principle but the general welfare. We owe no allegiance to any group which does not serve that welfare. By God's grace, the people's peace will usher in the Century of the Common Man.

# SHALL THE COMMUNIST PARTY IN THE UNITED STATES BE OUTLAWED? [4]

## Thomas E. Dewey and Harold E. Stassen [5]

Governor Thomas E. Dewey, of New York, and Harold E. Stassen, governor of Minnesota three times, engaged in this debate in the closing days of their Oregon campaign for nomination as the Republican candidate for the presidency. The debate was held in Portland, Oregon on May 17, 1948, and was broadcast over NBC and ABC, beginning at 10 P.M., Eastern Daylight Time.

Each occupied a glass-enclosed studio in station KEX. Donald R. Van Boskirk, chairman of the Multnomah County (in which Portland is located) Republican Central Committee, was moderator. Each speaker had twenty minutes for his original presentation and eight and a half minutes for his rebuttal.

Only members of the working press, picture men, still photographers, and the executive committee of the county central committe were admitted to the building to see and hear the debate. About forty reporters listened over the loudspeakers outside the glass enclosures.

Governor Dewey, losing out to Roosevelt in the campaign of 1944, had nevertheless been regarded as a highly effective campaigner in that contest with the wartime fourth term President. Dewey's preliminary campaigning and speaking in the state Republican primaries of the spring of 1948, including his canvass of New Hampshire, his last-minute appearances in Wisconsin, his Nebraska tour, and finally his Oregon drive, repeatedly demonstrated his practical skill on the stump. He opened in Oregon on May 1. With Stassen he gave "the greatest campaign the State has ever experienced." [6]

In the Portland debate, each repeated the arguments he had made frequently in previous months. In statement of issues, analysis of the problem, summoning of evidence, refutational skill, audience adaptation and appeal, language, and delivery, the two speakers were closely matched. Dewey, in the opinion of this critic, excelled in his management of concrete evidence, in statement of the essential argument, and in rebuttal he "won the debate."

[4] Text supplied through the courtesy of Mr. Robert Ray, speech consultant to Governor Dewey. Text corrected from recording made by this editor.
[5] For biographical notes see Appendix.
[6] *Sunday Oregonian.* p1. May 2, 1948.

In the primary election on May 21, Dewey also won the twelve delegates.[7]

## AFFIRMATIVE

## HAROLD E. STASSEN

Chairman Van Boskirk, Your Excellency Governor Dewey, My Fellow Citizens: During the recent war I saw many young Americans killed. I watched ships explode and burn, planes crash in flames, men—our men—my friends, fall. I met thousands of prisoners of war as they were liberated from indescribable conditions of imprisonment and suffering. I viewed the devastation of cities and of farms.

In the midst of these experiences, I thought more deeply than ever before of the way in which men should live, of the preciousness of freedom, of the future of America. I made a quiet resolve to do everything within my power after V-J Day to keep America free and to prevent a third World War.

Four principal objectives appeared to be essential. First, to maintain a sound and humanitarian free American economy, which would include avoiding inflation booms, with their out-of-reach prices, preventing depression crashes with unemployment, widely developing the superb natural resources of water, forests, and minerals, constantly improving housing and health, establishing a fair balance between capital and labor, assuring to agriculture a fair share of the national income, advancing in civil rights, decreasing discrimination and bigotry, constantly endeavoring to win happier homes throughout America; and, second, to keep America and other free countries strong in a military sense, especially in the air; and, third, to safeguard against the undermining and overthrow of free governments, and to defend the freedom of men; and, fourth, to establish a strong organization of United Nations for peace and economic progress without a veto, and with a real system of justice.

With a firm conviction that an open and frank discussion would lead to better answers of the manner in which to make

[7] For further comment on these speakers, see *Representative American Speeches*: *1943-1944.* p259-66; *1944-1945.* p56-67.

progress toward these objectives, I have talked directly to the
people of my views, and invited their questions and welcomed
any opportunity to meet with others in a joint discussion. This
is the background for my Oregon campaign. I have submitted
to the people of Oregon my position on the building of the
resources and the rapid development of the Columbia Basin
and the Willamette Valley, the need for long-range programs
in agriculture and forestry, the importance of that fair balance
between management and labor, and the progress in housing and
health. I presented my view of a strong foreign policy for
America with an alert and trained military, the Marshall
Plan, leadership toward amending and strengthening the United
Nations charter, the stopping of the shipments of machine tools
and electrical equipment to Russia, the direct outlawing of the
Communist organization in America, and in the free countries,
and positive action in ideals and moral standards and justice on
a worldwide basis.

I have presented my optimism, my hope that such policies
would lead to a future of peace and of progress for ourselves
and for others without the tragedy of a third World War. One
part of my proposed program for America has been directly
challenged. It has been challenged by a man for whom I have
great respect, a man who is a fellow Republican and who has
joined in campaigns in Wisconsin and Nebraska, and now in
Oregon. Tonight we meet in a joint radio discussion of that
one point. I will give you my position on this one point in
detail and give the reasons why I have reached this conclusion.

When World War II ended I felt that the key question as
to future peace would arise if bad policies were followed by the
Soviet Union of Russia and by the world Communist party
directed from Moscow. I, therefore, gave special study to their
actions to their methods, and their apparent intentions. I
journeyed to many of the European countries and to Russia,
questioned leaders of many nations, for a first-hand look-and-
listen trip. I followed closely the results of the peace conferences
of Potsdam and Yalta and the developments in country after
country. I have reached the conclusion that the Communist

organizations in the world are absolutely directed by the rulers of Russia in the Kremlin. I have reached the conclusion that the objectives of these Communist organizations in the world are to overthrow free governments, to destroy the liberties of men, and to bring other countries under the domination of the dictators of Russia. I have watched country after country in which these Communist organizations have taken every legal advantage, but have recognized none of the corresponding obligations and moralities. The most recent and extreme instance was Czechoslovakia. The Communists never had the support of a majority of the people of Czechoslovakia, but they were given full legal standing and Communists were appointed to some of the ministries of government. The people of the country were free, they were rebuilding from the war, there was no tyranny, there was no threat to Russia, there was a politeness and a friendliness toward the Communists, but the Communist organizations directed from Moscow took all of these legal blessings and at the same time moved underneath the surface, established Communist action committees in all the departments of government, in the big labor unions, in key industries, and in the universities and colleges. Then a few weeks ago the overground and underground moved together, Czechoslovakia was betrayed, the liberties of the people were wiped out, and another country was brought under the domination of the Kremlin.

These developments do give rise to a danger of war. Analyzing what they mean it seems clear to me that the free countries, including America, do not now have adequate laws to safeguard themselves in the face of this menace. I consider it to be clear that these Communist organizations are not really political parties. They are actually fifth columns. They are Quisling cliques. If we are to have the best chance of winning through for freedom, without the horror of a third World War, the free countries must take action to protect themselves against this fifth column in this unsettled period which has been called a cold war. I do not think it is generally realized in America that we do not now have any law to effectively oppose the actions of these Communist organizations, either overground or underground. There is now no law in America to prevent these Communist organizations from secretly developing organizations of hidden members, from carrying on secret conspiracies, to promote strikes, to stir up hatred between races and religions in America, and from following their directions from Moscow. Neither is there any present law to prevent the Communist organizations from maintaining large offices with telephone switchboards, and a network of communication to be used in reaching and coordinating these underground activities and in recruiting new members. In facing up to the problem we must maintain complete constitutional rights and liberties in America, the right of free speech, of free press, of freedom of conscience and freedom of religion must be kept inviolate. It must always be open for any individual in this country to protest, to object, to dissent, but there is no constitutional right to carry on organizations aboveground or belowground directed by the rulers of a foreign power for the purpose of overthrowing the government of the United States and taking away the liberties of its people. I, therefore, have urged for some months that we need a new law to directly outlaw these Communist organizations. Governor Dewey has insisted that our present laws are adequate. I submit that a new law is needed. It should directly make it illegal, after its passage, to carry on any organization, either aboveground or belowground, which is directed by the rulers of a foreign power for the purpose of overthrowing the government of the United States, destroying the liberties of its people, and bringing this country under domination of the rulers of a foreign power.

Such a law would not outlaw ideas. It would not outlaw thoughts. It would make illegal organized conspiracies of Fifth Columns. Such a law is constitutional under Article IV, Section 4 of the United States Constitution. A very eminent lawyer, the honorable William L. Ransom, past president of the American Bar Association, agrees on its constitutionality in an able article in the *American Law Journal* this month. The language of the Supreme Court of the United States in the case of Ohio versus Akron indicates that the Supreme Court would uphold its constitutionality. In fact, the national Congress is right now moving to do this very thing. A law has been introduced known as the

Mundt-Nixon Bill which provides that it shall be unlawful to attempt in any manner to establish in the United States a totalitarian dictatorship, the direction and control of which is to be vested in or exercised by or under the domination or control of a foreign government, a foreign organization or foreign individual, or to attempt to perform any act toward those ends. The report of the committee that had investigated the Communist activities before preparing that bill specifically found that the Communist organization was an organization whose basic aim, whether open or concealed, is the abolition of our present economic system and democratic form of government and the establishment of a Soviet dictatorship in its place. Now, the chairman and secretary of the Communist party of America have protested that this bill would outlaw their organization. I agree that it would, and I say that it should. The United States Congress indicated in a preliminary way their approval of the bill when they voted last Friday by a vote of 296 to 40 to bring it up for action on Tuesday. It might well be amended to some extent before it is finally passed by both houses, because in some clauses directed against individuals it goes even beyond what I have urged, but I do believe that it will pass in the near future in a form that will definitely outlaw these Communist organizations in both their underground and overground activities. I further believe that this will be a precedent for similar action by the other free countries of the world and that effective means will be developed to safeguard against the fifth column infiltration of the Communists.

Now, I recognize full well that there are some who very sincerely oppose my position in this matter. I am not certain of the reasons for Mr. Henry Wallace's opposition to my position, but I am confident that Governor Dewey's opposition is completely sincere. But I respectfully ask him to reconsider his opposition, as I believe he is mistaken. His position in effect, means a soft policy toward communism, and all the evidence around the world shows that a soft policy wins neither peace nor respect nor improvement from the Communists. We must not coddle communism with legality. They grasp every concession made and continue their undermining actions. Consider these facts: There are now eleven countries of the world under the domination of the Communist leaders in Moscow. They are Russia, Poland, Czechoslovakia, Hungary, Yugoslavia, Rumania, Bulgaria, Albania, Estonia, Latvia, and Lithuania. In none of these eleven did the Communists ever receive a majority support of the people in a free election. The last three were taken over by force during the war and held ever since. In every one of the remaining eight, the Communists used the legal recognition of Communist organizations as an overground nerve center and recruiting station for their underground movements, until they had seized power and brought the nation under the dictation of the Communist Politburo.

Russia was the first Communist-dominated nation. It came under this dictatorship through a combination of two main reasons: First, the bad government of the Czar; second, the organization developed by the legalized Bolshevik party which formed throughout Russia and elected six members to the Russian Parliament in the last election held in that country before the Communists came to power.

There seems to have been some mistaken idea that the Communists were outlawed in Russia. This is not correct. The Bolshevik party was active in Russia right up to the first war with Germany. The Communists carried on a nationwide election campaign in Russia in 1912, and elected six members to the Parliament or Duma. They used this means of developing their revolutionary organization, and when they were caught in the attempted revolution in 1905 and in various sabotage and train wreckings and bombings, they were severely punished, but they were not outlawed as an organization. When this present Communist party did come into power in Russia, they promptly wiped out all other political parties and took the whole people under a firm and dictatorial grip. In each of the other countries —Poland, Hungary, Yugoslavia, Bulgaria, Rumania, Albania, and finally Czechoslovakia, the Communists used the blessing of legality as an aid to organizing an underground movement, and finally betrayed the liberties of the people and brought them under the domination of the Kremlin in Moscow.

These are the facts which today cause a menace to Scandinavia and Western Europe. These are the facts which today present a danger of future world war.

Another mistaken impression is the claim that if we outlaw the Communist organization, we thereby endanger the liberties and civil rights of other people. This is not true. In Canada today the party was outlawed for years, and the people lost none of their liberties. In fact, the Communists were permitted to operate legally again under the name of the Labor Progressive party in 1943, and soon afterwards, in less than three years, it was found that the Communists were working directly with the Russian Embassy at Ottawa in a spy ring.

In order that we might narrow down our discussion and find out just exactly what the differences are in our positions, I should like to ask Governor Dewey specifically these questions:

(1) Do you agree that the Communist organizations throughout the world are directed from Moscow?

(2) Do you agree that the objective of the Communist organizations throughout the world is to overthrow free governments, destroy liberties, and bring the countries under the domination of the Kremlin?

(3) Do you agree that Communist organizations throughout the world are a menace to future peace?

(4) Do you agree that because of the menace to world peace it is necessary that we require American young men to serve in our armed forces and to take military training?

To make my position, then, clear, I say very definitely that it does not add up, to me, to say that loyal patriotic young Americans must of necessity be drafted; that their liberties must be taken away in order to make America strong in the face of the menace to peace caused by Communist organizations, but that none of the privileges and blessings of legality should be taken away from the Communist organizations, themselves, which, in fact, are causing the menace that makes the drafting necessary.

The fundamental principles of human liberty upon which this nation is founded are drawn from our basic religious concepts. Our founding fathers did believe that man has a spiritual value, that he is endowed by his Creator with certain inalienable rights, that he should have a human dignity, a respect for the welfare of others, that there is a brotherhood of man. The constitutional rights in America are based on that concept. When one speaks of the constitutional right of organizations that are seeking to destroy freedom, there is a misconception of the deep basis of constitutional rights.

There is no such thing as a constitutional right to destroy all constitutional rights. There is no such thing as a freedom to destroy freedom. The right of man to liberty is inherent in the nature of man. To win it and to maintain it requires courage and sacrifice, and it also requires intelligence and realism and determination in the establishment of the laws and the systems of justice to serve mankind.

I submit that the Communist organization in America and in the freedom-loving countries of the world should be outlawed.

## NEGATIVE

### THOMAS E. DEWEY

Mr. Van Boskirk, Mr. Stassen, Ladies and Gentlemen: I am delighted to participate in this discussion, with my distinguished confrere, and I have listened with good interest to his eloquent discussion of the subject and of all of the other matters which he brought up.

He asked me four questions:

One: Do you agree that the Communist organizations in the world today are under the direction of the Kremlin in Moscow? Certainly.

Second: Do you agree that the world Communist organization is a threat to world peace? Certainly.

Third: Do you agree that the objectives of these Communist organizations is to destroy the liberties of other men? Certainly.

Finally, fourth: If you agree to these things, under what provisions of the Constitution—as I took my quick notes here—

and what legal action are you against outlawing them when we are drafting young men in time of peace to build up the defenses against Communist aggression?

This last question, of course, entirely begs the question. The question is not whether anyone is interested in helping any Communist to preserve his liberties. No one in America has the slightest interest in the Communists. My interest is in preserving this country from being destroyed by the development of an underground organization which would grow so colossally in strength were it outlawed, that it might easily destroy our country and cause us to draft all of the young men in the nation.

Now, I find that the difficulty, here, tonight, is that Mr. Stassen has not adhered to his subject or his statements. He says he is for the Mundt Bill, because, says Mr. Stassen, it outlaws the Communist party. But the fact of the matter is, he is in grievous error. The only authority he quotes is the head of the Communist party, which is not exactly a very good authority for what is truth. Usually if a Communist says it does this, you know it does the opposite. So let's find out whether the Mundt Bill does outlaw the Communist party. That is the first job.

If the Mundt Bill did outlaw the Communist party, then we would be able to debate it. Here is what Mr. Mundt says, on May 14, 1948:

This bill does not outlaw the Communist party.

On February 5, 1948, Congressman Mundt said:

I have been one of those who has not looked with favor upon proposals to outlaw the Communist party or to declare its activities illegal, because I fear such action, on the part of Congress, would only tend to drive further underground the forces which are already largely concealed from public view. What I want to do is to drive the Communist functionaries out of the ground into the open where patriotic Americans of every walk of life can come to learn and understand their objectives.

Now, we have the head of the Communist party saying that it does outlaw them, and Mr. Stassen says so. Mr. Mundt, whose bill it is, says his bill does not outlaw the Communist party.

So, as between that debate, let us now see what the Committee says. After all, it is the Committee bill and the Committee presumably knows what its bill does.

In short, I have studied the bill. What it says is that it shall be a crime to endeavor to teach, to advocate, or to conspire to establish in the United States a dictatorship under the control of a foreign government. Well, if that isn't a crime now, then I greatly misread all of the sections of the laws as they now are. But before going to that, that is number one in the Mundt Bill. That certainly does not outlaw the Communist party. That simply says it is a crime to try to overthrow the government of the United States and establish a dictatorship under the control of a foreign power, and if that isn't good sound doctrine I don't know good sound doctrine. But it doesn't outlaw the party. It says that Communists cannot hold public office. Well, theoretically they aren't supposed to be allowed to hold it now. It provides they can't get passports, and of course everybody is for that. That is the Mundt Bill. Now, does that outlaw the Communist party? Mr. Foster, the head of the Communist party, and Mr. Stassen say it does. Mr. Mundt says it doesn't. So what does the Committee say? The Committee reports—this is the report of the Congressional Committee on Un-American Activities, whose bill this is. This Committee has been widely criticized in our country because it has been called a red-baiting committee. As a matter of fact, it has been doing a fine, solid, good American job for a great many months. It has done a fine job of exposing Communists and bringing them out in the open where they belong. Here is what the Committee says about the Mundt Bill, April 10, 1948:

Too often a cursory study of this problem leads people to believe that the answer is very simple; that all we have to do is outlaw the Communist party, or pass a law requiring its members to register, and that the problem will solve itself. This is not the case. The Communist party in its operations presents a problem which is something new under the sun. It changes its spots and tactics and strategy without conscience.

I am continuing to quote from the report:

Several bills before the Committee attempt to approach this problem by outlawing the Communist movement as a political party. The subcommittee has found it necessary [and mark you this] to reject this approach.

I think it is perfectly clear that the Mundt Bill does not outlaw the Communist party, and Mr. Mundt and the Committee say that it doesn't. But, just to complete it, let me give you the rest of the point so there can be no possible misundersanding that both Mr. Stassen and Mr. Foster, the head of the Communist party, are wrong. The report of the Committee on the Mundt Bill continues:

The Committee gave serious consideration to the many well-intentioned proposals which attempted to meet the problem by outlawing the Communist party.

Now I am skipping a little. No, I will read it all:

Opponents of this approach differed as to what they desired. Some wanted to bar the Communist party from the ballot and elections. Others would have made membership in the Communist party illegal *per se*. The Committee believes there are several compelling arguments against the outlawing approach. One, illegalization of the party might drive the Communist movement further underground, whereas exposure of its activities is the primary need; two, illegalization has not proved effective in Canada and other countries which have tried it; three, we cannot consistently [and this is of greatest importance] criticize the Communist governments of Europe for suppressing opposition political parties if we resort to the same totalitarian methods here; four, if the present Communist party severs the puppet strings by which it is manipulated from abroad, if it gives up its undercover methods, there is no reason for denying it the privilege of openly advocating its beliefs in the way in which other political parties advocate theirs.

It is absolutely clear that the Mundt Bill does not outlaw the Communist party, was not intended to, and that is the exact opposite of what the Mundt Bill was intended to accomplish, and does accomplish.

So, let's get back to the debate. Mr. Stassen said here in Oregon on April 27, "I hold that the Communist party organization should be promptly outlawed in America and in all freedom-loving countries of the world," and he repeated this in many states, all the way from New Jersey to Oregon. That is the issue. Not the Mundt Bill. The issue is, "Shall we pass a law outlawing the Communist party?" Now, I suppose if you say, "Let's outlaw the Communist party and preserve our liberties," and if you say it fast enough and don't think, it seems to make sense. But, my friends, it makes no sense. You cannot do both, and no nation in all the history of the world ever succeeded in doing it. The question before us is, "Shall the Communist party be outlawed?" The only way I know that could be done is to declare by law that people who call themselves Communists would be denied a place on the ballot and that anyone who is a member of that party after the passage of the law should be tried, convicted, and sentenced to prison for a crime. I believe in keeping the Communist party everlastingly out in the open so we can defeat it and all it stands for.

Now, this outlawing idea is not new. It is as old as government. For thousands of years despots have tortured, imprisoned, killed, exiled their opponents, and their governments have always fallen into the dust. This outlawing idea is as old as communism itself. It is the fact—and I might again refer, just to get our history straight, to the report of the House Committee on Un-American Activities; I quote from page 11—no, page 13 of the report dated—well, I can't find the date. It is the report of the hearings before the subcommittee on legislation, the Committee on Un-American Activities, 80th Congress, HR 4422 and HR 4480. I quote from page 13, "The Communist party was illegal and outlawed in Russia when it took over control of the Soviet Union." The fact is that the czars of Russia were the first people in the world to follow this idea of outlawing the Communist party. They whipped them and they drove them to Siberia, they shot them, they outlawed them, and in the very year, 1917, Lenin and Trotsky were exiles, and what was the result? This outlawing gave them such colossal following, such enormous force, such great loyalty on the part of the people that they were able to seize control of all Russia with its 180 million people, and the first nation to outlaw communism became the first Communist nation. That is what I do not want to happen to the United States of America. For twenty-five years Mussolini outlawed Communists, and they grew and flourished underground despite their punishment and their exile and their shooting. As a result, four weeks ago the Communists and their allies polled more than 30 per cent of the vote in the recent Italian election. In all of Nazi Europe the Communists were underground, and they emerged at the end of the war so strong that they were popular heroes. The French Maquis and others almost seized power in the governments of Europe at the end of this war because of the enormous strength that came to them from being underground. And Czechoslovakia is another beautiful example, and I am grateful to Mr. Stassen for bringing it up. For seven years in Czechoslovakia the Communists were underground by the Nazi tyranny and in those seven years they developed such enormous strength that they were able, shortly after the liberation of Czechoslovakia—which we could have done but our troops were pulled back and the Russian troops were allowed to go into Prague—they were able before long to take over the whole nation because they had flourished in the dark, underground.

Here is an issue of the highest moral principle and practical application. The people of this country are being asked to outlaw communism. That means this: Shall we in America, in order to defeat a totalitarian system which we detest, voluntarily adopt the methods of that system? I want the people of the United States to know exactly where I stand on this proposal because it goes to the very heart of the qualification of any candidate for office and to the inner nature of the kind of country we want to live in. I am unalterably, wholeheartedly, unswervingly against any scheme to write laws outlawing people because of their religious, political, social, or economic ideas. I am against it because it is a violation of the Constitution of the United States and of the Bill of Rights, and clearly so. I am against it because it is immoral and nothing but totalitarianism itself. I am against it because I know from a great many years' experience in the enforcement of the law that the proposal wouldn't work, and instead it would rapidly advance the cause of communism in the United States and all over the world.

Now, let's look at this: There is a war of ideas in the world, and we are in it. It is also a war of nerves. It is a conflict between two wholly different ways of life, the system of human freedom and the brutal system of the police state. On one side of this great world struggle are ranged all of those who believe in the most priceless right in the world, human freedom. We believe that every man and woman has a right to worship as he pleases, to freedom of speech or assembly and of the press; we believe that every man and woman has an absolute right to belong to the political party of his choice. We believe, in short, that human beings are individuals and that they do and should differ among themselves. We know that each of us has within himself a portion of error, and we believe each of us has within himself a touch of God.

On the other side of this struggle, hating us and all we stand for, are the advocates of the all-powerful totalitarian state. They believe human beings are cogs in a machine, Godless creatures, born to slave through life with every thought and every act directed by an overpowering, all-powerful government.

Everywhere these two conflicting schemes of life, the free system and the police state, are struggling for the soul of mankind. The free world looks to us for hope, for leadership, and, most of all for a demonstration of our invincible faith that the free way of life will triumph so long as we keep it free. Now, as in all the days of our past, let us hold the flag of freedom high.

As I have watched this proposal, this easy panacea of getting rid of ideas by passing laws, I have been increasingly shocked. To outlaw the Communist party would be recognized every place on earth as a surrender by the great United States to the methods of totalitarianism. Stripped to its naked essentials, this is nothing but the method of Hitler and Stalin. It is thought control, borrowed from the Japanese war leadership. It is an attempt to beat down ideas with a club. It is a surrender of everything we believe in.

There is an American way to do this job, a perfectly simple American way. We have now twenty-seven laws on the books, and I have the whole list of them in front of me, outlawing every conceivable act of subversion against the United States.

I spent eleven years of my life as a prosecutor in New York. That was in the days when they said nobody could clean up the organized underworld. They said we had to use the methods of dictators. We had to go out and string 'em up. I have had judges and people in high places tell me that. But a group of young men took it on, and week after week, month after month, year after year, they worked, and they delivered the City of New York from the control of organized crime, and they did it by constitutional means and under the Bill of Rights.

We can do that in this country. All we need is a government which believes in enforcing the law, a government which believes wholeheartedly in human freedom, and an administration of our government which will go ahead and do the job.

I have no objection to the strengthening of the laws. In fact, I have spent a good many years of my life endeavoring to strengthen the criminal laws of our country, and they should be strengthened; but let us remember for all time to come in these United States: we should prosecute men for the crimes they commit, but never for the ideas that they have.

Now, the times are too grave to try any expedients that have failed. This expedient has failed. This expedient of outlawing has failed in Russia; it failed in all Europe; it failed in Italy; it failed in Canada.

And let me point out that in Canada they tried it once, and the Communist party grew so powerful and so dangerous that they repealed the law in 1936, and in 1940 they tried it again and the Communist party came right up with a dozen new false faces exactly as it would do if you passed this ludicrous law to outlaw them now. They would come up with forty new fronts. They would then say, "We are not Communists any more," exactly as they did in Canada. "We are just good Canadians working to support our government."

And what happens? What has happened in Canada is exactly what would happen here. They became so strong that during the war, in the face of a law which said it is illegal to belong to the Communist party, they developed the greatest atomic bomb spy ring in history, and Canada had to repeal the law.

Let us not make such a tragic blunder in the United States that we build up these dangerous, venomous, subversive people with the power to overthrow our government. Let us never make the blunders that have been made throughout the history of the world. Let us go forward as free Americans. Let us have the courage to be free.

### Affirmative Rebuttal

### Harold E. Stassen

Mr. Van Boskirk and Your Excellency Governor Dewey, My Fellow Citizens: Apparently we have narrowed this question down very much, and it hinges now primarily on the Mundt-Nixon bill.

The Mundt-Nixon Bill says:

> It shall be unlawful for any person to attempt in any manner to establish in the United States a totalitarian dictatorship, the direction and control of which is to be vested in or exercised by or under the domination or control of any foreign government, foreign organization, or foreign individual, or to perform or attempt to perform any act with the intent to facilitate such end.

Now, I hold that that directly fits and applies to the Communist party organization in the United States and in the world today.

The question, then, is, Does it so apply? Obviously, you cannot and should not draft your law in such form that a mere name results in an outlawing. It is being directed by a foreign power for the purpose of undermining the liberty of the American people and overthrowing our Government, which is the key point.

They are so doing. There should be no doubt of that.

Here is a quote from Louis Budenz who left the Communist party. He said:

> We must understand, then, before we get to the meat of the matter, that we are dealing with a conspiracy to establish Soviet dictatorship throughout the world.

There are many such instances.

Generalissimo Stalin, himself, said in the speech to the American delegation in 1928, and they are now reverting to the policy:

The Communist party of America, as a section of the Third International, must pay membership dues to the Comintern. All the decisions of the Congress of the Third International are obligatorily carried out by all the parties affiliated.

In other words, the decisions in Moscow by the Kremlin must be carried out in America, so that definitely and directly the Mundt-Nixon Bill will outlaw the Communist party as it is now functioning in America and in the world.

In fact, perhaps we are coming down to a point where we can reach agreement. Although I heard the Governor say that he did not think the Mundt-Nixon Bill would outlaw the Communist party, I did not hear him say whether he would support that bill. Now, if he will say that he approves of and will support the Mundt-Nixon Bill I will be satisfied that we have reached an agreement, that we have thereby outlawed the Communist party as it actually operates, and therefore we can go on to these other very important issues in this campaign.

I reiterate, if the Governor feels that he can support the Mundt-Nixon Bill, I will agree that that is sufficient to outlaw the party as it is now constituted, and we can go on to other important issues in the development of Oregon and in America.

Now, then, on this matter of the Communist party in Russia: The actual report, *The History of the Communist Party,* which is an established work on what happened in Russia, states very positively that the Communists were not outlawed. The Bolshevik party, so to speak, were not outlawed in Russia and elected six members to the last Duma in the last elections which were held. So I have, of course, realized that we cannot, in these few minutes left in this debate, check references, but I submit to the Governor that he should look up his references in the history of what happened in Russia.

Now, then, the Governor says we have effective laws now, seventeen of them; that all we need to do is use them. May I ask, then, why is it that the Communist organization has been growing so strong in New York? New York is the national headquarters of the Communist party of America. New York, with 9 per cent of America's population, has 40 per cent of the Communists in America.

New York is the capital Communist center in America, and from that center, from the national headquarters in New York, they have been reaching out and infiltrating in the labor organizations of America. They have been prejudicing the sovereignty of this country and the harmonious relationships in labor. Clearly, does the Governor not agree that they have been operating underground now? It is not a matter of driving them underground by the passage of a law. They are underground and overground, and they themselves pick out which one best serves their purposes in each instance.

Now, I submit, so far as I have observed, there has only been one conviction of a Communist in New York in the last eight years, and that was the publisher or editor of the *Daily Worker,* and he was convicted for a libel against another editor that really had no connection with Communist activity. If there are these laws now that are adequate, why have they not been used in New York? Why have they not been used in the federal government? And has the Governor of New York called upon the federal government to use federal laws in cooperation with the State? We found in a limited way in Minnesota where we did have some Communist infiltration in 1938, which was causing strikes and violence and killings on the streets of Minneapolis, we found that we could make progress if we cooperated with the federal government and the state government and the local government moving together with the assistance of loyal, patriotic American workmen to gradually weed them out; but we found we were greatly handicapped in completing the job because there was no law that directly related to the manner in which the Communists took their orders from a foreign power. Let's be specific. If an underground order came from the Kremlin to the Communists in America and they held a secret meeting at which it was agreed that they were going to seek strikes in certain essential industries and stir them up, we will say industries that were going to develop some great dynamos for hydroelectric power, some great generators, or in any other way interfere with the potential of this country, even though every fact of that secret move was discovered, there is no law now under which we could act.

Or suppose this underground word came and said that the Communists should move in around the Panama Canal and in Alaska, just establish themselves in various jobs, and secret meetings were held where that was arranged, there is no law at this time in the books of this country that would permit us to move directly against that conspiracy. Under the present laws you would have to wait until a move of force was made or until they uncovered their hand in a very flagrant way. What we need is a law that goes directly to the problem of the way in which the Communist organizations have been operating since the end of the World War. They are the threat of war. We shouldn't stumble along with laws that are out of date. We should bring our thinking up to date. It is not a matter of outlawing any ideas. It is not a matter of any thought control. What constitutional provision would prevent a kind of a law like the Mundt-Nixon Bill? Which article of the Constitution would it violate? I know of none that says that an organization may carry on in the manner in which the Communist organization is carrying on now. Therefore, it is open for legislative action, and I submit to the Governor that he earnestly reconsider his position, and specifically if he will say that he will now agree to support the Mundt-Nixon bill unequivocably, then I will agree we have reached a point of union on this important issue, and we will go forward with a constructive campaign in Oregon on those other very important questions that are before the people of this great state and before our America in the wake of war.

NEGATIVE REBUTTAL

THOMAS E. DEWEY

Mr. Van Boskirk, Mr. Stassen, Ladies and Gentlemen: I gather from Mr. Stassen's statement that he has completely surrendered. The Mundt Bill obviously does not outlaw the Communist party. Mr. Stassen, in these words, has from Oregon to

New Jersey and back again, gone before audiences of the American people demanding in these words that the Communist party be outlawed in the United States and in the other free nations of the world. The Mundt Bill does not outlaw the Communist party. The only authorities Mr. Stassen cites for the fact for his claim that it does are the present head of the Communist party and a former Communist, whereas I point out very clearly, that the author of the bill, Mr. Mundt, and the Committee which sponsored it both say in the official record of the Congress of the United States that the bill does not outlaw the Communist party. Now, if Mr. Stassen says that that is all he wants, then he has completely surrendered because he admits that he didn't mean it when he has been demanding from one end of this country to the other that the Communist party be outlawed, and he is willing to settle now, when confronted with the facts, for a law which the author and the Committee say does not outlaw the party, which of course it doesn't.

Now, as a matter of fact, there are—I made a mistake a while ago—there are not seventeen laws, there are twenty-seven laws in the United States on this subject. There is the 1938 Act requiring all agents of foreign governments to register under penalty of five years imprisonment and $10,000 fine. The Voorhis Act of 1940 requiring the registration of all subversive political organizations. The Smith Act which makes it unlawful to teach or advise the desirability of overthrowing the government of the United States by force or to publish any literature teaching, advising, suggesting or conspiring to do so, all under penalty of ten years imprisonment and $10,000 fine.

All the things of which Mr. Stassen has spoken are covered by the Smith Act, by the Treason Bill, the misprision of treason, inciting rebellion—I am reading the titles of a few—criminal correspondence with a foreign government, sedition, conspiracy, subversive activity, sabotage, fraud, conspiracy, desertion, sabotage, non-mailable matter, inciting mutiny, espionage, mutiny, sedition, conspiracy to commit espionage and sedition, non-mailable matter, inciting mutiny, conspiracy, mutiny, sedition. That's about it—the list is endless.

The Mundt Bill is perfectly harmless, probably. I have some doubts about its constitutionality. It supplements these bills in a very small way. It doesn't outlaw the Communist party. It may have the virtue of helping to keep them out in the open because its main provisions are that the Communists must register, must register all their members and keep them everlastingly out in the open. That is a very good provision of the law. The other parts of it, if they are constitutional, are swell.

Now, let's get down to the rest of the subject. Mr. Stassen has surrendered. He is no longer in favor of outlawing the Communist party. He is now willing to be content with a bill which simply says what is practically already in the law, which all sponsors in the Congress say does not outlaw the party. But this is so dangerous, this idea; it is so fundamental to American liberties that I should like to enlarge upon it just a little. Mr. Stassen has spoken of New York; he has spoken of our history. Let me give you just a bit of history. One hundred and fifty years ago the French—the French were the Bolsheviks of the world—they had a violent revolution, and they beheaded their nobility just as the Communists did in Russia. First, they had purges of the old government; then they had purges among themselves; then they started rattling their swords for world conquest. It is all just like the movie we have been through, and this is where we came in. We see the same thing now 150 years later. Many people in the infant American republic were trembling in their boots just as some Americans now tremble in theirs. They were afraid for the cause of free government. The Federalist party was in power and it proceeded—but let me quote from Chafee, one of the great American historians. He writes:

In 1798 the impending war with the French, the spread of revolutionary doctrines, by foreigners in our midst, and the spectacle of the disastrous operation of those doctrines abroad [I am still quoting]— facts, all of which [says Mr. Chafee] have a familiar sound today—led to the enactment of the Alien and Sedition laws.

These laws punished false and malicious writings against the Government, the Congress, and the President, if they were intended to excite the hatred of the people or to stir up sedition, or to aid any hostile design of any foreign nations against the United States. The acts created such a furor and opposition that the whole country was in turmoil.

The only Federalist leader who dared speak out for the Bill of Rights was John Marshall, who later became the great Chief Justice of the Supreme Court. But the Federalists went bull-headedly ahead. The Act was used to punish even Republican editors who had criticized President Adams. And ten of them—all Republicans—were fined and sent to prison. Soon every person who was prosecuted, however violent the language he had used, was treated as a martyr and a hero.

Adopting what the historians, Charles and Mary Beard, describe in their *Basic History of the United States* as "underground political tactics," Thomas Jefferson wrote an indictment of the laws and persuaded the State of Kentucky to declare them null and void. At the next election Thomas Jefferson was elected President of the United States, and the Federalist party was utterly wrecked. Jefferson pardoned all the victims of these laws; Congress later refunded all the fines; and Thomas Jefferson's party held uninterrupted office in the United States for twenty years.

That was the result of an early American idea—of an early American attempt—to shoot an idea with a law. You can't do it.

And now that Mr. Stassen has surrendered on his outlawing idea, let's nail this thing down so hard no American will ever again seek to give the slightest impression to our people that it can be done. It can't. It is self-destructive.

Even in the midst of the Civil War General Burnside tried to suppress the newspapers that were hostile to our Government. General Burnside put them out of business, and Lincoln gave him orders to quit, saying, in strong language, "It is better that the people hear what they have to say than fear what they might say if they were suppressed."

Now, we have a lot of Communists in New York—we have a great many of them—and they cause us great trouble; but we lick them. The number in the country is down from 100,000 two years ago to 70,000 last year to 68,000 this year. In New York their influence is at the lowest ebb in their history. They ganged up with the Democrats, as the American Labor party, the miscalled Liberal party, and the PAC, to beat us two years ago. The Communists labeled me as their Public Enemy Number One, and we licked them by the biggest majority in history. Why? Because we kept them out in the open; because we everlastingly believe in the Bill of Rights; because we know that if, in this country, we always keep every idea that is bad out in the open, we will lick it. It will never get any place in the United States.

# EDUCATION AND CIVILIZATION

## SCIENCE AND CIVILIZATION [1]

### George D. Stoddard [2]

President George D. Stoddard, of the University of Illinois, de-livered this address at the forty-eighth annual conference of the Asso-ciation of American Colleges, at the State University of Iowa, on Friday, October 24, 1947. The three-day conference opened on October 23 and met in Iowa City in honor of the University of Iowa's centennial anni-versary. Highlight of the three-day program was the Friday afternoon session on the theme "Science and Civilization." Papers in addition to that of President Stoddard included those of Professor Robert F. Bacher, of the United States Atomic Energy Commission, and Dr. Archie Palmer, of the National Research Council.

"Repression of science and civilization alone cannot possibly solve the problem," Professor Bacher told the fifty-seven university delegates.

Dr. Stoddard analyzed the problem of the choice "between civiliza-tion and deterioration."

Structurally and syntactically the address was easily understandable to his audience—and is so to the reader. The context, however, probes basic issues. The speech contains much more than surface thinking and statement. The style is unhackneyed, connotative. The oral quality is apparent throughout. The exposition is reserved and com-bined with cautious prediction. The effect is persuasion but well grounded in logical and scientific analysis.

The speaker followed—but by no means merely read—the pages. His delivery was projective and conversational, heightened by his lively reaction to his philosophical-practical theme.

Dr. Stoddard was a member of the United Nations Educational, Scientific and Cultural Organization. In November-December 1947 he participated in the conference of that organization in Mexico City, and was selected as the United States representative on the Board of Di-rectors for 1947-48.

It is especially pleasing to me to reenter the circles of this Association, within which I spent six happy years. It was, in

---

[1] Text furnished through the courtesy of President Stoddard.
[2] For biographical note see Appendix.

fact, under the wise tutelage of Seashore, Richardson, Payne, Pierson, and Fred that I cut my eyeteeth as a graduate dean. I have discovered that to be president of a university is to endure a vast exercise in the art of frustration, of which the chief, it seems to me, is to be kept away from the main channels of teaching and research.

To be linked with a distinguished physicist under the general umbrella of "Science and Civilization," produced in me a slight "startle" reaction. I know that I am not nearly as civilized as Professor Bacher is scientific.

It can be held that, in the twentieth century, nobody can be civilized without being somewhat scientific. Obviously this was not always true. It is like saying that a man cannot be intelligent without a well-developed cerebral cortex. For this we have ample supporting evidence. There was a time when the brightest of animals could lay little claim to this crowning glory. The most intelligent were simply the subhuman animals who solved problems too hard for their companions.

Genetically and socially evolution is a one-way street. We change. We change not by going back to something that was once useful or that gave us supremacy, but by developing special traits. In man these traits appear to be two and two only— intelligence and an aptitude for social organization. There has been no apparent failure in intelligence, even in comparison with the great eras of the past. There is, however, a deep suspicion that social organization has not kept pace.

If we are set to kill, intelligence as expressed in science and engineering will improve our methods, leaving our morality unchanged. If we are set to endure, to heal, and to do right by others, science becomes our greatest ally. In the words of Louis N. Ridenour: [3]

Since we cannot guess how technology will use the still unknown results of a proposed scientific investigation, we must therefore conclude that either science as a whole is good for mankind or it is not. We can "plan" science only to the extent of turning it off or on. Since science, through technology, really means material civilization, the question becomes: Is material civilization good for mankind or is it not? There

[3] *Atlantic Monthly.* May 1947. p81.

are arguments on both sides of that question, but clearly its resolution is by no means the concern of the scientist alone.

It is so obvious that science is not culture, that we sometimes change the argument and say that the two are incompatible. This is a fallacy of the first water; when accepted it produces cynicism and despair. If civilization cannot be founded upon science, then we shall not be civilized. These are the new choices:

(1) Science and civilization
(2) Science and deterioration

We can no more lay away science and its household aid, technology, than we can eliminate the use of fire, the building of shelters, the domestication of animals or the growth of transportation and communication.

The choice, then, is restricted: it is between civilization and deterioration. Now, in the middle of the twentieth century, deterioration, while not proclaimed a winner, is a sufficient menace. All this is more frightening than it used to be, because increasingly we value life on this earth.

A strange paradox it is, too. Where life is cheap or readily consigned to the hereafter, as in some oriental populations, the means of intentional destruction are limited. One lack replaces another and the population increases; a lack of machinery and of health protection is neatly outwitted, as it were, by a lack of birth control. But in societies like our own where natural bounty, political doctrine, and Western religious concepts have worked together beautifully to build up man as a personality— to make him count, here and now—we have at the same time become terribly effective destroyers. We rip, burn, poison, and suffocate huge populations by remote control. The one among the many, for whom democracy and Christianity cry out, is in wartime not something that counts but something to be counted as a statistical item.

To say this is merely to return to a problem that is overcast with tragedy—how, fast and effectively, to close the gap between the physical sciences and the social.

Those who in the last century, seeing only the dark side of Darwinism, demanded a stop to scientific research had hit upon a half-truth. The people were not emotionally prepared for science. The revolution in thought that should have trickled down from the leaders into every journal, book, and school was delayed unduly and dangerously. The danger, of course, was not in the story of evolution which hurt only feelings, but in the swiftly mounting capacity for self-destruction. The physicist, chemist, and metallurgist were about to grind out some powerful weapons. The means of destruction were running ahead of social and political controls.

It is clear that we are about to confront science with values that are social and artistic in origin. There was a time when we could maintain a high civilization without benefit of science. Later, in our own time, an attempt was made—and it almost succeeded—to establish science and technology without benefit of civilization. It may yet succeed. Technology means physical power and control. If we place high among the values of civilization the concepts of liberty, freedom, and the supreme worth of human personality, it becomes clear that any form of dictatorship is in opposition.

The danger is twofold: (1) that the non-democratic forces may win and (2) that the democratic forces in achieving victory may themselves be diluted.

It does not seem plausible to me that a comprehensive solution can be dug out of the past. *Lower* and *higher* are invidious terms as applied to men or civilizations. For my purpose the term, *different*, will suffice. We are different from the men of the classical era or the Middle Ages. We are different, too, from the scattered groups in Asia and South America that achieved a high civilization. It is science, together with its handmaiden, technology, that has made us different. There is no evidence that we have improved physically, mentally, or ethically. Our graphic and plastic arts which depend upon skill of hand and eye coupled with a subtle interpretation of nature show no constant gain. We can say this because we have retained our criteria of excellence for two thousand years. Analogously, we can boast a bit about the musical maturity of modern man.

Of course, if we go back far enough, permitting genetic forces and the evolutionary process to get in their full weight, the picture changes markedly. The point is that the damage or the good done to us in two thousand years or, for that matter in twenty thousand years, is no by-product of evolution. The change is not in anatomy or physiology, except in so far as these respond, within the individual, to the demands of an activated nervous system. All that we have done is to uncover latent ability.

In the not too distant future we expect to survive under abnormal conditions ranging from deep-freeze to high boiling points—to gad about in the airless reaches of interplanetary space. We already have sufficient knowledge of nutrition and medicine practically to guarantee a long survival period, under normal conditions, if only we can control the necessary economic and political concomitants. We can say with assurance that more children will live—live so long that the hazards will derive increasingly from the external conditions of living. In the future if you want a person to die before age one hundred, you will have to kill him.

This brings us to a new line of expertness in human affairs. In the words of Whitehead:

> There is a curious illusion that a more complete culture was possible when there was less to know. Surely the only gain was, that it was more possible to remain unconscious of ignorance. It cannot have been a gain to Plato to have read neither Shakespeare, nor Newton, nor Darwin. The achievements of a liberal education have in recent times not been worsened. The change is that its pretensions have been found out.

It is time that pretensions were replaced by solid work, by new structures and discoveries. Discovery, we know, is more difficult than understanding. Turn the matter about, and it becomes a source of hope. The man of general learning can keep rather close to the frontier of science. He needs some access to science properly to follow the surveys, integrations, and special articles. He needs a good dose of the liberal in order to avoid unconscious rejection and conscious distaste. Persons who are aggressively ignorant will have to be treated as invalids—no step-climbing or solid food for a while and a whole series of tests to see how they are behaving.

My guess is that, under modern conditions of schooling, the common man will behave much like the uncommon specialist.

In a lecture given on the Sigma Xi circuit last year, Professor H. D. Smyth referred to the almost accidental discovery of radio-activity by Becquerel. The latter thought that phosphorescence resulted from a prior exposure of a substance to sunlight. He proved that a uranium salt thus exposed would affect a photographic plate. But one cloudy day he laid away uranium salt and plate without proper exposure. On developing the plate, he discovered that the uranium, without benefit of sunlight, had thoroughly blackened the plate. He had made one of the greatest discoveries in modern physics. Up to the time of these lucky circumstances Becquerel, keen and careful as he was, was in the same boat as the statistician who, having consumed rye and soda, bourbon and soda, and scotch and soda, only to feel bad each time, swore a solemn oath to stay away from the obvious common element—soda!

The truth is, that up to a point people are happy. Through science we get results satisfying alike to the scholar and the man in the street. Only the saint and the moralist remain unhappy. They are wary of this kind of progress, and they ought to be, for there is no turning back. The human race may go toward insanity or obliteration, but it will not again seek the befuddled half-life of the cave. Nor is it a free choice. Anatomy and physiology declare the cerebral cortex to be supreme, so far as *homo sapiens* is concerned; with it and through it, we arrange our affairs. To fear thought is to fear life.

For the time being, at least, the upper reaches of science, pure and applied, are contained within the study of nuclear physics. I am told that we are moving from a world of *electronics*, which still dazzles us, into a world of *nucleonics*. The more deeply researchers get into the core of matter and energy, the more startling the external, massive effects. Psychologically we have been prepared for this through disease in the human body. The most terrible afflictions are related to the smallest virus forms. Now the physical and biological may form a new partnership. For example, a tiny fraction of plutonium in the human system will cause severe damage. When no plutonium existed anywhere on earth, this condition rated zero among health hazards. Now, a means of maiming and killing, through a searching out by radiation of all living things in a given area, is on the agenda of every general staff. It is just one more item in the chamber of horrors.

In a paper given two years ago before the American Philosophical Society, J. R. Oppenheimer pleaded eloquently for a new morality springing from the fear of total destruction. He said:

> But as a vast threat, and a new one, to all the peoples of the earth, by its novelty, its terror, its strangely promethean quality, the atomic bomb has become, in the eyes of many of us, an opportunity unique and challenging.

I share this feeling. Nevertheless, as a psychologist I do not believe that the threat of death to others, no matter how many, will act as a deterrent to war. War has always used death as its not-so-secret weapon: what difference whether by sword, arrow, gun, poison, or bomb? The bomb is less fearful *to the individual* than the slower-acting agents, such as the hunger and torture of the prison camp. It takes a high-level morality, an extraordinary ethical projection, to give thought to suffering that occurs elsewhere in time or place. Without social allegiance there is no sorrow.

This far we may go with Oppenheimer and his apprehensive colleagues: to reduce the means and the occasion is generally an aid to inner resolution. The guns that go off when pointed are the guns that lie around handy. Frequently a man will not walk a mile for a smoke, a drink, or a fight. Those who profit by a knowledge of human inertia see to it that he need not.

It is not enough to identify war with murder, although we have been partially successful there. We have reduced the incidence of crime in certain cultural levels of the population. From crime somebody hopes to derive benefit, if it be only a release of intolerable tensions within himself. He will probably fail but he does not know this, being a neophyte, or worse yet, a hitherto successful operator: so with the reckless driver who also kills, and so with all persons who are blinded to the general welfare. Nowadays, the killing, short of war, while extensive, is a series of small events and we are numbed into fatalism. Were a city of fifty thousand inhabitants to be blotted out, we should take notice—at least for a time.

At this point the analogy to warfare breaks down. War is more than a mighty struggle with dangerous weapons. War is a vast intention. It is a considered risk on the part of the aggressor. That nation does not expect to lose. When the swift act occurs its people have already accepted, and sometimes have cheered, the wanton destruction of the enemy. We cannot forget the singing and the joyous marching of Fascists and Nazis as crowds of men, women, and children fell in blood before the conquering armies.

It is true that nobody in America cheered the dreadful fate of Hiroshima and Nagasaki. Nevertheless, in terms of actual physical revulsion—in loss of appetite or sleep or in the persistence of remorse—I doubt seriously if we could muster ten thousand Americans. Men of action were plainly glad that we had dealt such a beating to the enemy, while others reflected that the war had been shortened. They felt that we had exchanged the lives of Japanese for a far greater number of GI's whom we knew and loved. In this bitter world, few could regard the equation *one death = one death* as containing any true meaning. As to the Japanese, I believe from firsthand conversations that, for the most part, they cared little about the form of destruction. Under the right conditions, incendiary bombs were efficient and terrifying. The sight of a baby burned to a crisp does not make one think of fire, but rather of man's relationship to man.

If war comes, it will come with the bomb—fast, purposive, and incomparably destructive to both sides. The cities and strongholds will go first, followed by a penetration into the woods, caves, and mountains that shelter escaping multitudes. At least that is the picture painted by some scientists. They rarely exaggerate. More likely, in accordance with long tradition, their predictions are modest.

What then is the solution? How can we save ourselves? I suggest, as a first stage, that we follow the lead of the scientists who seek to control their own inventions. They report that fissionable material and its large-scale processing can be surveyed, supervised, and made safe. This makes sense to the layman; it is like keeping guns out of reach while setting up a system of license, manufacture, and distribution. Make the bomb hard to get, hard to use—in fact, of no value at all, except as a final almost never-to-be-used weapon invested in a sovereign world power. Like everybody else, I should like to say *never-to-be-made-or-used*, but we know that the production of nuclear energy will be accelerated.

If we reject the thesis that wars begin in the laboratories of scientists, that they emerge full-blown from wicked discoveries and inventions, we must turn elsewhere. Is the source in hunger, fear, hatred? Is it in sheer boredom? Is war an inevitable consequence of man's imperfect physical and social mechanism? The psychologists, in a formal pronouncement, have stated that the urge to make war is not a hereditary trait.

It is in a moral principle, manifest through insights independently arrived at, and seeking everywhere a world structure through which to operate, that we must put our faith. The inner man can approach the Golden Rule. What he needs now is external support through social and political institutions. The preamble to the Constitution of the Untied Nations Educational, Scientific and Cultural Organization clarifies this faith. It holds:

That since wars begin in the minds of men, it is in the minds of men that the defenses of peace must be constructed;

That ignorance of each other's ways and lives has been a common cause, throughout the history of mankind, of that suspicion and mistrust between the peoples of the world through which their differences have all too often broken into war;

That the great and terrible war which has now ended was a war made possible by the denial of the democratic principles of the dignity, equality and mutual respect of men, and by the propagation, in their place, through ignorance and prejudice, of the doctrine of the inequality of men and races;

That the wide diffusion of culture, and the education of humanity for justice and liberty and peace are indispensable to the dignity of man and constitute a sacred duty which all the nations must fulfill in a spirit of mutual assistance and concern;

That a peace based exclusively upon the political and economic arrangements of governments would not be a peace which could secure the unanimous, lasting and sincere support of the peoples of the world, and that the peace must therefore be founded, if it is not to fail, upon the intellectual and moral solidarity of mankind.

UNESCO itself may rise or fall, but if the ideas contained in its preamble are ever lost to mankind, we shall have failed in both science and civilization.

# THE YOUNGER GENERATION [4]

## HAROLD TAYLOR [5]

Dr. Harold Taylor, president of Sarah Lawrence College, Bronxville, New York, gave this address at Flushing, New York, before a Queens College graduating class of 255, on June 17, 1947.

Dr. Paul Klapper, president of Queens College, conferred the degrees. Other speakers included Ordway Tead, chairman of the Board of Higher Education, and Justice S. Colden, of the New York State Supreme Court. President Taylor was the chief speaker at the commencement exercises, held outdoors on the Campus Quadrangle.

Dr. Taylor, who became president of Sarah Lawrence in 1945, when only thirty-one, has gained prestige as one of the abler young college presidents. As a speaker he is at home with ideas and language, is effective in extempore delivery, has a sense of humor, an excellent voice. and good platform presence.

His educational philosophy is progressive. Stated Dr. Taylor, in criticism of Robert Hutchins of Chicago who emphasized great books as education: "In a work of the past [are] clues for dealing with the present. [But] an exclusive concern with the classical curriculum has failed in the past and will fail today. . . . The difficulty of living with the atom bomb is not that so few people have read Aristotle, but that so few people understand or care about the structure of contemporary society." [6]

The present address reveals the essence of his progressive educational philosophy. He believes in education that provides an understanding of and an interest in the structure of contemporary society; in the refusal to deal exclusively or mainly with the "folklore of society" and "past culture"; in teachers who are "centers of intellectual energy"; in college as a center of creative thinking rather than of acceptance of a set of beliefs framed "thirty years ago"; in college as a place of "free inquiry," free from "public pressures"; in a curriculum centering not in one hundred best books but in the "one thousand best human ideas"; and in the college as a place for training in modes of individual formation of standards of judgment rather than in the acceptance of absolute standards of value projected from above.

[4] Text and permission for this printing furnished through the courtesy of President Taylor.

[5] For biographical note, see Appendix.

[6] *Time*. 50:71. September 29, 1947.

I wish to speak on behalf of my generation. It is a difficult international generation. We were born into the first world war or shortly after it. In America, our childhood and adolescence was spent in the jazz age, in a time marked by a flood of money, illegal liquor, and frantic living. When we were fourteen to sixteen, we found ourselves in a desperate world economic crisis. My father lost his job, along with the fathers of many others, and we have been working our way ever since. At an early point in our lives, Hitler came to power, representing in his person, a symbol for the evil of our time. Under his leadership and that of others like him, the European youth were educated, in politics and moral philosophy, until the social diseases with which the young were inoculated grew to epidemic form in Germany and Spain. The destruction of European civilization having begun in Spain, a solemn ritual celebrating the high dignity of power and evil was performed at Munich by the older generation of European leaders. Over here, America set itself the task of reconstruction as best it could, with the aid of new forms of social organization in which the realities of a collective society were recognized for the first time.

Then as we began to move to a better life, Europe made its war more formal and declared it. This country began to seethe with more confusion and tension, until we were right back to the beginning with a world war in our lives and occupying our future.

Here we are today, full circle, in a period of greater conflict and confusion than that of our birth—having had war, the bilious twenties, the depressed thirties, and the confused forties. We also have the honor to escort into the world the atomic age, with its pretty little gadgets for knocking everybody off our planet. This is what I mean when I say ours is a difficult generation. Suckled in violence and weaned in destruction, it has had nothing to encourage it. It has entered a shocking world prepared for it by its elders, a world over which it has yet had no chance to exercise control except by fighting and dying and suffering.

The question I ask is, what can our generation do, not only for ourselves, but for the generation which will follow us?

I would like first to point out what happened to the postwar generation after the first World War.  Those boys who reached manhood at the close of that war became famous in American history for belonging to a lost generation.  Since I have no first-hand knowledge of that period, I shall have to agree with those who had, that the men who returned from the excitement of a shooting war to the drabness of peace in the 1920's became cynical, disillusioned, and bitter about America.  There was a shriveling of the spirit and a moral emptiness.  American democracy was said by them to be full of the faults and decadence of a dishonest society.  It was said to be in mortal danger from communism, labor unions, alcohol, and radical professors.  Our literature is full of the notion that America had lost a generation.

Whatever else may be true, it was a period of cynicism, of revolt against moral authority, and a final transition from the nineteenth century into a modern twentieth century, with all the faults and virtues of a new age.

Its intellectual character was for the most part negative. Young men and women criticized their country, they made fun of the business man as a Babbitt who had no values other than the profit motive and getting ahead with it.  They made of college life an impregnable defense against the intellect.  They made it a four-year escape from reality into the ballrooms, the bars, and the football fields of America.  When these men and women found that after graduation, there were no jobs, and that the American economy had broken down to the point where able young people could not be employed, this country was in the greatest danger in its history of democracy, since at that point the youth were ready for the partisan philosophy of the absolute state, at that time made attractive to some people in this country by the success of its operation in Europe and the East.

After this war, however, we have a different atmosphere, and a different kind of youth.  This is not a lost generation, this is a body of men and women made serious by war.  In Europe, amongst those who fought in the underground forces of France, Norway, or Belgium, there was a rediscovery of the solid values of freedom against the obscene domination of the Germans. These young men and women of Europe hated war and violence, hated the deceit of political control, yet found that only by violence and by clinging to a faith in freedom did their lives become meaningful to them. Even though the older moral values were broken, new values by which men and women could live were found in the struggle.

Similarly in America, the postwar youth is stronger and more serious because of its chastening. We can see it in the present generation of college students, who have learned to think for themselves and to act for themselves. They are interested in politics, in social reform, in marrying, in raising a family, in having a job, and, in a great many extreme cases, even in the academic subjects they study. Since the world is pressing closely upon them, they wish to know more about it in order to cope with it. We have for the first time a large proportion of married students on our campuses. For the first time in the history of American education, football players go home early from practice to mind the baby, husbands wash the dishes so that wives can type essays.

But in this virtue of seriousness in our youth lies the greatest responsibility for the rest of the country. What would happen, for example, if this new generation of college students and veterans found that there was no place for them, in America? Suppose that within three to five years, our economy breaks down, a depression arrives, and our youth, prepared for a career in the new America is faced with no opportunity for further advance? We have been accustomed to thinking that the advance of youth in a mobile society is automatic, that our high school and college graduates will move straight into jobs with no difficulty. Yet we now have more than two million men and women in colleges and universities, and more than twenty-six million youngsters in our high schools. The fact that our college students are more mature and that there are more of them means that in the event that America has not provided a place for them, they will form their own political allegiances, and take their own social action. All the forces of American society, government, labor, industry, and education must be turned towards that kind of expanding economy which will make a happy place for the energies and talents of our youth. In so doing it will make a happy place for everyone.

Yet the intellectual and moral climate of America today is not that of youth, but of a tired and fearful age. The muscles of the American mind seem to have stiffened, the self-confidence and the friendly assumption that others will be friendly has been replaced by hesitations and nagging doubts. There seems to be a mass conspiracy against expression of minority opinion, against anything except official views. The native bent of the young mind is towards liberalism and confidence in the powers of man for good. This youthful mind has been the secret of America's greatness—a boundless flow of vital energy and a willingness to try new things, combined with a deep faith in the goodness of man and the dignity of the individual. This is the most precious value which America has. With it, bold steps can be taken, whole countries can be reconstructed, men and women can be inspired to new heights of social achievement. Without it, we creep painfully from one timid mistake to the next into ultimate failure.

In this new postwar period, it is not the younger generation which is lost in cynicism. That label belongs to the older generation where there is fear of communism, fear of labor unions, fear of war, fear of depression, fear of new ideas. In education, as elsewhere, the fearful ones have given up the excitement of new ideas for the deceptive security of the old.

In thinking about education as a matter of books and minds, that generation has forgotten the human beings who do the teaching and the young people who do the learning. It is assumed that people become educated only by exposure to the folklore of society, presented in printed form, and that the function of the teacher is to transmit information, past cultures, and human values in the same way that the postman delivers the mail. Teachers are therefore hired at the lowest possible rates to deliver the word, and any attempt to look at the messages or to question their contents is actively discouraged as being outside the duty of the messenger, and a sign of radicalism in the postman. Those who receive the messages are accordingly viewed with suspicion, since they too might question the authenticity of the documents, or even refuse to accept the charges.

Our intellectuals in colleges and universities are not hired to carry out the policies of others. They are people to whom we have entrusted the making of new knowledge and the infusion of a spirit of honest enquiry in our students. They are the people who must make educational policy. One of America's philosophers, Max Otto, has written of his days as a student in Wisconsin's golden age of liberal education, when he studied with the great teachers, Jackson, Turner, Fish, McGilvary, and John R. Commons.

My professors [says Dr. Otto] were centers of aggressive intellectual energy, sources of cultural vision. They were not teachers of lessons, their classes were outposts in the recurring struggle between enlightenment and superstition, between knowledge and ignorance. And their students were apprentices in the same high venture. . . . I found myself in what seemed to me the very workshop of social reconstruction, permitted to participate in the attempt to expand and elevate the intellectual and moral life of our state, of our country, of mankind.

With this spirit in it, a college or a university is bound to be a center of active thinking, and an exciting place for American youth, where deep and significant education goes on.

For there are, in the main, two great forces at work in all institutions. There is the huge mechanical weight of things that have to be done, and all the practical details of carrying out a program. The program becomes static very quickly. Ideas which, thirty years ago, were new and produced changes, become part of regular policy, and are frozen into the structure of the institution. The school or college represents the ideas and the society from which it comes, and is usually considered to be the place from which the tribal laws, local customs, traditions and social habits are handed on to the coming generation. Quite naturally, once such a set of beliefs, body of knowledge, tradition, or curriculum has been established, it supports itself in its position by its own weight and opposes change or even critical examination.

Another force, more essential to the welfare of the institution, and of society, is that of a creative kind, which presses forward constantly searching for new ways of using the knowledge of the past in fresh situations, and building, revising, recreating from year to year the institution in which it operates. That force in education and society is represented by the minds and personalities of the people who teach in our universities. They are the centers of intellectual and moral energy around which institutions form themselves. Their responsibility to the young people they teach is to enable each of them to think for himself, to make wise choices amongst ideas and values, and to settle doubts and urgent questions by appeal to honest evidence.

The institution which stifles this free enquiry or which evades the conflicts and controversies which such free enquiry generates, has betrayed its mission as a university. It will succumb to the dead hand of the static and to the dictates of an authority. There are bound to be those who do not wish students and faculty to settle issues together by their own discussion and decision, and there are bound to be those who disagree with decisions taken after free discussion. It would be fatal to the growth of American society, however, if those who wish to prevent the free interchange of social ideas were to prevail, or if those who are frightened by the expression of dissidence and the discussion of radical ideas, were allowed to control education.

Education is a polite form of mental exercise unless the student feels for himself the tang of original thinking, the bite of new ideas, and the heat of social and intellectual controversy. For it is in the understanding of social forces and political doctrines in terms of the effect they have upon the society in which we live that our youth will become educated to live in the modern world.

This need is all the more pressing, since many people and powers are anxious to do our thinking for us. There are many who would like to divide all opinion into left and right wing, and to group all those who believe in free speech, or in anti-discrimination, or communism, or Franklin Roosevelt, or the TVA, or peace, as violent left-wingers. There are others who group in a dreadful right wing anybody who believes in free enterprise, fascism, American business, Winston Churchill, ownership of property, and the reconstruction of Germany. Each group then has a weapon for attacking any person of differing views.

The defense which young Americans have against such a weapon is to think straight through to the center of each social issue, without regard for the public pressures on either side. For in the long run, it is the private thinking of each of us which determines public attitudes, and each carries his own public community around with him. Each creates his own environment, and each has a direct effect on the people in that environment. The question is, what are the qualities of the ideal community which each can aid in building?

It would be one in which people helped each other to live happily together, without antagonisms and without hatreds. It would have housing in which only one family lived at a time. It would have nursery schools in which children could learn to play, to enjoy themselves, and to cooperate with others. It would have schools in which teachers were respected, well paid, and able to meet the varied needs of each child and to develop his talents. It would have colleges to which everyone who qualified might go, regardless of who his father and mother were, the color of his skin, or the social group to which he belonged. In those colleges would be intellectuals who believed that teaching and learning are in equal proportion a noble action which calls for the best that is in the human being. In those colleges, students and teachers would work cooperatively together to make of their lives an inspiration to the rest of society.

Their work together would not be a business of books and minds, nor would they try to find their knowledge from a group of one hundred best books. Rather they would try to understand the hundred best human actions, the thousand best human ideas, and the hundreds of different ways in which the world is seen by artists, scientists, poets, and philosophers. They would feel that the relation of books to minds and to life is one in which our great writers put into words the unspoken feelings and attitudes of an age. They would think those writers great because they speak for the people who can't speak for themselves, and give us all a view of life and of nature which we cannot reach by our own individual efforts. When writers tell about a past age, they do so as witnesses of events and values from which we may learn. It is only as we recognize the human qualities which they express, and the way those qualities have developed in our time, that they become valuable to us. We are still compelled to make up our minds about the good they express, and we still must choose amongst their ideas. Those choices are made, one at a time, by individuals who do the choosing.

Having made such a community, my generation would then be part of the older generation, and we would hand on to America, not a distrust of the young ones to whom we had given these new opportunities, but a faith that they too would create a new community according to these ideals.

# HAS TWENTIETH CENTURY CIVILIZATION IMPROVED MANKIND? [7]

## George V. Denny, Jr., Lin Yu-tang, Harlow Shapley, J. Herbert Smith, Lewis Browne [8]

This debate, presented on Tuesday evening, July 3, 1947, originated from an American Airlines DC-6 flying over Hollywood, from 8:30 to 9:30 P.M., Eastern Standard Time, and was broadcast over the American Broadcasting Company network.

These programs have been given continuously since 1935, the oldest series of this type on the air. Several millions usually listen. At least two sides of a current controversial subject are presented. In spite of the freedom with which each spokesman expresses his point of view, in spite of the strongly partisan refutation of some of the participants, and in spite of the sharpness of many of the issues, the program has retained a high level of impartiality and of public endorsement. Conservative intellecutals have criticized the "popular" oversimplification of the speeches and the other radio accompaniments of general interest and appeal. In defense Mr. Denny would remind the critics that it is better to have a presentation sufficiently interesting to catch and hold the attention of millions than to develop a more learned argument and exposition at the expense of popular listening. [9]

On this program were four outstanding platform speakers. Dr. Harlow Shapley is not only a well-known scientist, "perhaps the best known astronomer in the United States," but is a lecturer in great demand. An authority on photometry, spectroscopy, and galaxies, he has the rare gift of explaining simply and clearly the "complexities of scientific research." He has an excellent voice and platform personality. He is also popular as a radio lecturer and has several times appeared on programs of *America's Town Meeting of the Air*. [10]

Lewis Browne is also one of the outstanding lecturers of this decade. Born in England, he was educated in theology at the Hebrew Union College and Rabbinical Seminary at Cincinnati, Ohio. Later he studied at

[7] Reprinted from *Bulletin of America's Town Meeting of the Air.* Vol. 13, no. 10. July 3, 1947. By permission of the speakers, by special arrangement with Town Hall, Inc., and through the courtesy of the American Broadcasting Company.

[8] For biographical notes see Appendix.

[9] For other examples of debates presented on *America's Town Meeting of the Air* and for comment on this program, see "Should Industry Grant Labor's Demand for a 30 per cent Wage Increase?" *Representative American Speeches: 1945-1946.* p165-79; "Is The American Press Really Free?" 1946-1947. p159-76.

[10] For further comment on Dr. Shapley and a report of one of his lectures, see *Representative American Speeches*: 1944-1945. p245-71.

Yale. After ten years as rabbi in Free Synagogues in Connecticut and New Jersey, he decided to devote his time to writing and lecturing. He has delivered some two thousand public lectures not only before American audiences but in Japan, China, England, France, and many other countries. He was a lecturer on orientation for the War Department from 1942 through 1945. Dr. Browne writes:

"I never had any special training under a speaking teacher, but as a schoolboy in England, and later as a college student in this country, I engaged persistently and chronically in debates and oratorical contests, and that gave me an early start. Since then I have delivered an average of one hundred addresses a year, and in thirty years that adds up to considerable experience. For the past twenty years at least I have never prepared an address verbatim—except for the radio, of course, and even then I always interpolate and extemporize freely. I am always careful, however, to prepare two or three pages of outline, and usually the opening sentences.

"The two most helpful rules I know in lecturing are: (a) Believe what you are saying; (b) believe that what you're saying *must be said*." [11]

J. Herbert Smith is rector of All Saints Chuch, Beverly Hills, California. For thirteen years he was on the staff of the Calvary Episcopal Church in New York. He tells us that for the first three or four years of his ministry he preached from notes, and then decided that he would write his sermons fully in order to have the discipline of preparation and thought. During this period he took the full manuscript into the pulpit; "but," he says, "I was so thoroughly acquainted with it that I hardly needed to refer to it."

During the last five years, he has again gone back to the method of preparing his sermons with the use of very full notes. Usually he has an outline of five or six pages which he uses in the pulpit. Of his radio address he writes:

"This particular speech was written completely after many hours of reading and thought and preparation." [12]

Lin Yu-tang has also been in wide demand as lecturer. He attended Christian schools in his native China, was graduated from St. John's University in Shanghai, and taught at a Peking college. After the First World War he studied at Harvard, Jena, and Leipzig and returned to teach at Peking National University. Later he was Secretary to the Foreign Ministry of the Hankow Government. He has published numerous books in English that interpret his country for the West and that expound his philosophy.

He describes his speechmaking technique as follows:

"I make it a habit never to write out a speech in full text, because a speaker with his nose in his text always bores listeners. There is no

[11] Letter to the editor of this volume, May 10, 1948.
[12] Letter to the editor of this volume, May 5, 1948.

way to establish contact with the audience if the speaker doesn't look at them. Reading a speech robs the speaker of freedom and he usually loses his spark. I usually make out an outline, and fill in the rest extemporaneously. It keeps the audience on its toes for surprises, so they can't fall asleep." [13]

DENNY: Good evening, neighbors. Well, I've had a wonderful twentieth century vacation on the ancient Mojave Desert, here in California, and I'm delighted to be back with you as we continue our Town Meetings at this crucial time in the history of the world.

"Has Twentieth Century Civilization Improved Mankind?" All Town Meeting fans will wonder why we're doing this program over again which we did under the same title in February 1939.

But listen, friends, the world has grown a thousand years during the past eight. We've fought a second world war, we've snatched the fire of the atom from heaven, or hell, and we're not quite sure which. Our leaders tell us that we're standing on the brink of a third world war, if we cannot learn to live together in peace.

We're grateful to the American Airlines for furnishing us this beautiful modern DC-6, symbol of the twentieth century, that spans the continent in nine and a half hours regularly. We're continually indebted to the engineering staff of the American Broadcasting Company and its 226 affiliated stations, that make such a broadcast as this possible.

In a few moments you'll hear Dr. Lin Yu-tang, famous Chinese philosopher, and Dr. Harlow Shapley, celebrated American scientists, speak to us from New York. Then, Reverend J. Herbert Smith, well-known Beverly Hills minister, and Dr. Lewis Browne, distinguished author and lecturer, will speak from this high plane, high over the city of Los Angeles. All four speakers will be questioned by a representative audience along here with us.

This is another first for your Town Meeting. It's the first time a forum program has ever been presented from an airplane, and having two of our speakers in New York City further

[13] Letter to the editor of this volume, May 8, 1948.

emphasizes the scientific progress of this miraculous twentieth century.

Well, I'm going to begin with the first question, gentlemen. How can we assure ourselves that these products of twentieth century civilization will not be used to destroy twentieth century civilization itself?

Why do we live in constant fear that a plane such as this one will be used to carry a weapon that will destroy a city of a million people? Why do we fear so deeply the possibility of the use of radio as a means of enslaving millions of people through lies and propaganda?

While science and industry are busy forging one world, why are our politicians dividing humanity into two worlds? If we have the brains to produce such marvels, why can we not enjoy the fruits of man's genius and live in peace?

Dr. Lin Yu-tang, your countrymen have contributed enormously to our understanding during the past four thousand years, and your own books, beginning with the highly successful *My Country and My People,* have been read with warm appreciation all over America. Will you tell us, sir, what are we to do with this twentieth century civilization in the light of the appalling facts as we know them today. Has this age of science improved mankind? We are eager, sir, for your counsel. Dr. Lin Yu-tang, speaking to us from New York. (*Applause.*)

LIN: In regard to the question whether the twentieth century civilization has made mankind happier and wiser, my own answer is this: You can't have both.

In the present era, you can choose to be a happy idiot, or be a wise, but terribly worried man, that is, if you read the morning papers about what's going on in the United Nations, or at the Peace Conference in Paris this morning. No man can be happy when he feels he has to be responsible for the universe.

Now you know all the familiar answers to the question. On the one hand, there is progress of science, industry, medicine, sanitation, and a rising standard of living. On the other hand, people are suffering more from emotional conflicts. There is less home life, less religion, more social tension and unrest, more fear and hatred, and above all, the ever-present threat of war hanging over our heads.

This question of war overshadows all the other questions. We live better, it is true, but we kill and may be killed faster.

Since we are dealing with the question of happiness, we must distinguish between individual happiness, and the happiness of society as a whole. Individual happiness is largely a matter of the proper functioning of the endocrine glands.

In any society and age, an individual can, through wisdom and discipline, always arrange to have a happy life. But no man is an island. His individual happiness also depends upon the type of society in which he lives, and our society is changing fast.

Now, because man is both body and spirit, he can be happy only when both his material and his spiritual needs are satisfied. In other words, he needs both groceries and freedom. Now, in modern civilization we are threatened with an increase of groceries and a decrease of freedom.

Human civilization may be classified into four classes: (1) groceries with freedom, that is the American civilization; (2) freedom without groceries, that is generally and relatively true of the industrially backward nations; (3) groceries without freedom, that is true of white totalitarianism under Hitler; and (4) no groceries and no freedom, that is, Red totalitarianism under Stalin. There is every evidence that groceries are increasing in Russia, and that, given ten or twenty years of peace, the Russian people will move into Class 3 and have groceries without freedom.

Now because of the social and national tensions, modern mankind as a whole is decidedly unhappy under the threat of wars, which would wipe out all benefits from scientific progress.

If we think of America alone, where man has both groceries and freedom, civilization is moving straight toward its desired goal. If we only had peace, and the assurance of peace, when man's energies can be liberated for industrial production, scientific discoveries, and artistic creations, the possibilities of increasing human happiness are enormous; but Europe and Asia are also parts of the twentieth century. There, men are neither free from want nor free from fear. Therefore, another war is threatening to engulf us all. And the next war may destroy this civilization.

Therefore, the question is not whether this civilization has improved mankind, but whether there will be a mankind to improve after the next atomic war. We cannot be too happy if, in the next war, we are all driven to live in underground caves to avoid atomic bombs, although the caves may be perfectly air-conditioned and disinfected with ultraviolet rays. The very thought of it makes me unhappy.

What must we do? We must concentrate the highest human intelligence available at present to deal with the problem of world peace. No harm can come if we ban all scientific progress for five years, until we know what we can make of what we have got. Scientific discoveries can wait. The problem of peace cannot.

The United States spent two billion dollars and mobilized all scientific talent of the country to develop the atom bomb. It can well spend a hundredth part of that money, or twenty million dollars, to be raised by public subscription or private endowment, to mobilize ten or twelve of the best scientists of the world to study the question of peace. Such a congress of scientists will be a private but permanent institution, and it will have for its proper subject of study the whole problem of the mechanism of modern civilization for the specific purpose of achieving world peace.

We can have men like Einstein, Compton, Millikan of America, and, for instance, Haldane and Huxley of England; and thinkers like Thomas Mann and Toynbee, and some clergymen may be included. They will have no official power—no power except the weight of their opinion. We need such a concentration of human intelligence, and these men will wield a tremendous influence over this generation only by the power of their ideas.

I like this idea, because I am against official organizations, and because I distrust all politicians, and have implicit trust in scientists. (*Applause.*)

DENNY: Thank you, Dr. Lin Yu-tang.

And, now, Dr. Harlow Shapley, you were with us when we discussed this subject eight years ago, and you talked to us then about galaxy years equal to two hundred million earth years; but we impatient inhabitants of the twentieth century want to know what you scientists mean by giving us atomic power when we were so ill prepared for it.

Do you want us to think that we are ready for such dangerous toys as atomic bombs and radio-guided missiles of mass destruction? Are you as optimistic today as you were in February 1939? We seek your counsel as one of the leaders and outstanding spokesmen for the men of science who have contributed so richly to the building of this magic century.

May we hear now from Dr. Harlow Shapley, director of the Harvard Observatory of Harvard University, speaking from New York. Dr. Shapley. (*Applause.*)

SHAPLEY: You ask if mankind has improved in the past fifty years. The answer is, Yes! Mr. Denny. And may I go home now? Or, do you want me to fill in time by explaining, and lay myself open to criticism and contradictions?

Yes, not only mankind has improved, but cowkind, and pigkind, and turnips, and apples. Yes, apples have improved, notwithstanding the faulty memories of some of you old-timers.

But apples must be cared for in order to stay improved; also, mankind. The better we both get—apples and man—the more susceptible we become to blight. In all good apple country we must fumigate and sprinkle and spray. In our best human society we must exhort, and incite, and educate. If we do not, the bugs will get us—both of us.

Apparently one of the penalties of being improved and highly cultivated is increased susceptibility. Your healthy, rosy cheeks—you and the apples—your goodness, from tender skin throughout the whole interior, needs more conscientious care now than heretofore. Apparently, times have changed. We did not need to protect grandfather from "isms" so much, nor his apples from blight.

Yes, mankind has improved. But this statement does not necessarily hold if you are speaking of men and women in some parts of Poland, or if you define improvement in some special way. Dr. Smith doubtless will tell you that man could stand some still further improvements.

I'm willing to grant that changes for the better have not occurred in the character of political leaders, at least in some parts of the world; and in religious devotions, no improvement, in some parts of the world.

No, there have been, I admit, stagnations and recessions. It's in the average well-being of all people that steady improvement has come about, interrupted temporarily by a couple of world wars and some depressions. And there are good reasons why we should expect further improvement the world over, provided we do not get to fighting again and lose entirely the art of humanity. Among the good reasons for this hopeful human vista are the new resources which we have for the betterment of life.

Let me name some of the old resources that have helped get mankind into the somewhat civilized state in which we now find him. The instinctive combativeness of man has stood him in good stead—the thrill of competing and contesting is one of those nice inheritances from the jungle, like love, and our antipathy to snakes. Another resource, in ages past, has been the abundant mineral and vegetable supply that a bountiful planet has provided.

Perhaps the most useful resource up to now has been our confidence that the mind of man has indefinite possibilities for the higher decencies, providing we can control or appease sufficiently his emotions and hungers, and providing we remember that improved apples and mankind both recede if not taken care of properly.

We've got to spray, both with bug-killers and with education, for world civilization. In other words, ambition, energy, confidence in the human mind, and natural resources have got us nicely to the beginning of this century without too many disgraces and too many scars. Now we have additional resources, for instance, a world consciousness, and a widespread social sensitiveness—that is, we might say that we have a willful devotion to the whole of humanity. Our charities are less localized. The airplane, moving picture, and especially the radio, have brought about this planetary conscience and planetary concern.

Also, we have now a high degree of technical training, so that we tackle with confidence, and with reason, and with arithmetic such problems as soil erosion, poliomyelitis, static, and religious minorities.

In summary, therefore, not only has science, and the increased knowledge of social living, improved mankind during the first half of the twentieth century, but further improvement is inevitable if we do not make fools of ourselves by mishandling the tools.

I, too, worry, by the way, about the tools used at Paris today and yesterday. Were they bludgeons, stilettos, or gas?

We have had rich resources in the past. Science of all sorts, from electronics to psychology, is supplying us with additional resources for the good life that even a somber philosopher, Dr. Lin, cannot moan away, but we have got to watch out for the blights that beset the most advanced creations, whether they be creations of the human spirit or of the animal body; whether they be men or apples. We must fight off the pestiferous and pessimistic tendencies.

Let us maintain the advances. Let us watch for error and rust. Let us fight the blights. Let us spray. (*Applause.*)

DENNY: Thank you, Dr. Shapley. Now, let's turn to the speakers in our plane, flying high over Hollywood, the glamorous city whose moral life is constantly in the brilliant glare of the floodlights of publicity. We have with us tonight the rector of All Saints Episcopal Church in Beverly Hills, a residential city adjoining Hollywood in greater Los Angeles, who is in a position to give us his firsthand impression of tonight's question, "Has Twentieth Century Civilization Improved Mankind?" What do you say, Reverend J. Herbert Smith? (*Applause.*)

SMITH: Dr. Shapley, your gracious optimism makes me feel somewhat like the Pullman porter who took on a passenger at

Rochester. The man put a five-dollar tip in his hand with emphatic instructions to get him off at Albany in the middle of the night. The next morning, the fellow awoke in New York. Angry and frustrated, he called the porter and conductor and began to berate them both for their carelessness.

After he departed, the conductor said to the porter, "My! Did you ever see anyone so angry in all your life?"

"Yes, siree," replied the porter, "that fellow I put off the train in Albany last night." (*Laughter.*)

I want to agree with you, Dr. Shapley, and you, Lewis Browne, but facts will not permit me. No one can possibly deny that the twentieth century has blessed us scientifically. But technology has so far outdistanced our moral and spiritual growth that our civilization is imperiled. Our age is scientifically adult, but dressed in spiritual short pants.

Perhaps the late G. K. Chesterton described our embarrassing plight by a remark he made to a friend with whom he had been discussing the invention of the radio. "What a tragedy," said Chesterton, "that it was invented at a time when man had so little to say."

We must not lull ourselves into a sense of false security because our century has multiplied gadgets, has increased its speed, has made living softer. We are not happier. We have less security and peace of mind, and our human relationships seem to be more complicated.

The splitting of the atom ushered in a new age. But so far, it has done more to split men farther apart then to draw them closer together. I notice that you, Dr. Shapley, say that future world improvement will depend on our not getting involved in another war. Dr. Shapley, don't you think we are getting pretty close to such?

Two things have happened during the last week which would make me wonder. A few days ago, Dr. Urey and Dr. Einstein, speaking for a group of distinguished scientists, said that by 1955 Russia would have a stockpile of atomic weapons, and that after that, war might be a possibility any day. They made a strong plea for a world government and for international control of the atom.

Second, yesterday the Paris Conference ended in failure. Instead of dreaming about and working for one world, it looks as if we shall have to be realistic and face the fact that we are doomed to live in two. The big "if" which blocks our way to world unity and cooperation is the possibility of another war.

War means that people have not found a way to reconcile differences. This breakdown begins in the lives of individuals. Nowhere is this failure in relationships more graphic than in the deterioration of family life in America and in the shocking growth in the number of juvenile delinquents.

This tragic defeat in human relationship, beginning in the home, is magnified in our society in the form of racial antagonism, industrial strife, and rivalry between nations and their ideologies. This personal failure, raised to the nth power in social problems, multiplies intrigue, magnifies lust for power, makes for greater hypocrisy, and increases fear.

If we are to see brighter days, I believe with you, Dr. Lin Yu-tang, that you are right in saying that scientists must do their part to close the dangerous gap between our scientific accomplishments and our moral and spiritual potentialities. But this is a job for science and religion.

There are already encouraging signs that some of the leading scientists are losing confidence in science as a sufficient guide to life, and they are now turning to God. Dr. Arthur H. Compton says that "There can be no conflict between science and religion." Einstein said the other day, "Our defense against the atom bomb is not in armaments, nor in science, nor in going underground. Our defense is in law and order."

I am not one of those who think that it is too late to save our world. I do think, however, that time is rapidly running out on the basis on which we are now living.

I sincerely believe that the problems confronting us today could be faced and solved if America would undergo a genuine religious revolution. But religious revolutions begin in the hearts of individuals who are sincerely and wholeheartedly committed to faith in God and His plan for a united world.

The time has come for many of us so-called Christian Americans to forsake our pagan, selfish, and materialistic ways. A moral imperative and a divine authority, God Himself, must impel more of us to relate our Christian ideals to our own personal needs and to the needs of our world. Only on this basis can we continue to put the common good above that of any individual.

This revolution, conceived in the mind of God, begins in the hearts of men, and ends by transforming the world. Let religion and science join hands in this enterprise and reverse the moral trend. This is a challenge that faces you and me as American citizens. If we accept it, then the twentieth century will be remembered not only as the beginning of the Atomic Age but also as the dawn of a new and more glorious era. (*Applause.*)

DENNY: Thank you, Dr. Smith. Now we have saved our optimistic speaker until last. He is Dr. Lewis Browne, famous author, lecturer, and philosopher, whose books have, like Dr. Lin's, been widely read throughout this country. We shall want to hear from this highly provocative man of letters, who lives at the Uplifters Club here in sunny California, except for the brief rainy season when he goes to New York to lecture. Now, our old friend, Dr. Lewis Browne. (*Applause.*)

BROWNE: Thank you, Mr. Denny. The twentieth century is forty-seven years old—in other words, at the very most one ten-thousandth of the total history of mankind.

Asking, therefore, whether it has improved mankind is a little like asking whether the breeze that sprang up half an hour ago has improved the climate of California. Incidentally, as an old Californian, you couldn't improve the climate.

But the grave question has been asked, and if an answer must be given, I feel very strongly that the answer should be, yes; mankind has been improved.

You asked, Mr. Denny, a moment ago why we live in dread of war and all these other things now. It isn't the fault of the twentieth century. It's the fault of all the other centuries before the twentieth that we drag around with us now.

Now in this twentieth century, for the first time in history, there is a determined and universal revulsion against war.

Only the madmen romanticize it now, and that's a sign of improvement.

For the first time in history, there is widespread aversion to cruelty. Everything that happened in the German concentration camps and in the Japanese prison camps would have been taken for granted—it would have been accepted as normal—in former times. Today they arouse unspeakable horror, and that's a sign of improvement. The shocking thing is not that the atrocities occurred; the amazing thing is that we were so shocked by them.

At the moment we, in this country, are spending 10 per cent of the total national income on what used to be considered charitable activities, philanthropy, brotherly activities. More and more in this twentieth century we have the feeling that all men are our brothers, or at least our brothers-in-law, and that's some improvement.

We show more concern for the halt, for the lame, for the blind, for the aged than ever before in all of history. We are kinder to animals. We are more tolerant with eccentrics, more comradely with minorities than ever before.

Have you improved? Ask yourself. Aren't you kinder to the weak than your grandfather was? Aren't you more tolerant to people who have a different coloring than yours? Who happen to have a different outlook on life than you have?

Of course, you have changed, and you have changed for the better. If you haven't, you haven't really lived in the twentieth century. You have lived behind the times.

In this twentieth century, we have enfranchised the whole half of the adult population. We, at last, have woman suffrage, and that, too, it seems—to me, at least—is a sign of improvement.

Yes, brother, I can hear you snicker! You say, "What have females done with their votes?" Well, what have the males done with theirs? If you feel it is no improvement to give women the vote, then you must admit it was no improvement to give men the vote.

Perhaps you do make that admission—but would you be willing to surrender your right to vote? The achievement of woman suffrage—a twentieth century achievement—is like the acquisition of a pocket handkerchief. It won't necessarily keep your nose clean—but it certainly could help, couldn't it?

In this twentieth century for the first time we have begun to release the colonial populations of the world. Consider what has happened in the Philippines, and the East Indies, the whole sub-continent of India, and all of China. All this, in our day, is happening. These peoples—the millions, almost billions— were held in vassalage, or worse, until these last few years. Now they are becoming independent. See how imperialism has crumbled in this twentieth century, releasing millions, hundreds of millions, of colored people from the white man's yoke. That may seem no improvement to you, if you happen to be a white man. But if you're a white man, you're in the minority—and we are thinking of the majority at the moment.

And here we come to the crux of the question. For a minority, it cannot be denied that the twentieth century has been a disaster. It has ruined the kings and the lords and all the rest who enjoyed privileges, but for the rest it has meant at least the hope of triumph.

For a few, it has been possible to groan for the merry old days, but the rest of us should remember that the word "merry" originally meant "short," and those merry old days were short old days—short of food and short of clothing, short of roads to free the body, and short of schools to free the mind.

One final word. At the moment and on the surface, this twentieth century may seem pretty awful when compared with, let us say, the nineteenth century. But an adolescent, with a pimply face, and a strident voice, and a hobbledehoy boby-sox manner, looks even worse when compared with a sweet, gurgling, pink-faced baby. Nevertheless, we know that an adolescent is somehow an improvement over the baby.

Let's realize that the same is true of this world we live in. Dr. Smith said a moment ago that we are scientifically adult but spiritually in short pants. But it's better to be in short pants than in diapers, and that's what we were until this last minute or so.

This world of ours may look so awful in part because a new gland has begun to function in it rampantly—the gland of industrialism, which might be called the gland of the free, and the hormone of the brave. Don't groan because mankind is still so savage. Rejoice because in this twentieth century at last it has begun to see that it should be civilized. (*Applause.*)

DENNY: Thank you, Lewis Browne. I wouldn't be surprised if Walter Winchell and a few other columnists took you up on that last wisecrack of yours. It was very smart, indeed.

Now, gentlemen, let's imagine that Dr. Shapley and Dr. Lin are here with us in this plane, high over the city of Los Angeles.

You know, by this miracle of radio it would be just as easy for us to have Marshal Stalin and Tito join us by this same process, if it were not for certain ideological proprieties.

Now, let's see if we can't carry on a brief discussion before taking the questions from this audience, which is literally, if not figuratively, up in the air. Dr. Lin, have you a question for either of our speakers?

LIN: Oh, Mr. Denny, first I will tell you that I am very unhappy under the earphones.

I am glad there is enough difference of opinion, but I have one question that I would like to direct to Dr. Shapley. Dr. Shapley, if the next war, as the atomic scientists have warned us, is going to be an atomic war, and if, as is unavoidable, mankind is going to be wiped out, who will eat the apples?

SHAPLEY: Who will eat the apples? (*Laughter.*) Well, Dr. Lin, I'll tell you about the apples, who is the eater of them. There are people who have been civilized, say, fifty million years. They are the ants. They'll eat the apples, probably.

DENNY: Oh, boy! I think there you have your answer, Dr. Lin. Lewis Browne, have you a question for any of the speakers in New York?

BROWNE: I would like to ask Dr. Smith this question: He says that we've got to use religion in combination with science. A good idea, of course; but I should like to ask this question. There was a time when religion had all in its hands. They were ages of faith. Would he maintain that in those days we had a superior civilization to those which science, by itself, has been trying to create?

DENNY: All right, Dr. Smith.

SMITH: I would say that there was an imbalance in those days, as there is at this moment. There was a lag in scientific knowledge and understanding, and I think, today, science has gone so far ahead of religion that it still is imbalanced.

DENNY: Dr. Shapley, have you any questions for our speakers here in the plane?

SHAPLEY: Well, this is for any philosopher, whether in the plane or not. I once asked a philosopher for a definition of nonsense. He said it was what other philosophers talk. (*Laughter.*)

I want to refer to Dr. Lin's statement that no harm can come if we ban all scientific progress for five years. Now, that is some other man's philosophy, I would say.

Would Dr. Lin think that the science of psychiatry of individuals and of nations—that that should be banned and not used in these desperate days when we are seeking for peace?

DENNY: Dr. Lin?

LIN: In answer to that I can easily say that psychiatrists in modern days have many, many more patients than in the nineteenth century.

DENNY: Lewis Browne wants to comment.

BROWNE: Yes, but remember the psychiatrist has more patients in the twentieth century than in the nineteenth because nowadays people are recognized as needing psychiatric aid, who, in the past, were merely considered a little eccentric and weird. We used to, when they became very bad, put them in the attic and lock them up there.

Nowadays we are more civilized. We bring them out to some clinic. We haven't got more mad people. We've got more sane people who recognize that madness exists.

DENNY: But, gentlemen, let's wrestle with that question that Dr. Shapley threw back at Dr. Lin just a moment ago. He said that Dr. Lin proposed that we ban scientific progress for five years. Without a world government, Dr. Lin, how do you propose banning scientific progress? Do you think the Russians and the totalitarian countries are going to agree to ban scientific progress?

LIN: I must make that question clear. What I said was, scientific discoveries can wait, but the problem of peace cannot; and no harm will come if we ban scientific progress for five years, until we know what to make of what we have already got. I mean that all scientific intelligence should be devoted to the tackling of the problem of peace.

DENNY: Dr. Browne?

BROWNE: There is one problem there, Dr. Lin. Who is going to do the banning? You remind me of the mother who sees an adolescent child growing up and says, "I wish that girl would stop growing for five years. She's getting me embarrassed —she's showing off my age."

LIN: I can answer that question easily enough, but I have a more important question to ask Dr. Browne. I protest against Dr. Browne's insinuation that the nineteenth century man was wearing diapers, while the twentieth century man is wearing short pants. Materially that is true, spiritually that is decidedly not.

We speak of Mid-Victorianism as old-fashioned. Remember, the Mid-Victorian had a valid body of beliefs. The modern man is unhappy; he is confused because he has lost the good, old Victorian beliefs in certain things about the universe, about human life, the purpose of life, and the social decencies. That we have lost. We certainly cannot say that the nineteenth century was a pink-faced baby, while we are adolescents. I think that is not correct, historically.

SHAPLEY:   I think, Dr. Lin, that you have a little more defense about stopping the progress of science at this time not only from the standpoint of the use of psychiatry in curing us of our difficulties, but do you think that the one million people who are now suffering from cancer think we could now have science banned at this time?

LIN:   No, the question is—you don't understand what I said.   I said, the important thing is to concentrate human intelligence on the problem of peace.   The progress of science cannot be banned because it cannot be done; but even if it could be done, no great harm would come about.

# PERSONALITIES

## JOHN PETER ALTGELD AND THE BILL OF RIGHTS [1]

### William O. Douglas [2]

Associate Justice William O. Douglas, of the United States Supreme Court, gave this address in Chicago, on December 30, 1947, at a dinner in observance of the one hundredth anniversary of the birth of John Peter Altgeld.

The address is both biographical and interpretative. It analyzes not only the political philosophy of Altgeld but clearly reflects the liberal position of Mr. Douglas, for example, in his discussion of the Bill of Rights.

Justice Douglas, appointed to the Supreme Court by President Roosevelt in 1939, when forty-one years of age, "was the youngest member to be appointed to that court in 125 years." He had held a consistent record as a liberal. He was a graduate of Whitman College, school teacher, graduate of the Columbia Law School, member of a New York City law firm, teacher in the Columbia and Yale Law Schools. President Hutchins of the University of Chicago in 1932 described him as "the outstanding professor of law in the nation." Douglas' chief reputation came after 1936 when, as a member and later as chairman of the Securities and Exchange Commission, he led in the policing and "reformation" of the New York Stock Exchange.

As a speaker he is deliberate, "low voiced," physically somewhat awkward (like Lincoln), but dominating through voice, incisive language, and challenging ideas.

Mr. Douglas was an undergraduate debater and a member of Delta Sigma Rho, intercollegiate debate society. He also taught English, Latin, and public speaking in a Washington high school, and "coached" the debate teams. [3]

John Peter Altgeld is probably unknown to most Americans. He seldom figures in our history textbooks. Few adults or

---

[1] Text is from *Congressional Record*. 80th Congress, 1st session. 93:A2505-7. December 30, 1947 (daily edition). Permission for reprinting granted through the courtesy of Justice Douglas.

[2] For biographical note see Appendix.

[3] For an earlier speech of Justice Douglas, see *Representative American Speeches: 1940-1941*. p225-31.

school children identify him with the great human causes which have shaped the American character. His name has not yet become, as it should, a symbol of the clean, powerful force which we call American idealism.

He has, indeed, been an "eagle forgotten." But as Vachel Lindsay nobly said of him, "To live in mankind is far more than to live in a name." Altgeld does, I believe, "live in mankind." It was the cause of mankind which he pleaded. Though his name may no longer be identified with the issues which he espoused, their vitality in the years which followed him reflect the courage and faith with which he embraced them. Moreover, those who would not have seen eye to eye with him on many of the contentious issues of his era nevertheless gain inspiration from the character of his advocacy.

He feared no man. As a lawyer, his clients did not cause him to stand mute when his conscience urged him to speak out. As a politician, he did not follow the safe course of indecision or of ambiguous pronouncement when his instinct for justice told him to meet an evil head on. As a private individual, he did not turn his back and withdraw to the ease and comfort of his wealth when the victims of an industrial system cried out against its inhumanities.

The powerful social forces of his age moved him to action. He was blunt, outspoken, and at times indiscreet. Edgar Lee Masters once said that perhaps "his weakness was that he hated the bad so much that it obscured his love of the good." He certainly made up in daring what he may have lacked in discretion. His was the frontal attack—he stormed the walls of the enemy at high noon; he did not delay in order to infiltrate their fortress at midnight. He was, indeed, an expendable. The heat of his zeal, the tremendous demands of his nervous energy consumed him in a brief and hectic fifty-five years.

He lost almost every major cause he pleaded. But those were the skirmishes and the battles which were mere episodes in a larger and more far-flung campaign. His failures caused new recruitments. A full generation later men who never knew his name were summoned by the ideas which he had generated or espoused. They marched to great victories of which he perhaps had never even dreamed.

His activities were, in the main, restricted to Illinois. But the ideas which he represented spread throughout the land as seed travels on the great airways of the world. His platform power was potent, though his spoken word was carried by the tongues of men, not by the magic of radio. The issues of which he spoke later became national issues. Millions became advocates of his lost causes. A generation unborn at his death witnessed victory in the war of which his lost battles were a part.

One who follows a trail through the wilderness may not know who first laid it out, who blazed the trees that mark its course. The pioneer who went ahead and marked the trail may, like Altgeld, be unsung. Those who later come to know its rigors—the crags which it mounts and the treacherous lowlands which it skirts—will want to pay tribute to him who first dared walk it. As Irving Dilliard said, the State of Illinois paid such a tribute in a "literally inspired" way in 1941 when it chose Altgeld Hall as the name of the building to house its distinguished College of Law. Such monuments to his name do more than honor him. They help insure that his ideas continue as potent forces in our national life.

Altgeld came to maturity during the days of our robber barons. The great industrial and financial strength of the East had won a war and had grown stronger in the process. A large productive capacity, a huge reservoir of capital awaited new ventures. Men of vision saw untold opportunities in the exploitation of the western two thirds of the continent. Parrington has described the beginning of this Gilded Age in pungent terms:

A passionate will to power was issuing from unexpected sources, undisciplined, confused in ethical values, but endowed with immense vitality. Individualism was being simplified to the acquisitive instinct. These new Americans were primitve souls, ruthless, predatory, capable; single-minded men; rogues and rascals often, but never feeble, never hindered by petty scruple, never given to puling or whining—the raw materials of a race of capitalistic buccaneers. . . . The romantic age of Captain Kidd was come again, and the black flag and the gospel banner were both in lockers to be flown as the needs of the cruise determined. With all coercive restrictions put away the democratic genius of America was setting out on the road of manifest destiny. . . . It was an anarchistic world of strong, capable men, selfish, unenlightened, amoral—an excellent example of what human nature will do with undisciplined freedom. In the Gilded Age freedom was the freedom of buccaneers preying on the argosies of Spain.

Banker, industrialist, builder, and speculator were the driving forces in that tremendous undertaking. Some maintain that, at least in days of peace, the job never could have been done so fast any other way. However that may be, it is clear that it was extravagant in its cost, inhuman in its methods, corrupt in its influence.

The agrarian groups were exploited by the mercantile and industrial interests. A scourge of poverty and want—10 per cent interest and 10-cent corn—swept the farms. Out of such stuff grew the Granger movement and later the Populists and other groups bent on reform.

Jungle warefare was the technique that fashioned the trusts. Big business rose out of the ruins which it had made of little business.

The newly acquired wealth became, in part, a slush fund to corrupt legislatures, to purchase favors from public officers. The Credit Mobilier scandal and the Whiskey Tax frauds were typical.

The nation had just rid itself of chattel slavery, renouncing for all time the idea that men could be bought and sold and exploited like cattle. But it seemed to many that the nation was on the verge of embracing a form of industrial slavery, which in its consequences was almost as vicious as the slavery which had just been abolished.

The great industrial projects of that age required men as well as capital for their execution. But in the eyes of the promoters, men were as fungible as the ties of the railroad tracks which spanned the continent. There was at least some effort to protect the capital placed in the ventures and to give it rights against the day of loss and failure. But there was little or no effort made to compensate for the arms and legs and eyes and lives of human beings that went into these industrial undertakings. Workmen's compensation laws, employers' liability laws were still in the future. There were only a few who talked of social justice.

Many workers, living in company towns, were beholden as in feudal days to a master; and this time their master was a corporation.

Child labor was widespread. Long hours of work obtained for men and women alike. Unhealthy and unsanitary conditions of work were found on every hand. The eight-hour day was a radical idea. Trade unions were sabotaged. Collective bargaining was still largely a dream.

The claims of stockholders and bondholders against enterprises had long been recognized. But there was no similar recognition of the claims of labor. Workers had no right to work; they had no claim to a fair wage.

Men struck for more wages—so that they might live decent lives, so that they might raise sturdy sons. Strikebreakers were brought in; and the poorly organized strikers were usually defeated. A great industrialist handled his strike with these words: "There is nothing to arbitrate. The workers have nothing to do with the amount of wages they shall receive."

The reaction was severe. There were probably some men of violence on the scene who would destroy the system that gave birth to the new industrial oligarchy. But men of good will—zealots and reformers—were also pilloried as anarchists. So were those who only protested against the chains of their new slavery.

There were riots and bombs. Violence begat violence. Troops —federal troops—were called out to enforce injunctions issued by federal courts. These were injunctions not only to protect property but to keep plants open and to outlaw strikes. He who defied the injunction went to jail. He was in contempt of court.

A great restlessness swept the country. There was a depression in the early nineties and millions were unemployed. They swept over the Cascades and the Rockies on the move to Washington for currency reforms, for a public works program. Some stole trains and were jailed. So were the hitch-hikers who rode the boxcars. Strikers, too, were jailed. Contempt of court became a weapon in industrial warfare. It was a powerful weapon. It aligned the forces of government—the courts, the marshals, the troops—on the side of industry and against the workers.

Government was there not to adjudicate the justness of the claims, not to mediate nor to arbitrate the disputes, but to crush and suppress those who protested against the injustices of the new industrial era.

These issues were injected into local and national politics. A distinguished line of muckraking journalists, starting with Henry Demarest Lloyd, emerged and wrote in words that all could understand an indictment against the age of plunder and exploitation.

Anti-monopolists pressed their reforms. Those who protested against the great and uncontrolled power of industry often advanced as their cure-all the socialization of business. Many good people were alarmed. Mr. Justice Brewer, who severely criticized Altgeld, was of the view that "the cry for socialism comes largely from the dissipated, the lazy, the dishonest." Men stood condemned as un-American whose programs of reform were not more radical than the vision of our own Tennessee Valley Authority and Grand Coulee. The specter of socialism did indeed stalk the land. Mr. Justice Holmes, writing in 1897, observed that "when socialism first began to be talked about, the comfortable classes of the community were a good deal frightened"; in fact, the fear of socialism "influenced judicial action both here and in England." Many in high places believed that this society of ours was headed for a pitched battle along class lines.

It is easy in retrospect to draw a false picture of an age merely by emphasizing the extremes which history has recorded. The sketch of the Gilded Age which I present may suffer that defect. But whether it does or not, I think it fair to say that this is the view Altgeld had of the era. The enormous injustices which he saw violated his sense of social justice. He first wrote and spoke his protests; then he moved to action, giving and expecting no quarter.

As governor of Illinois he put through a law aimed at sweatshops, at the employment of children who were under fourteen, and at the employment of women over eight hours daily or more than forty-eight hours a week. The latter provision was held unconstitutional on grounds which reflected the dominant political philosophy of the age—that it violated both the employer's and the worker's freedom of contract. He put through a law in aid of collective bargaining, which made it a crime to dismiss an employee because of membership in a labor union, and thus sowed one of the first seeds out of which the National Labor Relations Act grew a generation or more later. He inaugurated a system of mediation and arbitration of labor disputes. He put through a law that outlawed limitation of production, price fixing, pooling agreements, and other restraints of trade. He got an inheritance tax law passed. He was offered $500,000 if he would sign a bill which would tighten the hold of the traction and other utility interests on the state. He vetoed the bill, stating it was a "flagrant attempt to increase the riches of some men at the expense of others by legislation." Thereafter he campaigned for public ownership of utilities.

He protested vigorously against the use of Federal troops to break strikes. He resisted the use of the injunction in industrial disputes. As Harry Barnard graphically shows, it was Altgeld who coined the phrase "government by injunction" and drove home at every opportunity the oppression which that practice fostered. The Norris-La Guardia Act, passed in 1932, thus can trace its ancestry to him.

As governor he put his influence behind the development of a strong, progressive university. He feared that monopoly capital might spawn its own seats of learning and dominate the minds of men as well as their bodies. He also knew that the character of a university is a "force that creeps silently over the land, and by day and by night molds the sentiment of men." He therefore wanted a university which would "represent the great common people of this country," which would be the "friend and the helper of the toiling masses, of those people who do the work of the world."

He well knew the workings of the judiciary because he had been a judge. So when he saw rulings of courts which seemed to him prejudiced and partisan, which tipped the scales against the common man and in favor of the vested interests of that day, he cried out in protest. In 1893 he said, "The men who administer the laws are human, with all the failings of humanity.

They take their biases, their prejudices, with them onto the bench. Upon the whole, they try to do the best they can; but the wrongs done in the courts of justice themselves are so great that they cry to heaven." He saw the "corrupt use of wealth" extending its influence so far as to create judges "who do its bidding."

Altgeld knew what we are apt to overlook or forget, that the procedural safeguards of the Bill of Rights were designed to protect the citizen against the tyranny not only of legislatures and of executives but of judges too. He knew that power could be abused, whether it was industrial power or judicial power. He knew his history and had read those chapters which reveal that even courts sometimes show a callous disregard for human rights. Their robes do not always conceal their tyranny. The Framers of the Constitution, knowing that, designed the constitutional requirement of a fair trial to protect the accused, not only against the police and the prosecutors, but against the judges as well. All these things Altgeld knew; and that is perhaps why, as Charles A. Madison says, "he was harshest on judges who abused the spirit of our laws to the hurt of the people."

When Altgeld became governor four of the men found guilty in the Haymarket Riots had been hanged. Three were still in prison. Altgeld reviewed their cases and granted them pardons. The pardon was for him a simple, uncomplicated act. For as he told Brand Whitlock, he knew he was "merely doing right." He felt that way because in his judgment "those fellows did not have a fair trial." Unfair attitudes of both judge and jury had, in his view, infected the trial.

The reaction was violent as Altgeld knew it would be. He at once experienced what many both before and after him experienced—that he who calls for the application of the Bill of Rights to unpopular minorities, as well as to the other groups of the community, often becomes himself suspect. Thus when Altgeld insisted that even anarchists were entitled to due process of law, he was dubbed an anarchist. But a man whose devotion to our system of government was so great that he did not want it to become the tool of a capitalist oligarchy was not even remotely related to the anarchists. He was merely seeking to apply the

philosophy of Jefferson to the workaday world of the nineties—
due process of law for every man, whatever his race or creed or
political faith; social justice for those at the bottom, as well as
those at the top, of the economic pyramid.

But the label stuck. Then came the bitter years. He lost
both his wealth and his health under the pressures of his enemies.
The man who had the courage to adhere to the spirit of our Bill
of Rights and extend its benefits to a despised and hated minority
was hounded to his death by powerful influences bent on his
destruction. Yet I am confident it will be recognized as true a
hundred years from now, as it is increasingly recognized today,
that of those on the public stage in that era it was Altgeld who
brought the brightest honor to the democratic ideal.

Some issues survive all ages. But most of them have a habit
of being redefined in the special context of the next generation.
Hence this review of the issues which drew Altgeld's fire has
relevancy here only as a reflection of his philosophy. It is that
philosophy which remains a vital factor in American problems
in at least two respects.

*First.* Altgeld placed human beings higher than the dollar
in the national scale of values. A nation's industrial plant represents not only the daring of capital and the imagination of
executives, but the blood and sweat of men. The men and
women who compose a nation are its greatest natural resource—
greater than its mines or forest or rivers. The nation is healthy
only if its people are strong. The state must concern itself
with their economic disasters. For the greater share of their
troubles are due not to laziness but to economic forces beyond
their control. There is in most men a lively sense of decency,
of good will, of fraternity. The poor have those instincts, as
well as those blessed with more wordly goods. The powers of
government should be directed to protect them in their struggle
to survive and in their efforts to live in dignity and to share
the fruits of freedom.

Altgeld felt with Cardinal Manning that even a starving
man had the right to eat. And he thought it was an "insult"
for those who "started in life with good brains, good training
and excellent advantages and who are now well-housed, well-

clothed and well-fed, who know nothing about the actual conditions or wants of the poor" to lecture them on "laziness or shiftlessness."

We will be wise if we carry that philosophy into the world problems which confront us today. There are active bidders for the good will and support of the common people of the world. There are emissaries of totalitarian regimes in the capitals of the world, bargaining with bags of wheat for the souls of men. They are our competitors; but we need not emulate their example.

The victims of war in Europe and Asia need and ask our aid. But these people must not be treated as if they can be purchased with the dollar. We must not manage this great crisis of democracy as if it were an auction; as if the peoples of the world were on the block and going to the highest bidder. The sensitiveness of people increases with their suffering. The peoples of the world have suffered beyond our comprehension. If we so manage this crisis as to leave the impression that our standards are mercenary, we will have generated a revulsion to our system which may well be irreparable.

As a result of their struggles all peoples of the world are closer together. Their common interests have made them parts of something which is bigger than their own country. That is true of us, too. We have wider horizons, greater obligations. So when we come to the aid of the distressed people of the world, we act not out of charity alone but in answer to a responsibility to support in peace the ideal for which we were willing to wage a war.

Someway, somehow, we must let the peoples of the world know that. We must reach behind the facade of ministers and cabinets and commissions and let the common people feel our warm handclasp. We must let them know that we understand their suffering. We must make sure they know that our desire is not to make them our satellites but to meet them as equals in a world where standards of decency and justice prevail.

My remarks are not directed to agencies of government. I refer more particularly to the role which all groups—civic, cultural, and religious—can play in keeping close ties with the peoples of the world. Behind even the iron curtain of Eastern Europe are human beings whose thirst for freedom is as great as our own. We must manage to let them feel the warmth of our understanding and friendship. We must not let them become the forgotten people of the world. They must know that their problems are our concern too, that we respect their worth as human beings, that they also are part of the brotherhood which we have come to symbolize in the world. Governments may be imposed on these people. But the people themselves are the ultimate source of political power in every state. The pattern of an enduring peace will be found only in their hopes and aspirations.

Altgeld once said that "All great reforms, great movements, come from the bottom and not the top." That is true in the international as well as the national field. Thus it is doubly important that we do not lose the link which we have with all peoples whose dream is political, intellectual, and religious freedom.

*Second.* There is another current problem to which Altgeld's philosophy is relevant. On the domestic scene his courage and steadfastness of purpose are needed for protection of the civil liberties of our people.

We are apt to leave that task to the faraway court in the state or national capital. Those courts, by their examples, exert a great influence. But the great percentage of the grist is found in the lower courts. A more accurate measure of the vitality of our Bill of Rights is not in the sporadic rulings of our highest tribunals but in the day-to-day attitudes of the lower courts. Moreover, it is not in the courts alone that the strength of our civil liberties is to be ascertained. The executives and legislative branches of government also have responsibilities for enforcement of the Bill of Rights. The administration of the voting booths, the habits of the police in law enforcement, the nature of the city's ordinances—these all are indices of the vitality of the Bill of Rights in the life of the community. So is the attitude of the community. For an indifferent community, like a misguided one, will surely breed disrespect for the standards embodied in the Bill of Rights.

We may never reach perfection in our practice of the ideals of the Bill of Rights. But there is no earthly reason why with education and organization it cannot become an increasingly potent force in the everyday lives of our people. The extent of a community's respect of the human rights of all of its citizens is in fact the measure of its progress in civilization. Altgeld broke the trail—making it easier for every man of conscience who followed.

The creation of a healthy community attitude is not the exclusive task of any one group. The task starts in the home, in the schools, and in the churches. But city and state officials, editors, lawyers, and other groups of citizens have an important share of the responsibility. I remember recent instances where tyrannical judges sitting in local courts rode roughsod over the civil liberties of defendants charged with crime. In one case it was a doctor, in another an editor who thundered personal disapproval and started campaigns to rid their cities of those oppressive practices. They were indeed the ones that alerted the local bar associations and caused civil liberties committees to be formed to patrol the local scene.

These are not always easy steps to take. When Altgeld insisted that even anarchists were entitled to due process of law, he himself was labeled a subversive influence. That will often be said today when one insists that the safeguards of the Bill of Rights be extended to all groups, including any minority group in our midst that may be at the whipping post or the subject of temporary hysteria.

Yes, it takes courage to stand between an unpopular minority and the community, insisting that our Bill of Rights was designed for the protection of all people whatever their race, creed, or political faith. The lawyer may feel uneasy when it seems that important clients may slip away because of his attitude. The editor may be tempted to stand mute by reason of the views of important advertisers. Even the clergyman may be under pressure to hold his tongue because of the influence of some of his parishioners.

But those who are devoted to the democratic ideal expressed in our Bill of Rights will take the direct and daring course.

Once they are sure of their facts and know they are doing right they will, like Altgeld, espouse the cause of the victims of ignorance, prejudice, or passion. They, too, may be pilloried or cursed. But institutions become great by the greatness of the men who champion them, by the greatness of the advocacy that defends them. A people indifferent to their civil liberties do not deserve to keep them, and in this revolutionary age may not be expected to keep them long. A people who proclaim their civil liberties but extend them only to preferred groups start down the path to totalitarianism. They emulate either the dictatorship of the right or the dictatorship of the left. In doing this they erase a basic distinction between our system of government and totalitarianism.

To allow that to happen is to lose by default. Far better to lose pleading the cause of decency and of justice. Then we win greatness even in defeat, and leave behind a rich heritage for those who later rebuild on the ashes of our lost hopes. But there will be no failure if we adhere steadfastly to our faith. For the goal of people of all races is toward a system which respects their dignity, frees their minds, and allows them to worship their God in their own way. None has yet designed an article of political faith more suited to those ends than our own Bill of Rights.

# JAN MASARYK [4]

## EDWARD R. MURROW [5]

Edward R. Murrow broadcast this talk over the Columbia Broadcasting System at 7:45 P.M., Eastern Standard Time, on March 10, 1948.

Jan Masaryk, non-party Foreign Minister of the new Communist-dominated Czechoslovak Cabinet, "jumped to his death" at six o'clock on the morning of March 10, 1948. According to the Prague government, he "leaped from the bathroom window of his third floor apartment in the Foreign Ministry."

Late in February the Czechoslovakian Communists in a five-day bloodless putsch took over the nation. Premier Gottwald demanded that President Eduard Benes approve a new government composed almost entirely of Communists. Communist parades demonstrated their power. Benes succumbed.

The victors controlled press, factories, education, and all other representative phases of the national life. Confidence was given to the new regime by reason of the appointment of Jan Masaryk as Foreign Minister. He was the son of the first president of Czechoslovakia and was popular both at home and abroad.

When the new parliament assembled, Masaryk was scheduled to appear. Apparently the reproaches of his friends at home and abroad influenced him to commit suicide rather than accept power in the Soviet-controlled state.

The reaction throughout the world was bitter. Secretary of State George Marshall said, "It is a reign of terror in Czechoslovakia." Dr. Jan Papanek, the Czech delegate to the United Nations, broke with his government. He asked the Security Council to look into the Czechoslovakian case as a "threat to peace and security." Chile took up the issue and asked for action by Secretary General Lie.

On March 17 the United Nations debated the issue. Mr. Andrei A. Gromyko declared that Chile was a "puppet" and that consideration of the complaint would constitute gross intervention in the internal affairs of Czechoslovakia. The charge of Soviet domination there was "pure slander." The British and American delegation replied. The Council voted, 9 to 2, to put the question on the agenda.

Sir Alexander Cadogan, United Kingdom delegate, said: "Country after country on the confines of the Soviet Union has succumbed to the rule of the ruthless Communist minority." Replied Gromyko: "The

[4] Permission for this reprint granted by the Columbia Broadcasting System and by Mr. Murrow.

[5] For biographical note see Appendix.

policy of the United States and Great Britain [was] the subjugation of Czechoslovakia to their political and economic control . . . to drag Czechoslovakia into the Marshall Plan aimed at the enslavement of other nations."

Because it was difficult to prove direct Russian manipulation of the coup and because Russia could veto any action the Council might vote, the investigation bogged down in a welter of violent crimination and recrimination.

Mr. Murrow continued to sustain his reputation as an outstanding radio commentator. His material is usually related—as this broadcast illustrates—to his personal experiences.

His European broadcasts, after he became chief of the CBS European bureau in 1937, were colorful, sensitive, at times vivid, always personal, and yet accurate as reporting. His *This is London* program gained a large wartime radio following, especially among his British listeners. The London *Morning Telegraph* called him "America's unofficial ambassador."

After the war Murrow returned to New York as vice president of the Columbia Broadcasting System. He soon, however, was again in Europe to report such events as the betrothal of Princess Elizabeth, and the Italian election of March 1948.

Mr. Murrow has an unusually good radio voice. He is always conversational, comparatively objective, free from the kind of vocal passion that pervades the tones of other representative radio commentators.[6]

This is the news! Secretary of State Marshall says the world situation is very, very serious. Some hours after the Communist government in Czechoslovakia announced that its non-Communist Foreign Minister, Jan Masaryk, had committed suicide, some hours after the chief Czech delegate to the United Nations filed a charge against Russia, Mr. Marshall faced reporters in his office. One of them asked a question. He said recent events in Europe have caused great alarm in this country. There are many fears ranging from the possibility that Italy may fall to the Communists in the April election to talk of war. The reporter asked the Secretary for his assessment of the situation. Mr. Marshall replied, and he permitted his words to be quoted:

There are great fears as to the developments. There are also very strong feelings regarding these developments and a considerable passion

[6] For further comment on Mr. Murrow and for examples of his broadcasts, see "Spring Comes to England." *Representative American Speeches: 1940-1941.* p157-62; "Orchestrated Hell." *1943-1944.* p37-46; "Farewell to England." *1945-1946.* p33-8.

of view on the part of a great many in this country. The situation is very, very serious. It is regrettable that passions are aroused to the degree that has occurred.

What is this passion the Secretary referred to? The best sources in Washington say they are these—that too many people in this country want action quickly. They overlook the value of cool, logical, considered action. The Secretary is also said to fear the effect of statements made by some public officials, such as last night's story about selective service plans. Some people may think that indicates war plans. That is not so. Mr. Marshall said something else at his news conference. He said the death in Prague of Jan Masaryk indicates very plainly what is going on in Europe. He said: "It is a reign of terror in Czechoslovakia, and not an ordinary due process of government by the people." That same thought was made clear today to millions of free people throughout the world. The Communist government in Prague is the source of all news about Mr. Masaryk's death. This is its version. The sixty-one-year-old son of the founder of the Czech Republic, wounded by telegrams and letters from his friends in the Western world, who did not approve his going along with the Communists, took his own life. He jumped, say the Communists, from a third-floor window at his home, fell thirty-five or forty-five feet. The only other word from Prague comes from the United Press reporter who says members of Mr. Masaryk's family have noticed his deep mental depression ever since the Communists took over. I should like to discuss Masaryk, the man, with you in a few minutes.

Among the many, many government officials in the free countries who doubt the Czech government's story is Jan Papanek, chief of the Czech delegation at the United Nations. He says it could not have been suicide. He filed a thousand-word note with the United Nations, indirectly accusing the Soviet Union for his best friend's death, directly accusing the Soviet Union of organizing and directing the Communist coup in Prague two weeks ago. Mr. Papanek says Russian troops were on the Czech northwest frontier, ready to enforce the plans made by Russian leaders who conspired with the Communists in Prague.  He says Russia, therefore, used the threat of force against Czechoslovakia, a violation of the United Nations Charter.  The legal experts of the United Nations have decided that this is a non-governmental communication, that it will not be presented to the Security Council.  Any other member nation may make the charge.  Secretary Marshall spoke of aroused passions in this country.  Chairman Eaton, of the House Foreign Affairs Committee, says true, but it's because of the pending presidential elections.  He asks all of us to approach foreign problems without passion and with calm, cool judgment.

Today, Mr. Eaton's Committee heard General Chennault, the former head of the Flying Tigers.  He proposed that we spend from one and a half to two billion dollars to help China with economic as well as military materials.  The alternative to military help, he said, could be Communist control of all Asia and a third World War.

In the Senate, Glen Taylor's move to have the United States give the United Nations five billion dollars for world recovery was defeated decisively.  Only Senator Taylor, Senator Pepper, of Florida, and Senator Langer, of North Dakota voted for it.  The next big hurdle for the Marshall Plan will be the amount to be appropriated.  Senator Taft says he favors cutting the program from five billion three hundred million to around four billion.

In Denmark today, the Foreign Minister told Parliament: "If attacked, we will defend our liberty with all available forces." He said:  "The Soviet Union is at present striving to attach Finland to the East European system."

In Vatican City, Pope Pius told the Catholic people of Italy to vote in April for candidates who will safeguard the rights of God and of the souls for the true good of individuals.  He said: "The Church doesn't want to interfere in politics, but it cannot remain silent at this moment of such consequence."

And, now, this reporter would attempt to say a few words about an old friend.  They say he committed suicide.  I don't know!  Jan Masaryk was a man of great faith and great courage. Under certain circumstances he would be capable of laying down his life with a grin and a wisecrack.  For more than two years he had hidden a heavy heart behind that big smile and a casual, sometimes irreverent, often caustic comment on world affairs. I knew Jan Masaryk well, before, during, and after the war. I say that, not in any effort to gain stature in your eyes, but, rather, as a necessary preface to what follows.

I sat with him, all night, in his London embassy the night his country was sacrificed on the altar of appeasement at Munich. He knew it meant war, knew that his country and its people were doomed, but there was no bitterness in the man, nor was there resignation or defeat. We talked long of what must happen to Europe, of the young men that would die, and the cities that would be smashed to rubble, but Jan Masaryk's faith was steady. As I rose to leave, the gray dawn pressed against the windows. Jan pointed to a big picture of Hitler and Mussolini that stood on the mantel and he said: "Don't worry, Ed. There will be dark days and many men will die, but there is a God and he will not let two such men rule Europe." He had faith and he was a patriot and he was an excellent cook. One night during the blitz he was preparing a meal in his little apartment. A bomb came down in the middle distance and rocked the building. Jan Masaryk emerged from the kitchen to remark: "Uncivilized swine, the Germans! They have ruined my soufflé." I once asked him what his war aim was, and he replied: "I just want to go home."

He always knew that in a world where there is no security for little nations, there is neither peace nor security for big nations. After the Munich betrayal, the British made a conscience loan to Czechoslovakia. Benes and Masaryk used a considerable part of that money to set up an underground news service. It was functioning when the Germans overran the country. And all during the war those two men were the best informed on matters having to do with middle Europe. They had information out of Prague in a matter of hours, from under the very noses of the Germans. Jan Masaryk took to the radio, talking to his people at home, telling them that there was hope in the west, that Czechs and Slovaks would again walk that fair land as free men. When the war was over he went home, certain that his country had to get along with the Russians, or as he used to say, "they will eat us up." His faith in democracy was in no wise diminished. He became Foreign Minister in a coalition government. As the Communist strength increased, Jan saw less and less of his friends when he came to this country.

His music no longer gave him comfort. No more were there those happy late-nights hours with Masaryk playing the piano, hours of rich, rolling Czech and Slovak folk songs. I asked him why he didn't get out, come to this country, where he had so many friends. He replied: "Do you think I enjoy what I'm doing? But my heart is with my people. I must do what I can. Maybe a corpse, but never a refugee."

Did he make a mistake in this last crisis? I don't know! He stayed with Benes. Who knows what pressures he was subjected to. It is unlikely that he could have altered the course of events. Perhaps it was in his mind that he could save some of his friends, some small part of liberty and freedom, by staying on as a non-party foreign minister. I talked with him on the phone on the third day of the crisis, before the Communists had taken over. He thought then that Benes would dissolve parliament, call a national election, and the Communist strength would decrease. It would appear that the Communists moved too fast.

Did the course of events during the last two weeks cause Masaryk to despair and take his life, or, was he murdered? This is idle speculation. Both are possible, but, somehow, this reporter finds it difficult to imagine him flinging himself from a third-floor window, which, as I remember, and as the news agencies confirm, is no more than forty-five or fifty feet above the flagged courtyard. A gun, perhaps poison, or a leap from a greater height would have been somewhat more convincing.

It may, of course, be that Jan Masaryk made the only gesture for freedom that he was free to make. Whichever way it was, whichever way it happened, his name, with that of his father, will be one to lift the hearts of men who seek to achieve or retain liberty and justice.

And now, a brief word about what I am told is a widely syndicated newspaper column. It is written by the brothers Alsop, Joseph and Stewart. Under date of March 3, Washington dateline. In the course of chronicling the cause of the Communist coup in Czechoslovakia, they stated that Jan Masaryk, the salon favorite in New York, has played perhaps the most morally shabby game of all. What arrogance, fathered by ignorance. What a profound moral judgment delivered from such a distance. If the brothers Alsop were looking for a martyr they have found his name in today's news from Prague. So far as salons are concerned, if they have them in the next world, this reporter will count himself fortunate to be permitted to sit on the floor in the one where Jan Masaryk will be found.

We've come down to Philadelphia to make a small reconnaissance concerning the plans for the political convention, but in view of the news from Prague, it seemed to us more appropriate to talk about Jan Masaryk—the conventions can wait.

These words are from Jan Masaryk, spoken at San Francisco in 1945. He said: "Let us see to it that our lofty aims are carried into deed, worthy of the memory of our heroic, beloved youngsters."

Good night—and good luck!

# RELIGION

## AN ADEQUATE FAITH FOR THE WORLD CRISIS [1]

### REINHOLD NIEBUHR [2]

Dr. Reinhold Niebuhr gave this address on Tuesday, October 21, 1947. The occasion was the second session of the Sixteenth Annual Forum, conducted in the Grand Ballroom of the Waldorf Astoria Hotel, New York City, under the auspices of the *New York Herald Tribune*.

The Forum theme was "Modern Man: Slave or Sovereign?" Four sessions were held on October 20, 21, and 22. The theme of the second session was "Spiritual Contributions to the Strength of Man." Harriet Hiett was chairman; Ralph Linton talked on "Why Men Believe"; Chaim Weizmann, "Judaism"; Barbara Ward, "Catholicism"; John Foster Dulles, "Protestantism"; Bidhan Chandra Roy, "Non-Violence for Modern Man"; Charles Morris, "Testimony of American Youth." Dr. Niebuhr was the closing speaker.

This address is no mere popular religious appeal or surface application of religious philosophy. It has little of the prosaic directness of a George Marshall speech or the brisk radio appeal of America's Town Meeting of the Air.

Niebuhr's well organized discourse moves from comparatively simple to highly complex propositions related to "three dimensions of the world crisis."

Each is discussed from his approach as a "neo-orthodox" theologian. This speaker, with his *Nature and Destiny of Man* and ten other works, his magazine articles, lectures, and sermons has become recognized as one of America's outstanding theologians.

His is a pessimistic but vigorous Christianity. His teaching at Union Theological Seminary is "based on the conservative traditions of Lutheran and Reformed churches, on the philosophy of John Dewey, and on the economic approach of Karl Marx." [3]

His interpretation takes account of contemporary logic, science, political ideologies, history, and economics, as well as Christian ethics.

---

[1] Permission to reprint was given through the courtesy of Dr. Niebuhr and of the *New York Herald Tribune*. For full proceedings of the Forum, see *New York Herald Tribune*. Section X. October 26, 1947.

[2] For biographical note see Appendix.

[3] *New York Herald Tribune*. Section X. p33. October 26, 1947.

He invests these concepts of man and his destiny with new significance. "Niebuhr has restored to Protestantism a Christian virility." [4]

Something of his religious philosophy appears in the first and second divisions of his treatment of the world crisis when he argues for "humility" and "imagination." In the third division he more clearly grapples with the problem of the way to salvation—secured not by succumbing to history as a meaningless movement of investigation nor yet by assuming the progress of mankind upward and onward, but by appropriating "a tragic sense of life and a recognition of the Cross [with Niebuhr's full implication of that word] as the final center of life's meaning."

The address was probably by no means easy to listen to—even for his highly intelligent audience. It calls for rereading and thoughtful review. Its language is comparatively abstract and academic. It is, however, an address of high ability, "representative" of one type of public discourse.

We might profitably distinguish between three dimensions of the world crisis and consider what resources are required to meet our situation in each of these dimensions. In the narrowest dimension, the crisis we confront consists of the peril in which a democratic civilization stands.

The second dimension of the crisis consists of the peril in which the whole of civilization stands, whether democratic or no. It is the dimension of the crisis which would exist, even if Russia were not a difficult partner in the world community. It would exist in any event because we have not yet developed the moral imagination or the political instruments for creating a world community.

The third level of the crisis is more explicitly religious and spiritual. It is created by the fact that the vicissitudes of our generation were not anticipated in our culture. We are experiencing tragic realities for which the optimism of modern culture had not prepared us, and we are consequently threatened by despair and the sense of the meaninglessness of life. Our perils are most obvious and most immediate in the first dimension and least so in the third: but the perils in the third dimension may be ultimately the most serious.

Perhaps it may seem foolish to speak of moral or religious resources for overcoming the peril in the first dimension. We

[4] *Time.* 51:76. March 8, 1948.

face a truculent and ruthless foe, who is probably not as intent upon world dominion as some people imagine but who is certainly driven by peculiar dogmas and by a probable inferiority complex to defend himself against fancied or real enemies by rejecting every offer of cooperation and by stirring up as much confusion in the world community as possible.

It would seem that what is required to meet such a foe is not some great resource of imagination but simply common sense: the common sense which counsels us to be well armed and not to allow the foe to gain the strategic advantages in any part of the world which might prompt him to risk a martial adventure against us. But though the bitter experiences of the last decade have taught us that power is inevitably a factor in international relations, we would lack wisdom if we followed these precepts of common sense alone.

The defense of a civilization requires military strategy but it also requires political and moral strategy. The best political strategy is prompted not so much by ordinary common sense as by humility—if you will, by religious humility. We call our civilization a democratic one and believe it worth defending. And so it is. But no civilization is as just, and no cause is as persuasive as it seems to its defenders and proponents. Our business is to make our cause more deserving of defense, even though we must defend it strategically without reference to its virtues but because it is ours.

This is particularly true in facing a great center of power, a nation which has become a holy land of a secular religion. To millions of devotees, including many in our Western world, Russia has falsely become a fixed point of international virtue. This is a highly implausible faith. It is made the more implausible by the fact that this holy land seems increasingly involved in every kind of political chicane and skulduggery which we once attributed only to Nazi tyrants. The fact that millions should still hold to this faith must be partly attributed to generosity of the dream of a classless and just society which originally animated the Marxist cause.

Modern communism is corruption of utopianism and is thus different in principle from the moral cynicism of nazism. We are therefore in a more difficult ideological battle than when we engaged the Nazis. It is a battle which we cannot win among the impoverished and insecure people of Europe and of Asia if we do not make it clearer than we have done that we stand for freedom and justice, and not for the preservation of privilege. To win the ideological battle against communism it is not enough to point to the crass corruptions of the original dream of justice which we see in the police states of Eastern Europe. It is more important to make our cause so just that it will win the allegiance not of the comfortable but of the insecure and the impoverished.

It is particularly important that America, as the most powerful and wealthiest of the nations in the Western World, should acquire a higher degree of humility. Without it we will insist upon political creeds and political forms which Europe regards not as the creed of democracy but as the characteristic prejudice of a very wealthy nation. Europe is a vast ideological middle ground between communism and American libertarianism. We are quite wrong if we think that it does not cherish freedom as much as we do.

But it needs economic security more desperately than we. Its creeds are colored by that fact even as our creeds are colored by the fabulous character of our productivity and our immediate, though not ultimate, lack of anxiety about economic security. Without the humility and the imagination to think beyond the characteristic prejudices of American life we cannot win the ideological battle against communism.

But even if the world's hopes had not been frustrated by the irrelevancies and the truculence which the Communist creed has introduced into our situation, we still would have been in a world crisis. For there is another dimension of the crisis. A technical civilization has produced a potential world community, but not an actual one. There would be great centers of power in the world not easily brought under the dominion of a law higher than their own will, even without this conflict between a Communist and capitalist, a totalitarian and a democratic world. Even if we survive the present tensions we will face for decades the problem of achieving moral strength and political imagination to bring moral and political order in a world now related only by technics.

Our immediate perils tempt us to forget our more ultimate danger, caused not by Russian policy but by the inability of all nations and peoples to face new responsibilities. By clinging to ancient securities they make themselves increasingly insecure in a new situation. It is a tragic aspect of human history that men learn so little from the lessons of history. They are, as one of the prophets observed, wounded by the Divine Judge but they do not grieve; they are consumed but they will not receive correction.

An adequate faith for such a day as this must be a faith which induces repentance on the part of all nations and all peoples; and a consequent readiness to sacrifice any privilege or prestige, incompatible with community on the new and wider level of human community. No dreams of world constitutions or contrivances of international law will avail if there is not a wider and more resolute will to achieve world community than is now apparent.

The first and the second level of the world crisis—the peril in which a democratic civilization stands and in which civilization as such stands—engage the minds of our generation. These perils are obvious and immediate. I should like to suggest, however, that there is a third level or dimension of the crisis which is not so obvious but which may be more important than the others. It is the crisis in our culture caused by the fact that the faith of modern man has not prepared him for the tragedies which he experiences and does not help him to interpret his urgent tasks as meaningful.

Our culture has been dominated by one idea: the idea that history would solve all our problems. We hoped that historical growth and development would eliminate methods of force and bring all politics under the dominion of reason; that it would bring victory to democracy everywhere and eliminate tyranny; that it would abolish poverty and injustice; and that it would move inevitably toward a parliament of mankind and a federation of the world. These are false hopes.

Contemporary experience proves that history creates as many problems as it solves by creating human power and freedom. A technical civilization created a vast interdependence of nations but not a world brotherhood or even world community. It did not abolish methods of force but ushered in total wars, engaging the total resources of nations. It did not insure man's increasing security. Rather it transmuted the perils of nature into perils of history and society. It made us safer against death by epidemic and less safe against death by atomic destruction. It did not gradually change our position from that of slavery to historical process to mastery over our own destiny. We remain now, as we have always been, both masters and tools of history. We are moved by forces vaster than our own power and are yet called upon to make fateful decisions.

It is because we had so completely miscalculated the character of human history that we are so frequently threatened by despair in this day of frustration and disappointed hopes. We fear atomic destruction partly because it is a great peril but also because it is the old peril of death in a new form. We thought we had banished the peril of death. We are driven to despair because the last war did not result in a stable peace, because we falsely thought that every task had to be justified by some completely new tomorrow. But no tomorrow is ever completely new. We must learn all over again not only that "sufficient unto the day are the evils thereof" but also the duties thereof and the hopes thereof also. We must learn to exploit the qualitative meaning of our duties and tasks today without too much regard for what tomorrow may bring forth.

We are driven to despair because we cannot build out of hand the kind of stable world we desire, having discovered that recalcitrant forces in history stand against our will and our purposes. We must again acquire a faith which finds meaning in human life, even though no person or generation ever has the power to complete the ideal meaning of life. Our modern culture moved from a too simple optimism to a too deep despair: This cultural and religious confusion is dangerous for us, even on the lower levels of the crisis, because the distraction of alternate moods of unjustified hopes and unjustified pessimism prevent us from doing our duties amidst the pressing and urgent tasks of today.

An adequate faith for a day of crisis will contain what modern men have completely dismissed, namely, a tragic sense of life and a recognition of the Cross as the final center of life's meaning. The Scripture describes the works of the night, as those of sleep and drunkenness: "They that sleep, sleep in the night and they that be drunken are drunken in the night." Let us who are of the day watch and be sober. We cannot afford either the sleep of complacency or the drunkenness of hysteria. We must watch and be sober. But this watchfulness and sobriety is the fruit of a profounder sense of the meaning of our existence, than any of the credos which have recently guided us. A much more modest estimate of human power and of human virtue might bring us nearer and quicker to the goal of a tolerable peace and a sufferable world order for all nations.

Finally, we had hoped that it was a fairly simple matter to achieve a universal culture or a universal religion as the basis of a universal community. Now we realize that the universal community remains full of partial and particular elements. It is characterized by differences in political, moral, and religious ideas. There is no possibility of achieving complete unity or identity of conviction. We must learn therefore that community with our fellow men and other nations requires not so much a common culture as a recognition of the partial and particular character of our truth and our interest.

A religion adequate for community building or a world scale must cease to identify God with any particular culture or civilization, but sense, as the prophets of Israel did, that the judgment of God stands over all nations and that His mercy is available to all who are moved by that judgment. We can achieve accord with our fellow men in the proportion in which we recognize that both they and we hold facets of the truth and are loyal to aspects of justice imperfectly.

The wide variety of human aspirations is an old fact. We now face it in the new dimension of a world community. Every form of fanaticism has achieved new proportion of evil in this wider dimension. Religious forbearance of our fellow men has become even more urgent than when the words were spoken, "Let us judge not that we be not judged."

# COMMUNISM AND CHRISTIANITY [5]

## John A. O'Brien [6]

The Reverend John A. O'Brien gave this address before the Harvard Law School Forum, Cambridge, Massachusetts, on November 14, 1947. The setting in late October and early November 1947 was that of Paris Communists rioting as they attempted to break up an anti-Communist demonstration.

Moscow was systematically closing the gap in the iron curtain. Nicola Petkov, leader of the anti-Communist Agrarian party in Bulgaria, was convicted of treason and hanged. The Serbian Peasant party leader and an opponent of Tito of Yugoslavia was imprisoned. Stanislaw Mikolajczyk, anti-Communist Peasant party chief, had managed to escape from Poland to England. The head of the anti-Communist Peasant party of Rumania was placed on trial (and later convicted). The leader of the anti-Communist Slovak Democrats of Czechoslovakia was forced out of his vice-premiership—a prelude to the taking over of Czechoslovakia. Zoltan Pfeiffer fled Hungary as the Communists consolidated their control over the government. Communist attacks on the United States, via radio and press, rose in crescendo. Vishinsky, before the United Nations General Assembly, made a famous speech condemning this country for "warmongering."

In October the Communists and their followers had officially announced that they would do their best to wreck the Marshall Plan. In early November, on the thirtieth anniversary of the Bolshevik Revolution, Molotov bitterly denounced the United States. Western Europe was facing a hard winter with much prospect that the Communists in France and Italy might seize control. The "Big Four" were preparing for another, and as it turned out, futile attempt to draw treaties of peace for Austria and Germany. In Greece and China the Communist versus anti-Communist struggle continued.

In the United States the Henry Wallace movement was rapidly developing. Communistic struggles within the labor unions continued. In Washington, the Senate War Investigating Committee was attempting to prove that certain screen writers were Communists. The American press, Congress, schools and colleges, busines, labor, and the church discussed Marxism at length, with its present ramifications and its possible power in this country.

---

[5] Permission to reprint given through the courtesy of the Reverend John A. O'Brien, S.J. The text is corrected from the version in *Vital Speeches of the Day*. 14:174-6. January 1, 1948.

[6] For biographical note see Appendix.

What were the results of Father O'Brien's address and many similar ones? This formal indictment at Harvard was symptomatic of a considerable movement within and without the Church to identify Marxism with anti-Christianity. Before the April 1948 elections in Italy, for example, the Vatican formally urged Catholics to vote against the Communist-led Popular Front, led by Palmiro Togliatti. That factor was presumably one explanation for the defeat of communism in the Italian political crisis.[7]

Apart from the communism of Plato's philosopher-kings, the voluntary poverty and common life of some early Christians, and the doctrinal opposition to private property of some medieval Christian groups, communism is a distinctly modern ideology and social phenomenon whose beginnings are discovered about the time of the French Revolution. After the French Revolution and before the publication of the Communist Manifesto of 1848, there are traces of communism in the theories and social proposals of such French socialists as Babeuf, Fourier, Saint Simon, Enfantin, and Bazard. To Karl Marx however, who died in 1883, and to his friend and collaborator, Frederick Engels, must be attributed the essentials of the doctrine and the impetus as an historic fact and movement of what is known in our day as communism.

Vladimir Ulianov, better known by his pseudonym, Nicholas Lenin, was an enthusiastic student and interpreter of Marx. When he seized political power in Russia in the revolution of 1917, he immediately set about to introduce by governmental decree and violence his idea of what a Marxist state and society should be. After Lenin's death in 1924, the present Russian government inherited the mantle of his political power. The communism then of the Soviet Union and its satellite states, as well as that of the Comintern and the Communist parties throughout the world, comes from Marx and Engels through Lenin.

Modern exponents of the doctrine may have departed in some minor points from Marx's teachings. The strategic tactics and practical policies of Communism have been adjusted frequently to the emergencies of a critical political or social situa-

[7] See also "Shall the Communist Party in the United States Be Outlawed?" Harold E. Stassen *vs.* Thomas E. Dewey. p144-67 of this volume.

tion. But its essential doctrines remain substantially those of Marx and its ultimate goal as an historic fact and movement, namely worldwide revolution, bloody or unbloody, and a worldwide collectivist society in the Marxist meaning of the term remains.

It is in the Marxist meaning that I understand both the words, socialism and communism. To Marx, socialism was the first phase after the overthrow of capitalism in the inexorable evolution of society towards communism. It was communism in swaddling clothes catastrophically born from the womb of a dying capitalistic society that would grow up to be the world-embracing man, communism. We need not concern ourselves with the progressive steps in this necessary evolution as envisioned by Marx. It is sufficient to say that "the dictatorship of the proletariat" was one such step, and that in the final phase of the evolution society would be classless, and its motto would be the famous Marxist dictum: "From each according to his ability, to each according to his needs."

To understand the irreconcilable opposition between Marxist communism and the barest minimum of the essentials of Jesus' teachings in the Gospels, it is necessary to realize that in the secularized Europe of the nineteenth century, Christian faith was at a low ebb. Supernatural revelation in and through Christ was widely considered, especially in intellectual circles (and Marx was an intellectual) to be an exploded myth. Heaven and Hell were fanciful superstitions. The scientists and philosophers dissected and analyzed man, and man who had thought himself to be "a little less than the angels" found himself much less than a man. God might be admitted to be a "necessary hypothesis" or "a becoming" or a "totally other," but it was fashionable, if not vociferously to deny His existence, at least to regard Him as an "unknown and unknowable," who, if He did exist, had no concern with man and man's world.

Man thought himself self-sufficient. He had no need of God. With the aid of natural scienece and its technical discoveries, whose achievements in the sphere of economic production amazed man, he set about to assist the evolutionary process in making for himself a heaven on earth. It was in this milieu that Marx proposed his doctrines that would remedy, so he thought, existing social ills and give mankind the hope of a new heaven on earth in the absence of any substantial reality to the Christian Heaven of Jesus and St. Paul.

There are four essential points to Marx's teachings. These four remain part and parcel of twentieth century communism. Without them, communism is not communism. With them, despite certain apparent similarities such as the universalism of both, communism and Christianity are necessarily incompatible in the ordinary meaning of the word; that is, they cannot exist together in agreement or harmony. The Communist cannot be a Christian and the Christian cannot be a Communist.

The first essential of Marxist communism is its materialism. "Materialism" is an ambiguous term in Marxist writings but Marx certainly adopted the materialism of Ludwig Feuerbach in the sense that matter in motion is the only reality. Spirit as a reality that is not matter, and can exist and act independently of matter, has no place in Marxist thought. At the most, spirit is only a phenomenon of matter, or as Feuerbach says, "Nature in its otherness."

Philosophy begins, where materialism ends. Much more so does Christian theology. If matter and motion are the only realities, there is no Christian God, Who is spirit, and communism is necessarily atheistic; there is no human soul, which is spirit; there is no personal immortality, since matter of its nature is corruptible. God and the human soul as spiritual beings, and a personal immortality for man, are so clearly certain doctrines of Jesus that one cannot deny them and remain a Christian in any real meaning of the word. To attempt to do so, it would be necessary to strip Christ's teachings of all doctrinal content and to reduce Him to the status of a mere social reformer and practical moral teacher. Such an interpretation of Him is completely at variance with the historic account and interpretation of His life and teachings. Christian sects may and do argue about the nature of His person, His claims to divinity and His teachings on such doctrines as the Trinity, the Incarnation, the Atonement and the Sacraments, but to deny that He unequivocally taught the existence of a God and a soul that were not matter but spirit, and a personal immortality, is untenable.

Matter in motion is evolving, according to Marx. He was not, however, concerned primarily at least with the evolution of matter in the Darwinian sense of the evolution of natural species, but rather with the evolution of matter in the ambiguous sense of social institutions. This evolution was proceeding in the spiral motion of the Hegelian dialectic, which Marx borrowed from German idealism. Existing social institutions such as religions, forms of government, economic systems, legal and moral codes were being negated, and new forms were coming into being. The new forms were a synthesis of the previously existing forms and their modifications in the antithetic stage of the evolution. They were then the old ones in more perfect form.

This evolution of social institutions as Marx conceived it was inexorable, necessary, deterministic and mechanistic. It was proceeding according to laws as necessary as the law of motion of the planets and the law of growth of plants. Matter and its motion alone determined the process and its term. Since there was no God, a Divine Being had no control over it, and while man's mind and will could accelerate the process, man could not arrest the process or change its direction. Its term was the Marxist classless, worldwide, collectivist society. Why the process should then cease, Marx never explained. Nor did he demonstrate that there was such a process, but he assumed it. These are glaring weaknesses in his thought. In any event, the dialectic was proceeding and communism was its term. It was the factors and the laws that governed the process that Marx sought to discover and verify by experimental observation.

This materialistic dialectic of history remains an essential of communism. The false faith in its truth of even the rank-and-file Communist is an explanation to my mind of his relentless, fanatical zeal for his cause. His cause, he believes, cannot fail. Communism must come.

This doctrine, however, and Christ's doctrines of the Fatherhood of God and His loving Providence over His creatures are mutually exclusive. The Communist cannot pray at all, or if at all, certainly not as Jesus taught His disciples to pray—"Thus therefore shall you pray: 'Our Father Who art in heaven, hallowed be Thy name. Thy kingdom come. Thy will be done on earth as it is in heaven.' " For the Communist, there is no Father in heaven, Whose will should be done on earth. There is only the blind motion of matter and its forces towards an utopian collectivist society.

The words of Our Lord in the sermon on the Mount, "Behold the birds of the air, for they neither sow, nor do they reap, nor gather into barns; and your heavenly Father feedeth them. Are not you of much more value than they?" can only be and are to the Communist arrant nonsense. In the Marxist doctrine, there is no place for any concept of sin and redemption by Christ. Society and man in society are borne along like flotsam and jetsam in the tide without moral responsibility towards a mechanistically predetermined millenium where the state, an instrument of oppression, will wither away and the brotherhood of man will be realized without the Fatherhood of God.

That the prime factors in this evolutionary process are economic factors, that is factors that result from man's relation to material nature, is the third Marxist essential. To meet his bodily and other needs, man works with the material of nature and is thrown into certain relations with nature and with other men. This totality of "the production relations" is what Marx means by "the economic structure of society." The change in these production relations, as they are operated on by the dialectic process of history, determines in general the social, political, and intellectual processes of life and the consciousness of the individual. "It is not," Marx says, "the consciousness of human beings that determines their existence, but conversely, it is their social existence which determines their consciousness."

Surely man in common with other animals has material needs. The urge to satisfy them is a powerful motivating force in human affairs. The impact of his social existence on his person exerts an influence on man's mind and spirit. These are readily admitted truths with which the Christian can have no quarrel. But to overemphasize economic factors in human affairs and more especially to attempt to explain man's nature and destiny primarily in terms of man's animal urge to satisfy his bodily needs is to oversimplify and hence to misunderstand the complexities of human nature.

To the Christian, man is a curious, mysterious, if you will, mixture of matter and spirit, animal and angel. He needs food like the animals. He is, as it were, immersed in matter and nature. But with his spirit, he yearns and strives to transcend matter and nature. His feet are on the ground. His spirit reaches for the stars. Material goods alone will not satisfy the restless craving and yearning of man's spirit. The Scriptural words, "Not in bread alone doth man live, but in every word that proceedeth from the mouth of God," remain eternally true. Material values and progress are desirable, to be sure, and they should be an aid to spiritual values and progress, but the former are no substitute for the latter and in the Christian view of life must always remain subordinate to the things of the spirit. Man's nature and end must be sought in the nature and perfection of his soul and spirit. St. Augustine's expression of this truth is classic: "Thou hast made us for Thyself, and our hearts are restless till they find rest in Thee."

Communism's doctrine of the class struggle is its fourth essential. "The history of society is the history of the class struggle." To substantiate its importance and necessity, Marxist writers stress the conflict of master and slave in Roman times, of baron and serf in medieval, and of capitalist and worker in modern times. To the Marxist, class war is an essential factor in the dialectic motion of society. It is necessary and it is good. Although man's mind and will cannot arrest or control the dialectic process, it can and should accelerate it. This man can do by sharpening and fomenting the natural and necessary antagonism of class for class. Since this incitement to hatred will hasten the arrival of communism, whose coming in any event is inevitable, any means employed to pit class against class in mortal combat is justifiable and morally good. This is a blatant expression of the pernicious ethical error that "the end justifies the means." Means, evil and harmful in themselves, are made to be justifiable to attain a good end. They even

become morally good because of the supposed goodness of the
end. The doctrine is utterly destructive of all moral order.
Communist advocacy and practice of it—all too manifest today—
is the explanation of the ruthlessness, unscrupulosity, injustice,
violence, fraud, deceit, false and unfair propaganda that the
movement and its followers have manifested.

Such a doctrine is a gospel of hate and as such diametrically
opposed to Jesus' gospel of love and His perfect sacrificial
practice of it in His own personal life. Christians may and
should regret that Christian states, societies, and individuals have
miserably failed even to approach the perfection of the ideal of
love of God and fellow men of Christianity's founder. But it is
one thing to acknowledge in our heart of hearts the perfection
of the ideal, to sorrow that in our individual and social lives it
has not been attained, and try again to attain it. It is quite a
different thing to abandon it, to make a virtue of hatred and
a vice of love, and to make the law of the jungle, the law of
human life. Such a perversion of moral values can eventuate in
the complete destruction of civilization. That so dire a catas-
trophe is not beyond the realm of possibilities, the discovery of
the atom bomb and the harnessing of atomic energy has begun
to make us realize.

Christianity has not been tried and found wanting. It has
not been tried. In our day of the atom bomb, we had better
try to reject any gospel of hate and every manifestation of it
and try the unitive power of Jesus' ideal of love of God and all
fellow men.

Christianity and communism are then irreconcilably in com-
patible. The latter is atheistic, materialistic, mechanistic, and deterministic. It seeks to explain man's nature and end too exclusively in terms of his animal urge to supply his material needs,
and it inculcates a gospel of hate in the minds and hearts of
men. Christianity teaches the existence of God, the Creator of
Heaven and earth, the Father and Redeemer of man. It believes
man to be the image of God, and like God spiritual and free.
Its gospel is one of love.

Without such faith in man and God, Christianity believes
that man is divorced from reality. He is living in the dark and

all his intellectual and political systems become distorted. This is the case with communism. It is attempting to build its new world in the dark. Hence, the house that it would build for the new humanity, is not a palace but a prison, since it has no windows. For what man will always need and in his heart desire is the coming of "a dayspring from on high to give light to them that sit in darkness and the shadow of death, to guide our feet in the way of peace." For the Christian, that light must always be Christ and not Karl Marx or Nicholas Lenin.

# APPENDIX

## BIOGRAPHICAL NOTES [1]

BROWNE, LEWIS (1897-    ). Born in London, England; came to the United States, 1912; B.A., University of Cincinnati, 1919; B.H., Hebrew Union College, Rabbinical Seminary, 1920; student at Yale, 1920-22; rabbi, Waterbury, Connecticut, 1920-23, Newark, New Jersey, 1924-26; free-lance writer and lecturer since 1926; lecturer at various colleges and universities, including Columbia University, 1938-43; author, *This Believing World*, 1926; many other volumes; radio commentator and world traveler; Civilian Lecturer on orientation, War Department, 1942-45.

DENNY, GEORGE VERNON, JR. (1899-    ). Born in Washington, North Carolina; B.S., University of North Carolina, 1922; LL.D., Temple University, 1940; instructor in dramatic production, University of North Carolina, 1924-26; actor, 1926-27; manager of W. B. Feakins, Inc., 1927-28; director, Institute of Arts and Sciences, Columbia University, 1928-30; associate director, League of Political Education, 1931-37; founder and director, America's Town Meeting of the Air; treasurer, Economic Club of New York; member of executive board, American Association for Adult Education; president, Town Hall, Inc.; served, Students' Army Training Corps, 1918. (See also *Current Biography: 1940*.)

DEWEY, THOMAS EDMUND (1902-    ). Born in Owosso, Michigan; A.B., University of Michigan, 1923, LL.M., 1937; LL.B., Columbia University, 1925; honorary degrees at Tufts, Dartmouth, and other institutions; admitted to New York bar,

---

[1] The chief sources of these notes are *Who's Who in America, Current Biography, Religious Leaders in America, International Who's Who, Who's Who in American Education, Directory of American Scholars*, and the *Congressional Directory*.

1926; chief assistant, United States Attorney, 1931-33; special prosecutor, Investigation of Organized Crime, New York, 1935-37; elected District Attorney, New York County, 1937; Republican governor of New York since 1942; defeated as candidate for the presidency, Republican ticket, November 1944; Republican presidential nominee, 1948; author, *The Case Against the New Deal,* 1940.  (See also *Current Biography: 1944.*)

DOUGLAS, HELEN GAHAGAN (1900-    ).  Born in Boonton, New Jersey; studied at Barnard College, New York, 1920-22; married Melvyn Douglas, 1931; appeared in many Broadway plays, including "The Cat and the Fiddle," "Moor Born," "Mary, Queen of Scotland"; also in motion pictures and operas; toured Europe in concerts; member of 79th and 80th Congresses, 1945-49; prominent in Democratic national politics; member of Foreign Affairs Committee, House of Representatives.  (See also *Current Biography: 1944.*)

DOUGLAS, WILLIAM O. (1898-    ).  Born in Maine, Minnesota; private in United States Army, 1918; A.B., Whitman College, 1920; LL.B., Columbia, 1925; honorary A.M., Yale, 1932; honorary LL.D., Whitman, 1938; with law firm in New York City, 1925-27; member of faculty, Columbia Law School, 1925-28; Yale Law School, 1928-39; active as a member of various governmental agencies, including Securities and Exchange Commission; appointed by President Roosevelt to Supreme Court, 1939; author of various works, including *Cases and Materials on the Law of Management of Business Units* (with C. M. Shanks), 1931; member, Delta Sigma Rho.  (See also *Current Biography: 1941.*)

DULLES, JOHN FOSTER (1888-    ).  Born in Washington, D.C.; B.A., Princeton, 1908, LL.D., 1946; Sorbonne, Paris, 1908-09; LL.B., George Washington University, 1911; LL.D., Tufts, Wagner, Northwestern; began law practice, New York City, 1911; director, Bank of New York; trustee, Rockefeller Foundation; chairman, Carnegie Endowment for International

Peace; chairman, Federal Council of Churches Commission on a Just and Durable Peace; secretary, Hague Peace Conference, 1907; captain and major, United States Army, 1917-18; counsel, American Commission to Negotiate Peace, 1918-19; member, Reparations Commission and Supreme Economic Council, 1919; member, United States delegation, San Francisco Conference on World Organization, 1945; Council of Foreign Ministers, London, 1945; General Assembly, United Nations, 1946; Meeting of Council of Foreign Ministers, Moscow, 1947; London meeting of "Big Four," 1947; Phi Beta Kappa; writer and speaker on international affairs. (See also *Current Biography: 1944.*)

GOLDSBOROUGH, T. ALAN (1877-    ). Born in Greensboro, Maryland; A.B., Washington College, 1899, LL.D., 1935; LL.B., University of Maryland, 1901; State's Attorney, Carolina County, Maryland, 1904-08; member of Congress, 1921-41; resigned to accept appointment as United States District Judge for District of Columbia, 1939.

LILIENTHAL, DAVID ELI (1899-    ). Born in Morton, Illinois; A.B., Depauw University, 1920, LL.D., 1945; intercollegiate orator; LL.B., Harvard Law School, 1923; admitted to Illinois Bar, 1923; in practice of law, Chicago, 1923-31; edited Public Utilities and Carriers' Service for the Commerce Clearing House, 1931; director of the Tennessee Valley Authority, 1933-46; appointed chairman of Board of Directors, 1941; appointed Chairman of the Atomic Energy Commission, 1947, reappointed, 1948; Phi Beta Kappa, Delta Sigma Rho; author, *T.V.A.: Democracy on the March,* 1944. (See also *Current Biography: 1944.*)

LIN YU-TANG (1895-    ). Born in Changchow, Fukien Province, China; B.A., St. John's College, Shanghai, 1916; student, Harvard Graduate School, 1919-20, M.A. 1922; student at Jena, Germany, 1921; Leipzig, 1921-23 (Ph.D.); Litt.D., Elmira, 1941, Rutgers, 1942; professor of English, Peking National University, 1923-26; secretary, Foreign Ministry, Hankow Government, 1927; editor of various magazines; author (in

English) of *My Country and My People,* 1935; *The Importance of Living,* 1937; *Wisdom of Confucius,* 1938; *Between Tears and Laughter,* 1943; various other books; lecturer; now lives in the United States. (See also *Current Biography: 1940.*)

LIPPMANN, WALTER (1889-    ). Born in New York City; A.B., Harvard, class of 1910 (degree taken, 1909), graduate student, 1909-10; associate editor, *New Republic,* and editor, *New York World;* after 1931 special writer for *New York Herald Tribune* and other newspapers; assistant to Secretary of War, 1917; captain, United States Army Military Intelligence, A.E.F., 1917-18; member, Board of Overseers, Harvard, 1933-39; column, "Today and Tomorrow," in about 180 papers; member, Phi Beta Kappa; author, *A Preface to Politics,* 1913; *Liberty and the News,* 1920; *The Phantom Public,* 1925; *A Preface to Morals,* 1929; *The United States in World Affairs,* 1931; *Interpretations,* 1933-35; *The Good Society,* 1937; *The United States Foreign Policy,* 1943; and other books. (See also *Current Biography: 1940.*)

MARSHALL, GEORGE CATLETT (1880-    ). Born in Uniontown, Pennsylvania; student, Virginia Military Institute, 1897-1901; honorary graduate, United States Infantry-Cavalry School, 1907; graduate, Army Staff College, 1908; honorary degrees at Washington and Jefferson, Pennsylvania Military College, William and Mary, Trinity, and elsewhere; mounted through the grades to major general, 1939; served in the Philippines, 1902-03, 1913-16; with A.E.F., 1917-19; on General Staff, and in Meuse-Argonne operations; in China, 1924-27; chief of staff with rank of general, 1939-1945; awarded the D.S.M. and many other military awards from United States and various other countries; on military mission to China, 1945-46; "One of the principal brains and powers behind the vast military effort of the Allies in World War II"; appointed Secretary of State, 1946; author of *Selected Speeches and Statements of George C. Marshall,* 1946. (See also *Current Biography: 1940; 1947.*)

MURROW, EDWARD R. (1909-    ). Born in Greensboro, North Carolina; graduate of Washington State College, 1930; student at Stanford University and University of Washington; President of National Student Federation, 1930-32; assistant director of Institute of International Education, 1932-35; with Columbia Broadcasting System since 1935; chief of European service, 1937-46; vice president, Columbia Broadcasting Company since 1946. (See also *Current Biography: 1942*.)

NIEBUHR, REINHOLD (1892-    ). Born in Wright City, Missouri; student, Elmhurst College (Illinois), 1910; Eden Theological Seminary (St. Louis), 1912; B.D., Yale Divinity School 1914, A.M., 1915; D.D., Amherst, Yale, Oxford; ordained in ministry, Evangelical Synod of North America, 1915; pastor, Detroit, 1915-28; associate professor of philosophy of religion, 1928-30, professor of Applied Christianity, Union Theological Seminary, since 1930; author, *The Nature and Destiny of Man,* 1941; other books on Christian ethics and philosophy. (See also *Current Biography: 1941*.)

O'BRIEN, JOHN A. (1897-    ). Born in Chicopee, Massachusetts; A.B., Holy Cross College, 1918; M.A., Woodstock College, Woodstock, Maryland, 1924; Ph.D., Gregorian University, Rome, 1933; instructor, Holy Cross College, 1924-27; assistant professor, Boston College, 1933-35, professor of philosophy, since 1935; chairman, philosophy department, since 1938; member, American Philosophical, American Catholic Philosophical, and Jesuit Philosophical Associations; past president, Jesuit Philosophical Association; contributor to various educational and philosophical journals.

REUTHER, WALTER PHILIP (1907-    ). Born in Wheeling, West Virginia; apprentice tool and diemaker, Wheeling; employee, Briggs Manufacturing Company, Ford Motor Company (a foreman), Detroit; attended Wayne University for three years; traveler, by bicycle, through Germany, Russia, China, Japan; student of auto plants and machine shops, 1933-35; organized auto workers in Detroit, 1935; member of the executive board, International Union of Automobile Workers, 1936-46; vice president of the International Union, United Automobile, Aircraft and Agricultural Workers of America of the Congress of Industrial Organizations, 1942-46; president, since March 1946; led General Motors strike, 1945-46; severely wounded by assailant, 1948. (See also *Current Biography: 1941.*)

SHAPLEY, HARLOW (1885-      ). Born in Nashville, Missouri; A.B., University of Missouri, 1910, A.M., 1911, LL.D., 1927; Ph.D., Princeton, 1913; honorary degrees at Missouri, Princeton, Harvard, University of Pennsylvania, and elsewhere; astronomer at Mt. Wilson Observatory, 1914-21; director of Harvard Observatory since 1921; research in photometry and spectroscopy; member of Council of American Association for the Advancement of Science; officer in other learned societies; recipient of various medals for distinguished contributions in the field of astronomy; president, Council of American Association for the Advancement of Science, 1947. (See also *Current Biography: 1941.*)

SMITH, J. HERBERT (1899-      ). Born in Homewood, Kansas; Ph.B., University of Chicago, 1921; S.T.B, General Theological Seminary, New York, 1926; on the staff of Calvary Episcopal Church, New York, for thirteen years; rector of All Saints Church, Beverly Hills, California, since 1942; consultant to motion picture studios in preparation of movie scripts; technical director of "The Flame," "Life with Father," and "The Bishop's Wife."

STASSEN, HAROLD E. (1907-      ) Born in West St. Paul, Minnesota; student, University of Minnesota College and Law School, 1923-29; began practice of law in Minneapolis, 1929; County Attorney, 1930-38; Governor of Minnesota, 1939-41; reelected Governor for the terms 1941-43 and 1943-45; resigned to enter United States Navy, 1943; keynote speaker of the Republican National Convention, 1940; member of Delta Sigma Rho; selected as one of the seven delegates to represent the

United States at the United Nations Security League Conference, San Francisco, 1945; candidate for presidential nomination on Republican ticket, 1948; appointed president, University of Pennsylvania, 1948; author, *Where I Stand*. (See also *Current Biography: 1940; March 1948*.)

STODDARD, GEORGE D. (1897-    ).   Born in Carbondale, Pennsylvania; A.B., Pennsylvania State College, 1921; diploma, University of Paris, 1923; Ph.D., University of Iowa, 1925; LL.D., St. Lawrence, Hobart, New York, Union, and various other colleges and universities; associate in psychology and education, University of Iowa, 1925-26, assistant professor, 1926-28, associate professor of psychology, 1928-29, professor, 1929-41; director, Iowa Child Welfare Research Station, 1928-41, and dean of the Graduate College, 1936-42; second lieutenant, Field Artillery, Reserve Corps, 1918-23; member of Delta Sigma Rho; executive officer of various educational societies; president of the University of the State of New York and commissioner of education, 1942-45; president, University of Illinois, since July 1946; United States representative, UNESCO, 1947-48; author, *Tests and Measurements in High School Instruction* (with G. M. Ruch), 1927; *Study Manual in Elementary Statistics* (with E. F. Lindquist), 1929; *Child Psychology* (with B. L. Wellman), 1936; *The Meaning of Intelligence*, 1943; *Tertiary Education*, 1944. (See also *Current Biography: 1946*.)

TAFT, ROBERT ALPHONSO (1889-    ).   Born in Cincinnati, Ohio; attended public schools of Cincinnati and the Taft School; A.B., Yale University, 1910; LL.B., Harvard University, 1913; attorney at law; assistant counsel for the United States Food Administration, 1917-18; counsel for the American Relief Administration, 1919; Republican member of the Ohio House of Representatives, 1921-26, speaker, 1926; Ohio State Senate, 1931-32; United States Senate, since 1939; candidate for presidential nomination on Republican ticket, 1948. (See also *Current Biography: 1940; April 1948*.)

TAYLOR, HAROLD (1914-    ).   Born in Toronto, Canada; A.B., University of Toronto, 1935, M.A., 1936; studied at

Cambridge, 1936; Ph.D., University of London, 1938; came to United States, 1939; naturalized, 1946; instructor in philosophy, University of Wisconsin, 1939-42, assistant professor, 1942-45; armed forces representative, 1943; Office of Scientific Research and Development, 1944; president, Sarah Lawrence College, Bronxville, New York, since 1945. (See also *Current Biography: 1946.*)

TRUMAN, HARRY S. (1894-    ). Born in Lamar, Missouri; student, Kansas City School of Law, 1923-25; captain, Field Artillery, World War I; judge, Jackson County Court, 1922-24; presiding judge, 1926-34; United States Senator from Missouri, 1935-41, reelected for the term 1941-47; elected Vice President on the Democratic ticket, November 1944; sworn in as President of the United States on the death of President Roosevelt, April 1945. (See also *Current Biography: 1942; 1945.*)

VANDENBERG, ARTHUR HENDRICK (1884-    ). Born in Grand Rapids, Michigan; studied law at the University of Michigan, 1901-02, honorary A.M., 1925; LL.D., Hope College, 1926; editor of *Grand Rapids Herald,* 1906-28; United States Senator from Michigan, since 1928; Chairman of Republican Senate Legislative Committee, 1933-34; received 76 votes for Republican presidential nomination, 1940; American delegate, United Nations Organization Conference, San Francisco, 1945; United States Delegate to United Nations, 1945-47; chairman, Senate Committee on Foreign Affairs, 1947; candidate for presidential nomination on Republican ticket, 1948; member, Authors' Club, London, England; author, *Alexander Hamilton, the Greatest American,* 1921; *If Hamilton Were Here Today,* 1923; *The Trail of a Tradition,* 1925. (See also *Current Biography: 1940.*)

WALLACE, HENRY AGARD (1888-    ). Born in Adair County, Iowa; B.S., Iowa State College, 1910, honorary M.S. in agriculture, 1920; editor of *Wallaces' Farmer* since 1910; Secretary of Agriculture in cabinet of President Roosevelt, 1933-40;

Vice President of the United States, 1941-45; visited Latin America, 1943; defeated for nomination for reelection as Vice President on the Democratic ticket in 1944, but campaigned actively for Roosevelt; appointment as Secretary of Commerce confirmed in March 1945, after vigorous Senate opposition; resigned, September 1946; spoke in England, France, and other European countries, April 1947, in opposition to Truman policies; candidate for the presidency on the Progressive party ticket, 1948; author of books and articles on agricultural, political, and religious topics. (See also *Current Biography: 1940; 1947.*)

WAYMACK, WILLIAM WESLEY (1888-    ). Born in Savanna, Illinois; A.B., Morningside College, 1911; honorary degrees, Morningside College and Drake University; vice president, The Register and Tribune Company, 1939-46, editor, 1942-46; Pulitzer Prize for distinguished editorial writing, 1937; member of the United States Atomic Energy Commission, since October 1946; chairman, Economic Policy Commission; National Resources Planning Board, 1942; adviser, Department of State, 1942; member, Board of Directors of Twentieth Century Fund, since 1942; board member of many other agricultural, economic, social, and philanthropic organizations. (See also *Current Biography: 1947.*)

# CUMULATED AUTHOR INDEX

An author index to the volumes of *Representative American Speeches* for the years 1937-1938 through 1947-1948. The date following the title of each speech indicates the volume in which it appears.

Willkie, W. L. Acceptance speech.
1940-41: 93-112; Economic freedom
for the world. 1942-43: 105-15;
The function of a political party.
1943-44: 267-76; Isolationism and
the League of Nations. 1941-42:
251-8; Lidice. 1942-43: 163-7;
Why are you unemployed? 1939-
40: 306-15

Wise, S. S. Fifty years of Zionism.
1946-47: 262-70
Woll, Matthew. Labor's contribution
to American democracy. 1939-40:
327-34
Wriston, H. W. Free enterprise.
1943-44: 230-41

Young, O. D. Science of better
living. 1937-38: 190-7